The Futility of Family Policy

GILBERT Y. STEINER

The Futility of Family Policy

THE BROOKINGS INSTITUTION
Washington, D.C.

Copyright © 1981
by the Brookings Institution
1775 Massachusetts Avenue, N.W.
Washington, D.C. 20036

Library of Congress Cataloging in Publication data:
Steiner, Gilbert Yale, 1924–
The futility of family policy.
Includes bibliographical references and index.
1. Family—United States.
2. Family policy—United States.
I. Title.
HQ536.S74   306.8'0973   80-26448
ISBN 0-8157-8124-5
ISBN 0-8157-8123-7 (pbk.)

THE BROOKINGS INSTITUTION is an independent organization devoted to nonpartisan research, education, and publication in economics, government, foreign policy, and the social sciences generally. Its principal purposes are to aid in the development of sound public policies and to promote public understanding of issues of national importance.

The Institution was founded on December 8, 1927, to merge the activities of the Institute for Government Research, founded in 1916, the Institute of Economics, founded in 1922, and the Robert Brookings Graduate School of Economics and Government, founded in 1924.

The Board of Trustees is responsible for the general administration of the Institution, while the immediate direction of the policies, program, and staff is vested in the President, assisted by an advisory committee of the officers and staff. The by-laws of the Institution state: "It is the function of the Trustees to make possible the conduct of scientific research, and publication, under the most favorable conditions, and to safeguard the independence of the research staff in the pursuit of their studies and in the publication of the results of such studies. It is not a part of their function to determine, control, or influence the conduct of particular investigations or the conclusions reached."

The President bears final responsibility for the decision to publish a manuscript as a Brookings book. In reaching his judgment on the competence, accuracy, and objectivity of each study, the President is advised by the director of the appropriate research program and weighs the views of a panel of expert outside readers who report to him in confidence on the quality of the work. Publication of a work signifies that it is deemed a competent treatment worthy of public consideration but does not imply endorsement of conclusions or recommendations.

The Institution maintains its position of neutrality on issues of public policy in order to safeguard the intellectual freedom of the staff. Hence interpretations or conclusions in Brookings publications should be understood to be solely those of the authors and should not be attributed to the Institution, to its trustees, officers, or other staff members, or to the organizations that support its research.

Foreword

IMPORTANT changes have taken place over the last ten or fifteen years in the way American public policy addresses some fundamental questions of domestic relations. For example, the general easing of divorce law and the constitutional protection afforded abortion brought public policy closer to social reality than it was when terminating a marriage or terminating a pregnancy was either discouraged or virtually proscribed in most of the United States. But the fusion of law and practice in these matters does not stop many Americans from regretting present realities, or from searching for ways to reduce the incidence of separation and divorce, abortion, and such other deviations from traditional family life as unmarried cohabitation, adolescent parenthood, and neglect or abuse of dependents. One manifestation of that search is interest in a national family policy.

In this book, Gilbert Y. Steiner explores the prospects for defining a national family policy. He traces the uses of the family policy idea by several national administrations, and weighs its value as a political theme. Part two of his book turns to hard cases, what Steiner terms "intractable problems" that nonetheless must be confronted by a national family policy. In part three, a discussion of European responses to the family problem focuses on their transferability and relevance to the American political situation. Finally, Steiner sums up the evidence to suggest the futility of an overarching political solution to the complex value questions raised by the range of family troubles.

Gilbert Y. Steiner is a senior fellow in the Brookings Governmental Studies program. For thoughtful review of and critical comment on a draft of the manuscript, he acknowledges particular indebtedness to Martha Derthick, director of Governmental Studies at Brookings, Mary Jo Bane of Harvard University, and Robert Lampman of the University of Wisconsin. Louise Steiner assisted in the interviews of European respondents reported in chapter 6. The text was typed by Donna

Daniels Verdier, the footnotes by David Morse. The index was prepared by Diana Regenthal.

The Brookings Institution is grateful to Carnegie Corporation of New York and to the Robert Sterling Clark Foundation, Inc., for grants to support this work. Neither organization took any part in the direction of the research, nor has any responsibility for the views expressed. The author's views are his alone and should not be ascribed to the trustees, officers, or other staff members of the Brookings Institution.

BRUCE K. MACLAURY
President

October 1980
Washington, D.C.

Contents

PART ONE

Family as a Public Issue

CHAPTER ONE

The Evolution of a Political Theme

FAMILIES are an aspect of human existence that American politicians usually avoid or bury under platitudes rather than address as a public policy problem. Two weeks after the Democratic convention of 1976, however, in a statement during a campaign tour of New Hampshire, Jimmy Carter deplored what he called "the steady erosion and weakening of our families," and promised "to construct an administration that will reverse the trends we have seen toward the breakdown of family in our country."[1] At that same time, the candidate revealed that he had appointed a special adviser "as an immediate step toward developing a pro-family policy." And in his inaugural address in 1977 President Carter returned to the family problem with the assertion that strengthening the family would be an important administration goal.

That exemplary goal appears unique in the litany of presidential objectives. Reviewing its evolution and disposition shows how one social cause achieved listing on the public-issues agenda, illuminates the kind of planning for implementation that may precede or follow adoption of what a president terms an important administration goal, and allows for judgment of the total process by which good intentions for families are to become good deeds for families.

Most of this book deals with the evolution of the family problem as a public—that is, political—issue, with various perceptions of the dimensions of the problem, with the ways politicians and policies have responded to the family problem as an abstraction and in some of its most troublesome manifestations, and with the practical and political limits of responsibility for the way families function. An underlying question throughout the work is whether and how the evolution of family as a political theme contributes to improved policies that help dysfunctional families.

1. "A Statement in New Hampshire, August 3, 1976," *The Presidential Campaign, 1976*, vol. 1: *Jimmy Carter* (Government Printing Office, 1978), pt. 1, p. 462.

Doleful Judgments

Once just taken for granted, families now as often as not are thought of as an endangered species. If families, in Mary Jo Bane's phrase, are here to stay, they are also said to be changing, with consequences approaching the calamitous. "Gone increasingly," says the psychologist Urie Bronfenbrenner, "are family picnics, long Sunday dinners, children and parents working together fixing the house, preparing meals, hiking in the woods, singing and dancing with other families or friends."[2] Though the family problem becomes absurd when reduced to nostalgia for a walk in the woods that most urban families probably never took, it is not a trivial problem to be dismissed flippantly. No massive scholarly documentation is required to appreciate that Americans are basically dedicated to a pattern of social organization characterized by discrete family groups. If, for whatever reason, the strain on such groups leads to the bifurcation of families against their will or to a widespread loss of satisfaction in family life, the social system loses an important stabilizing element.

A strong and stable family is the voluntary association most consistently admired by politicians as well as by philosophers. Fear of its breakdown has "haunted American society," from "early settlers in Plymouth to modern reformers and social scientists."[3] The use of civil authority to strengthen the family can be traced to roots as old and honorable—if not democratic—as the Puritans. They believed that civil government was necessary, Edmund Morgan has written, because after the sin of the first Adam "family governors could not be trusted to maintain the order that God had commanded."[4] In the Puritan era, family incapacity produced the chief problem for the state: to see that family governors enforced the laws of God, which covered the minutest details of personal action. Jimmy Carter's reminder that "the family

2. Urie Bronfenbrenner, "The Calamitous Decline of the American Family," *Washington Post*, January 2, 1977.

3. Tamara K. Hareven, "Family Time and Historical Time," *Daedalus*, vol. 106 (Spring 1977), p. 69. About Plymouth, John Demos has written, "Since the entire community had an interest in the smooth performance of these various [family] tasks, it seemed only natural that there should be a certain amount of direct governmental supervision over the family." *A Little Commonwealth: Family Life in Plymouth Colony* (Oxford University Press, 1970), p. 183.

4. *The Puritan Family* (Harper and Row, Harper Torchbook, 1966), p. 142.

was the first government" and his conclusion that "if we want less government, we must have stronger families, for government steps in by necessity when families have failed"[5] appear to be consonant with Puritan conviction expressed 300 years ago in Massachusetts law.

Modern philosophers of the family commonly emphasize its importance as the basic caring institution that provides the emotional support necessary for adjustment to a crass society. On that count, sociologists and psychologists agree. The family is, according to Christopher Lasch, a "haven in a heartless world,"[6] and, according to Otto Pollak, "a place of intimacy in a world of loose and depersonalized relationships."[7] Family ties, Bane writes, are "persisting manifestations of human needs for stability, continuity, and nonconditional affection."[8] Bronfenbrenner characterizes the family as "the foremost influence in . . . 'character formation,' " but finds it "clear that the American family is disintegrating," and worries about a new "uncaring society."[9]

To be fair, predictions of the total demise of family life are less likely to be heard than are doleful judgments that debilitating ailments sap strength from families. To those making such judgments, cohabitation, divorce, abortion, and family violence all indicate debility. Families are said to be not what they used to be, and public policymakers are being challenged or think they are being challenged to make necessary repairs. Politicians tend to respond to the challenge by exalting the glories of the family that took care of its own and did things together in a spirit of joy—the family few people ever knew in quite this idealized form—and to yearn for its rehabilitation. The vision of the extended family is a case in point. "As part of the family program which we will put together, we will provide the incentives or ability for older Americans to live either with their families as part of extended family or to live in their own homes," Joseph A. Califano, Jr., told a Senate committee that was considering his nomination in 1977 as secretary of the Department of Health, Education, and Welfare (HEW).[10] No such

5. "A Statement in New Hampshire," *The Presidential Campaign*, p. 463.

6. *Haven in a Heartless World: The Family Besieged* (Basic Books, 1977).

7. "The Outlook for the American Family," *Journal of Marriage and the Family*, vol. 29 (February 1967), p. 199.

8. Mary Jo Bane, *Here to Stay: American Families in the Twentieth Century* (Basic Books, 1976), p. 141.

9. Bronfenbrenner, "Calamitous Decline."

10. *Joseph A. Califano, Jr. to be Secretary of Health, Education, and Welfare—Additional Consideration,* Hearing before the Senate Committee on Labor and Public Welfare, 95 Cong. 1 sess. (GPO, 1977), p. 40.

incentives or ability were actually provided—"the family program which we will put together" never having been "put together"—and if they had been, Califano might have found less enthusiasm than he anticipated for the idea of an extended family under one roof. Helping the aged to live independently is one thing; encouraging the aged to live with their children as part of an extended family is swimming against the tide.

Some of those who warn that American families in general are weakening under pressure also assert that increasing numbers of people—especially children—are harmed by the historic disposition to insulate family matters from public policy. The obvious prescription is a body of public policy to strengthen families. All who care about children, the Carnegie Council on Children concluded in a report it subtitled "The American Family under Pressure," must take on "a new set of responsibilities": to concern themselves with "the public facts of the society that impinge on . . . families." According to the council, responsible parents must become public advocates for children's interests, and that cause must be interpreted broadly. What it described as a broad, integrated, explicit family policy became the council's central goal, and failure to support it was likened to deferring a heavy tax to the next generation.[11] Yet this gloomy view of the family world is not reflected in any of three annual surveys of satisfaction with family life that were undertaken independently of the Carnegie Council but were coincident with its working life. Rather than massive discontent, 94 percent of those sampled in 1975 by the National Opinion Research Center reported either a very great deal (44.1 percent), a great deal (32.9 percent), quite a bit (10.5 percent), or a fair amount (6.6 percent), of satisfaction. Less than 2 percent answered "none."[12] Responses scarcely varied from those reported for 1973 or 1974.

Believing changes in traditional patterns of family relationships to be a cause of widespread anxiety and a challenge to government, Jimmy Carter introduced a family-strengthening theme during his presidential campaign in 1976, and periodically replayed it in subsequent years. For example, Carter told Congress in 1979, "Our government must never impede nor work against the American family, but

11. Kenneth Keniston and The Carnegie Council on Children, *All Our Children: The American Family under Pressure* (Harcourt Brace Jovanovich, 1977), pp. 214, 216.

12. U.S. Department of Commerce, Office of Federal Statistical Policy and Standards, *Social Indicators, 1976* (GPO, 1977), p. 68.

rather we must design programs and policies that support families and ensure that future generations of American families will thrive and prosper."[13] The hortatory language may conceal an impractical objective. Political history, after all, discloses proposals to impede or work against the family to be no more common than proposals to impede or work against the Constitution. As for designing programs and policies that support families now and into the future, caution is appropriate. Like the proverbial free lunch, there is no such thing as free support for families now or free insurance of families' future growth and prosperity.

The failure of the Carter administration to put together the promised family program is matched by the virtual absence of specific family-strengthening proposals by most politicians. Since politicians express anxiety about the state of the family, the shortage of proposals is puzzling. One explanation may be that whereas only a handful of politicians may know of Nathan Glazer's observation that social programs that come about in consequence of a weakening in social structure invariably weaken the social structure even further, a good many others share the belief. Of course, an alternative explanation for the absence of a family policy agenda could lie in the widespread acceptance of deviations from the traditional model of family. Though many deplore the deviations, many others applaud them, making it foolhardy for a politician to try to manipulate things toward a return to the status quo ante. For example, it is now understood that cohabitation is common and that marriage may not last for a lifetime, or even a decade—6.5 years is the median duration of marriages ending in divorce. One might prefer that things were not so, but there is no evidence that having them so presents a clear and present danger to the future of democratic society. Forty-five percent of the couples divorcing in 1977 reported that no children under eighteen were involved in the divorce.[14] If a coherent family policy includes programs to forestall marital dissolution, that 45 percent might reasonably wish to be excluded. Whatever the explanation for the reticence to propose and to legislate, the result is continued uncertainty over whether family

13. "The Supplemental State of the Union—Message From the President of the United States," *Congressional Record*, daily edition (January 25, 1979), p. H302.

14. U.S. Department of Health, Education, and Welfare, National Center for Health Statistics, *Final Divorce Statistics, 1977*, Vital Statistics Report, vol. 28, no. 2, DHEW (PHS) 79-1120 (HEW, 1979), p. 3.

policy should be a policy that accepts family relations as they are and eliminates legal or social barriers to a variety of family life-styles, or should be a policy that posits a goal—for example, a permanent and self-sufficient family relationship for every American—and programs to implement the goal.

Family Dysfunction

The design of policies that can positively affect the quality of family life challenges the inventive capacity of any government. Problems of design present only the first difficulty. In a libertarian democracy that prizes privacy and rejects the primacy of the state, further constraints stem from constitutional limits to permissible government action. In addition, good inventions that are within constitutional boundaries may pose insuperable difficulties of delivery.

To begin with, the intangible sentiments that are the foundation of strong family relations can neither be legislated nor set forth in executive order or court decree. Government has no mechanism to enforce love, affection, and concern between husband and wife, between parent and child, or between one sibling and another. Because intangibles are so important to family relationships, even identifying the characteristics of strong families and of failing families poses problems. No one knows, for example, how many persons who live together in family groups, sharing resources and chores, nursing one another as necessary, and celebrating or commiserating with one another as the occasion requires, do so for practical reasons rather than out of deep emotional attachment. Nor does anyone know how many seemingly stable families are really composed of incompatible parents, sustaining family life temporarily "for the sake of the children." If such families could be identified, it is a safe bet that one observer would characterize them as strong, since they hold together, and another would characterize them as failing.

Whatever the route to the conclusion—statistical data and scholarly analysis, personal experience and observation, or reports in the media and from opinion leaders—a decision to countenance family policy implies a belief that a valuable institution is in jeopardy, that the family model is a good one, and that it needs more shoring up than private agencies can manage. Were it not believed that the model is a good one, government could be indifferent to its deterioration. Were families not believed to be in jeopardy, government would be expected to respect the privacy of these voluntary associations through which people share emotional, physical, and economic strengths and weaknesses and re-create themselves.

The path from private institution to public responsibility can readily be traced. Each family remains an essentially private institution so long as the various needs of family members are met by the working of the idiosyncratic and volatile formula that defines family relationships. When the needs of individual members cannot be satisfied by changes in the formula, the family becomes dysfunctional. When enough families become dysfunctional, public or quasi-public support systems try to take up the slack, that is, meet unfulfilled economic, physical, or emotional needs.

Family policy has to do with mechanisms for identifying family dysfunction, and with the organization of responsibility in public support systems: decisions about when public programs will take up the slack and the conditions under which they will do so. In the ideal world there would be no slack to take up—every child would be planned and wanted, would be physically and emotionally healthy, and would live with economically self-sufficient parents who maintained affectionate, interdependent relationships between themselves and with their child or children—and there would be no need for family policy. In the real world dysfunctional families are not uncommon and are perhaps inevitable. Indeed, the Carnegie Council on Children has characterized the "self-sufficient, protected, and protective family" as a myth. As policies to help dysfunctional families have come to command more money and more services, it seems sensible to ask not only how these policies are working but also whether policy should be designed to forestall family dysfunction rather than only to mitigate its consequences after the fact.

Dual objections, one philosophical and one practical, are quickly raised to the idea of family policy designed to forestall dysfunction. The philosophical objection holds that family is a last bastion of privacy in an already overregulated and overorganized society and should not be the object of policy that would surely be intrusive but might not be useful. The practical objection is that the diversity of family forms and styles is simply too great to be encompassed by a national policy, that what is dysfunctional in one family may be quite tolerable in another.

Since both objections are compelling, the burden is on proponents to make the case for family policy that is preventive in intent.

On this subject politicians, sensing trouble, are hard to persuade. The politician who will jeopardize his or her election or reelection prospects by subjecting family relations to public intervention wants to be able to identify the specific goal and to be able to explain why it is an appropriate one. Programs that even imply the idea of a "model family" are unacceptable to a society devoted to maintaining numerous cultural and religious heritages, each carrying its own view of how a family should function.

In the bad old days dysfunctional families were a problem for voluntary charity or local government. A pregnant adolescent, for example, might be sheltered in a Florence Crittenton home until delivered of a child for whom adoptive parents had been arranged. The unfortunate adolescent could be reported to be visiting grandparents on the farm. Alternatively, a pregnant adolescent of the lower class, in a family without appearances to keep up, waited out her time at home, then added her child to the household for collective care. In either case, congressmen and cabinet officers were not expected to worry about it.

Dysfunction stemming from economic weakness was formally recognized as a national problem only in 1935, when the Social Security Act made provision for money payments to children deprived of parental support because of death, continued absence from the home, or incapacity of a parent. That same act recognized dysfunction stemming from emotional weakness in authorizing limited services to some children—homeless, dependent, and neglected—deprived of intimate ties to their biological parents. For twenty-five years afterward neither the money side of public assistance nor child welfare services got more than cursory attention. For an even longer time no federal government response whatever developed to such other manifestations of family dysfunction as abusive behavior, incest, delinquency, adolescent pregnancy, and runaway youth. Not all these unpleasant matters lend themselves to a case count, but as adolescent pregnancies, runaways, divorces, cohabiting couples, and abortions each approached or passed the million a year mark, increasing numbers of families may have come to sense it could happen to them.

Any such sense would have been reinforced by the gush of commentaries on the state of the family that began to appear in the mid-1970s. An example is the sweeping judgment rendered by a Columbia

University psychiatrist in August 1976: "Drug abuse, alcohol abuse, minor and violent crimes are increasing problems not just in poor black families, but in affluent white families, not just in broken families, but in seemingly intact families, not just when mothers work, but also when they stay home. The American family is being undermined by the divisive forces at work in society."[15] If no data were offered to support the judgment, it still sounded right. Family dysfunction became a public issue less because of actual evidence of massive numbers of new cases than because of a general uneasiness about family stability with which numerous families could empathize.

Even for those who are persuaded that families are more troubled than they used to be, what government might do to help them and how it will do it are political questions of considerable complexity. One problem is that as a target of public policy, family takes on the characteristics of a kaleidoscope. Its most common form is the nuclear grouping of father, mother, and minor children within a single household, but it is also more and it is less and it can be none of these and it is different at different times. In both 1977 and 1978 the Bureau of Labor Statistics reported that the so-called typical American family of working father, homemaker mother, and two minor children accounted for only 7 percent of husband-wife families.[16] Yet, as the report's compilers point out informally, at some time in their histories most families do take on that configuration. If public policy is addressed to the 7 percent, it has immediate effect on only that small fraction of families, but—like high-school enrollment, which involves a comparable percentage of the population at any moment—it deals with a period through which most Americans have or will have passed.

Family forms change not only as an inevitable consequence of the passage of time but also as a consequence of free choice. The two-parent nuclear grouping may include either a homemaker mother or a working mother; the trend is clearly toward the latter, although there are still more of the former. Variations on the basic nuclear theme are extensive. Single-parent households resulting from death, desertion, separation, divorce, unwed motherhood, and single-person adoption

15. Herbert Hendin, "The Ties Don't Bind," *New York Times*, August 26, 1976.

16. U.S. Department of Labor, Bureau of Labor Statistics, *Employment in Perspective: Working Women*, Report 531 (April 1978), p. 1. Beverly L. Johnson and Howard Hayghe, "Labor Force Participation of Married Women, March 1976," *Monthly Labor Review*, vol. 100 (June 1977), p. 34. The 7 percent figure would obviously be even smaller if the base were all families rather than husband-wife families only.

obviously constitute a family. So do households in which a child or children live with a grandparent or some relative other than parent or parents. And although a marital relationship or the presence of a child is usually thought of as a sine qua non of family, many cohabiting couples—including some homosexual ones—consider themselves to be as much a family as a legally married, childless couple. An early lesson learned by politicians who recently took on the issue as a policy problem was that policy would have to recognize and accept the varieties of families and of patterns of behavior within families, that there could be a useful conference or a bureau on *families*, but not on *the family*.

Big numbers help explain the interest in families. Problems of families become public problems when there is fresh thinking about old issues as in foster care or when the presumably deviant population can actually be counted in the millions. In some other areas like family violence, where data are soft, estimates that range into the millions and terms like "epidemic proportions" are accepted as surrogates for hard numbers.

Another explanation of the national interest in families is the identification in middle-class families of behavior once associated only with the welfare class. For example, among the latter, significant numbers of deserting fathers and unmarried mothers were long taken as evidence of unstable family patterns. High rates of divorce—since 1975 the annual divorce rate has been exactly half the marriage rate—and of abortions now offer evidence of a comparable instability in middle-class family patterns. Again, though data on family violence are fragmentary, disorderly, and even suspect in some respects, what there are suggest that no socioeconomic class or ethnic group may be ignored. "Studies of the incidence of domestic violence," the Senate Committee on Human Resources reported to the Senate in 1978, "have found that it permeates all socio-economic levels."[17] Growth in the number of working mothers of young children has created a child care problem by no means limited to the poor. Although society may be disposed to accept marital dissolution and out-of-wedlock births as part of the regular order of things, the fathers involved do not tend to make child support payments part of their regular order, even when they can afford to do so.

17. *Congressional Record*, daily edition (August 1, 1978), p. S12248.

It develops, in short, that loving, mutually supportive, traditional, long-lasting family relationships are no more certain outside the welfare population than within it. Politicians willing to address families as a policy issue come to understand that the political stakes are high because the affected population is not isolated by geography, class, or race.

Family Policy as a National Issue

Walter Mondale, when senator from Minnesota, was among the first American politicians to pick up the theme of government responsibility for the family as an institution. If there is no caring family mechanism, the argument goes, human problems proliferate. "I have worked on practically all the human problems," Mondale said in 1973, "—the hunger route, the Indian route, the migratory labor route, the equality of education route, and the housing route; all of them—and increasingly reached a conclusion that is not very profound. It all begins with the family. That is the key institution in American life. If it breaks down, if it is unable to do what society has assumed it will do, then all of these other problems develop. They are symptoms I think of more fundamental family breakdown."[18]

Mondale provoked little public or political interest in his discovery of the family problem, partly because the Senate Subcommittee on Children and Youth, then his forum, was no bully pulpit, and partly because relating government action to family stability had never been in style in America. Neither his early sponsorship of child development legislation nor his identification of the family as the key institution in American life benefited Mondale's short campaign for the presidential nomination. In fact, Mondale's known association with issues of family and children's policy even appears to have been an impediment to his selection as vice-presidential nominee in 1976. Explaining how he selected a running mate, Jimmy Carter made it clear then that Mondale's record of support for day-care centers (a subject that Carter said had earlier involved him with Mondale "in a nonpersonal way"), his

18. *American Families: Trends and Pressures, 1973,* Hearings before the Subcommittee on Children and Youth of the Senate Labor and Public Welfare Committee, 93 Cong. 1 sess. (GPO, 1974), p. 123.

chairmanship of the Subcommittee on Children and Youth, and his airing of trends and pressures on the American family were not regarded as important strengths:

Q. If somebody said the name Mondale to you at the time this [selection] process started, what thoughts and what image would have flashed in your mind?

Carter. Let me just tell you two or three concerns that I had at the beginning that have been alleviated and I think long ago. I had the impression that Senator Mondale was primarily concerned with peripheral issues in the federal government.

The more I got into his voting record, his committee assignments, his involvement, congressional deliberation, the more I found that was not true. I did not, for instance, know that he was on the Finance Committee or the Budget Committee. And when I began to talk to the leaders of the Senate, that is where they felt that his contributions had been greatest.[19]

Whether or not it fell under the heading of "peripheral issues," interest in family policy in the United States clearly escalated when Carter—first as Democratic nominee, then as president—chose to express concern about a perceived erosion and weakening of families. "There can be no more urgent priority for the next administration," Carter said three months before his election, "than to see that every decision our government makes is designed to honor and support and strengthen the American family. . . . We need a government that thinks about the American family and cares about the American family and makes its every decision with the intent of strengthening the family."[20] Two months later, Carter's approach seemed no less aggressive: "I believe that government ought to do everything it can to strengthen the American family because weak families mean more government."[21]

A stated interest in using government to strengthen families represented a new departure for an American president. Throughout the twentieth century the dominant ethic discouraged civil intervention in family affairs. Without legal question or even expressions of moral anxiety, recent generations of political leaders accepted interpretations of a constitutional system that left domestic relations, including most aspects of child rearing, as a concern of the individual states or as beyond the concern of any government.

19. *The Presidential Campaign, 1976*, vol. 1, pt. 1, p. 345.
20. "A Statement in New Hampshire," ibid., pp. 463, 464.
21. Speech at New York Liberal party dinner, October 14, 1976, in ibid., pt. 2, p. 1012.

Nonrecognition of national government responsibility for family stability had survived even the New Deal's incursion into social policy. Divorce, desertion, illegitimacy, and abortion were no competition for unemployment and old-age dependency. Attacks on the last two problems through social insurance and other New Deal techniques no doubt had a trickle-down effect on the family, but the authors of the program were not thinking "family stability." They were thinking "protection of the individual" against dependency and distress.[22] One consequence was the failure to make special provision for family dependency—as against individual worker dependency—in unemployment insurance; another was the failure to provide assistance to dependent, intact families. Later, Presidents Kennedy, Johnson, and Nixon did address government's role in strengthening poor families, and Johnson its role in strengthening black families, but only Carter imposed no comparable limiting condition of poverty or race. Because Carter was the first president to address the family cause generally, without class or race qualifiers, the Carter administration could define the issue, organize on its behalf, and measure results according to its own standards.

In the mid-1960s Daniel Patrick Moynihan called attention to the important differences between and the different consequences of policy that focuses on the individual and policy concerned with the family. "American social policy until now has been directed toward the individual," Moynihan wrote. "Thus, our employment statistics count as equally unemployed a father of nine children, a housewife coming back into the labor market in her forties, and a teen-ager looking for a part-time job after school." Noting that the pattern is almost uniquely American, Moynihan suggested that "it has something to do with the extraordinarily diverse pattern of family systems in the United States, which results from the no less extraordinary pattern of immigration." Immigrants brought so wide a variety of family structure that "it was impossible to prescribe family programs that would meet the needs or desires of all groups." But now, Moynihan concluded, the time had

22. "The field of study to which the committee should devote its major attention is that of the protection of the individual against dependency and distress." "Preliminary Outline of the Work of the Staff," approved by the Committee on Economic Security, August 13, 1934. The typescript is quoted by its author, Edwin E. Witte, executive director of the committee and principal author of the Social Security Act of 1935, in *The Development of the Social Security Act* (University of Wisconsin Press, 1963), p. 21.

come to overcome a great shortcoming of the past, and to proceed to a national family policy:

A national family policy need only declare that it is the policy of the American government to promote the stability and well-being of the American family; that the social programs of the Federal government will be formulated and administered with this object in mind; and finally that the President, or some person designated by him, perhaps the Secretary of Health, Education and Welfare, will report to the Congress on the condition of the American family in all its many facets—not of *the* American family, for there is as yet no such thing, but rather of the great range of American families in terms of regions, national origins and economic status.[23]

Earlier, Moynihan (together with Richard N. Goodwin) had drafted an important speech for President Johnson that drew on the findings and the argument of a report Moynihan had prepared as assistant secretary of labor for policy planning and research. That report proclaimed the Negro family to be "in the deepest trouble" and referred to its weakness as a "tangle of pathology."[24] Johnson's Howard University speech—planned as a major event for civil rights progress in America—was especially designed to announce the president's intention to convene a White House conference with the theme and title "To Fulfill These Rights." In building up to the conference announcement, however, Johnson adopted Moynihan's position about the central importance of family stability:

The family is the cornerstone of our society. More than any other force it shapes the attitudes, the hopes, the ambitions, and the values of the child. When the family collapses it is the children that are usually damaged. When it happens on a massive scale the community itself is crippled.

So, unless we work to strengthen the family, to create conditions under which most parents will stay together—all the rest: schools and playgrounds, public assistance and private concern, will never be enough to cut completely the circle of despair and deprivation.[25]

Propounded within the context of a civil rights initiative, suggestions for strengthening the family as a precondition for the success of accompanying social policy submissions implied a collective abnormality

23. "A Family Policy for the Nation," *America*, September 18, 1965; reprinted in Lee Rainwater and William L. Yancey, *The Moynihan Report and the Politics of Controversy* (MIT Press, 1967), pp. 387, 393.

24. U.S. Department of Labor, Office of Policy Planning and Research, *The Negro Family: The Case for National Action* (GPO, 1965), p. 29.

25. Lyndon B. Johnson, "Remarks of the President at Howard University, June 4, 1965," in Rainwater and Yancey, *The Moynihan Report*, p. 130.

among black families—or so the package was read by some black activists and some black intellectuals. Subtitled "The Case for National Action," the Moynihan report provoked the question "What kind of action?" If strengthening the family meant national action to preclude continued growth of matriarchal black families, the costs to pride and race consciousness would exceed the benefits even of economic and education programs. The Moynihan report–Howard University speech became a *cause célèbre* of the Great Society. Moynihan, the White House conference as originally conceived, and further discussion of family policy retreated or were banished from highest level consideration.

The first and last—Moynihan and family policy—rose again after a decent interval. (In the interval Moynihan wrote in his foreword to a new edition of Alva Myrdal's *Nation and Family*: "The United States is paying a great price for having failed, or refused, to accept the subject of family as a legitimate object of social policy."[26]) The momentum of civil rights progress was unaffected by the evaporation of the grand-scale conference first planned and the substitution of a scaled-down planning conference. For those who stayed and for those who would come back, however, the lesson was that family policy is a complex political question, unexplored and therefore attractive to a leader in search of new issues but susceptible to interpretation as a slur on some families and repugnant if applied selectively.

Family policy now connotes different things to liberals and to conservatives. Family policy, in liberal circles, is understood to mean economic assistance and social services that will put a floor under family income and lead the way to self-sufficiency. There is a tendency for conservatives to read a different meaning into national programs directed to the family, a reading that equates family policy with acceptance of indolence, promiscuity, easy abortion, casual attitudes toward marriage and divorce, maternal indifference to child-rearing responsibilities. If family policy means accepting these behavior patterns, indeed facilitating them by minimizing resulting economic hardship and social stigma, conservatives want none of it. For them, family policy appears to involve the use of national resources to legitimize behavior not consistent with behavior of the typical American family. Right-minded national policy should reinforce traditional American patterns, not abide deviations that smack of irresponsibility.

26. MIT Press, 1968, p. xvi.

On the other side of the ideological divide, many liberals view proposals for national government aid and services to the family as a way to redress old wrongs to blacks, to the poor, and to women. These liberal proponents are persuaded that federal support is necessary to relieve the economic and social pressures that discourage family stability. To the contrary, opponents reply, measures that inject federal dollars into family services are more likely to invite family instability than the reverse. Family policy is a theme in need of definition.

CHAPTER TWO

A Theme in Search of a Definition

STIMULATED by the apparent interest of a president, a vice-president, and a secretary of health, education, and welfare, the idea of "family" as a social policy focus so titillated academics, philanthropic foundations, and policy research groups as well as politicians that a kind of family policy industry rapidly developed, complete with first-ever conferences, newly created study centers, retitled federal agencies, redesigned old ideas to give them a family cast, and investment of private foundation resources. "'Family' has become the new buzz word," Nancy Amidei wrote in 1977, shortly before her appointment as HEW deputy assistant secretary for legislation. "Everybody seems to be getting on the 'family' bandwagon."[1] But though the bandwagon is fashionable and crowded, its destination remains uncertain.

Family or Families: An Ambiguous Policy Objective

"As an area of recognized and reasonably coherent social policy," Senator Daniel Patrick Moynihan said in 1977, much as Professor Daniel Patrick Moynihan had said in 1967, "family policy eludes us."[2] An important distinction is implicit in the observation. Family policy does not necessarily elude us; family policy as an area of recognized and coherent social policy does. The former is discernible, only the latter is really elusive.

1. "The Role of the (Federal) Community," in *Child Abuse and Neglect: Issues on Innovation and Implementation*, Proceedings of the Second Annual National Conference on Child Abuse and Neglect, April 17–20, 1977, DHEW (OHDS) 78-30147 (HEW, 1977), vol. 1, p. 314.

2. *Public Assistance Amendments of 1977*, Hearings before the Subcommittee on Public Assistance of the Senate Committee on Finance, 95 Cong. 1 sess. (Government Printing Office, 1977), p. 55. Compare Moynihan's foreword in Alva Myrdal, *Nation and Family* (MIT Press, 1968), pp. v–xvii.

19

Even though some family-related issues, as Senator Mark Hatfield has said of abortion, are marked by such intensity and divisiveness as to invite abstention on the part of the politician, abstention has become increasingly difficult. Public policies are inevitable in response to pressure from a growing number of people who believe themselves or the nation disadvantaged by government neutrality in family matters. Thus, in the 1970s, Washington policymakers decided whether the national government provides or withholds education and materials for family planning, prohibits or pays for abortions, furnishes or turns aside demands for child care facilities and services, sustains poor families adequately or niggardly, discriminates for tax purposes in favor of or against marriage, enforces or shrugs off child support obligations, ignores or treats abused and abusive spouses and parents, accepts or rejects unconventional patterns of family composition, encourages or remains indifferent to permanent placement of foster children. Policies in each of these areas may seem fainthearted, trial efforts that do too much or too little. They are often ambiguous if not contradictory—but they do constitute family policy.

So understood, family policy avoids judgments about "good" families and "bad" families. Whether black families have been stronger or weaker than other families, whether the interests of children and the interests of working mothers are compatible, whether abortion is morally defensible or indefensible are questions that family policy need not answer. Family policy can address the legitimate concerns of those groups organized on behalf of out-of-home child care and the legitimate concerns of those groups that shy away from further government action in connection with child care. All things to all people, family policy offers a way to keep diverse legitimate interests within the same political camp.

By contrast, recognized and reasonably coherent family policy makes choices. It became a public issue in the mid-seventies because Jimmy Carter took it up as a surrogate for one cause and as a spin-off from another—surrogate for the child development, child care movement for which Walter Mondale had served as political godfather and spin-off from the remains of the various approaches to social policy for black families that politicians had anguished over since Moynihan's analysis of the black family. Adverse reactions to those earlier approaches discouraged sponsors from renewing them but did not diminish the conviction of supporters that the social problem involved

demanded governmental action. Cast in broad terms, that social problem is the problem of children in need—in need of a father, of financial
assistance, of care and supervision, of cognitive development, of moral
and ethical guidance, or of a combination of these advantages. All of
them—and others—will be provided under the happiest circumstances
in the intact, traditional, self-sustaining family that appears to have
been Carter's ideal image, as it appears earlier to have been Moynihan's.

Widespread condemnation of abortion, divorce, unmarried motherhood, and adolescent sexual activity, together with routine acceptance of women as homemakers, describe the recognized and
reasonably coherent practice of American family life until the beginning
of the 1970s. Moynihan's report, making the case for national action on
behalf of black families, serves as the most explicit proposal for national
action to turn recognized and reasonably coherent practice into policy.
But the report's emphasis on black families as deviants from the norm
made it a political liability. Similarly, to have pursued Carter's initial
interest in recognized and reasonably coherent social policy to sustain
and strengthen "the American family" would only have invited a
replay of the great uproar that resulted from Moynihan's characterization of deviants from "the family" model as caught in a "tangle of
pathology." Blacks, feminists, and social liberals, at least, see strong
families as possible in forms other than the stereotypical American
family. Responding to these important elements of his political constituency, Carter fused his model into theirs, blurring the differences
between a reasonably coherent family policy and family policy—differences between policies to restore a particular style of family and
policies to assist various styles of families.

As the presidential interest in family became widely publicized, and
the purposes to be served by policy became ambiguous, scholars and
politicians recast a plethora of old social policy questions—child development, social services, public welfare—as issues of family policy.
For example, where children's cognitive processes or deserted mothers
might have been focal points earlier, the whole family now became the
subject of interest. Commissions and committees that were organized
early in the 1970s to think about children or social services reported
later in the decade in terms of families and family policy. Some of these
groups followed the data as they read the data; others simply followed
fashion.

Illustrations of the shift in emphasis and attitudes abound. Consider the comment made in 1971 to a congressional subcommittee by the psychiatrist who chaired the Joint Commission on Mental Health of Children: "There is serious thinking among some of the future-oriented child development research people that maybe we can't trust the family alone to prepare young children for this new kind of world which is emerging."[3] Then consider the comment made in 1978 to the same subcommittee by the psychologist who chaired the later Carnegie Council on Children: "One of our central recommendations is that parents need to regain control over the forces and institutions with which they share the bringing up of their children, and that programs and institutions must have a built-in accountability to parents."[4] The different titles given to comparable legislative proposals considered by the subcommittee over the years also reflect the shift to a family strategy. For example, bills titled "Comprehensive Child Development" in 1971 and 1972 became in 1974 and later "Child and Family Services."

Two prestigious study groups, the Carnegie Council on Children and the National Research Council's Advisory Committee on Child Development, both years late in reporting, finally did report as President Carter began to play the family theme.[5] Both study groups recognized that child development was too weak an issue to serve as a

3. *Comprehensive Child Development Act of 1971*, Joint Hearings before the Subcommittee on Employment, Manpower, and Poverty and the Subcommittee on Children and Youth of the Senate Committee on Labor and Public Welfare, 92 Cong. 1 sess. (GPO, 1971), p. 184. Compare the statement by Nicholas Hobbs, in *The Futures of Children: Report of the Project on Classification of Exceptional Children* (San Francisco: Jossey-Bass, 1975), p. 261: "The family in America is in deep trouble. It may or may not prove adequate to its child-rearing responsibilities. If it is to survive as the basic structural unit of our society, the family must be strengthened or replaced by some new structural unit fully adequate to its child-rearing responsibilities."

4. *White House Conference on Families, 1978*, Joint Hearings before the Subcommittee on Child and Human Development [formerly Children and Youth] of the Senate Human Resources Committee [formerly Labor and Public Welfare] and the Subcommittee on Select Education of the House Committee on Education and Labor, 95 Cong. 2 sess. (GPO, 1978), p. 329.

5. In distributing the National Research Council report, the director of the Office of Child Development observed that "several years were required by a distinguished and balanced group of scholars to do justice to the inherent complexity and controversy of the task." Letter from John Meier to the author, December 16, 1976. In fact, discord within the committee and between committee and staff effectively ended committee deliberations three years before a new National Research Council administrator drafted a lowest common denominator report as a matter of institutional honor.

focal point for national policy on behalf of children, and though neither group was created to deal with family policy, each reached out to include "family" on the title page of its report and in its discussion. None of the four tasks given the National Research Council's Advisory Committee in 1971 mentioned the word *family*. Yet the committee's 1976 report barely touched on the child development questions of 1971. Its core recommendation for comprehensive policy sounded less like the Society for Research on Child Development and more like the National Conference on Social Welfare:

> The Committee recommends that the federal government take the lead in developing a comprehensive national policy for children and families, the essential components of which include: (a) employment, tax, and cash benefit policies that assure each child's family an adequate income, (b) a broad and carefully integrated system of support services for families and children, and (c) planning and coordination mechanisms to ensure adequate coverage and access of families to the full range of available services.[6]

The just-as-blue-ribbon Carnegie Council on Children, created in 1972, implied the prior existence of some, but not enough, family policy in its 1977 report recommending that "the nation develop a family policy as comprehensive as its defense policy." The council's enumeration of components that would constitute a "broad, integrated, explicit family policy"[7] included jobs and income for the working poor as well as income for a parent choosing to provide full-time care of a child under six; health programs that emphasize prevention and primary care of children; family services—conveniently located—to help all those who need them in the prevention or alleviation of family crisis; and own-family or substitute-family care of children in preference to institutional care.

Among others aboard the family bandwagon, there is an understandable difference of opinion about whether or not family policy already exists. Sheila Kamerman and Alfred J. Kahn, indefatigable cross-cultural surveyors of family-related programs, say of the United States: "The absence of coherent, comprehensive, explicit, intensive federal policy does not signify that there is absolutely no family policy in the U.S. True, there is no comprehensive, overall national policy,

6. National Research Council Advisory Committee on Child Development, *Toward a National Policy for Children and Families* (Washington, D.C.: National Academy of Sciences, 1976), pp. 4–5.

7. Kenneth Keniston and The Carnegie Council on Children, *All Our Children: The American Family under Pressure* (Harcourt Brace Jovanovich, 1977), pp. 76, 216–20.

clearly. Yet there are many social policies relating to family concerns and . . . they are often recognized and dealt with as such."[8] These academic observers found a body of policies, "some implicit and some explicit, policies which address the family and would appear to affect its status, role, and well-being."[9]

Other proponents of family policy equate the absence of "strong" or "comprehensive" or "coherent" family policy with the absence of family policy deserving the name. In 1970 the United States Catholic Conference took the position that there had been no family policy and there had been bad family policy. The Reverend James T. McHugh said to a House subcommittee: "The United States is long overdue in establishing a family policy for the Nation. Such a family policy must be comprehensive, positive, supportive of family life. . . . In the absence of such a family policy, family planning, and birth control programs are a limited and negative approach to family life."[10] In 1976 Jimmy Carter also had it both ways, claiming that there had been no family policy and that there had been bad family policy: "It is clear that the national government should have a strong pro-family policy, but the fact is that our government has no family policy, and that is the same thing as an anti-family policy. Because of confusion or insensitivity, our government's policies have often actually weakened our families, or even destroyed them."[11]

Unless income support, food relief, health programs, family planning services, and home care of children do not constitute family policy, Carter was clearly wrong in concluding that the government had no family policy. Moreover, members of the recent advisory councils who called for comprehensive policy can now declare victory. Many if not most of the fundamental elements of what the latter describe as a comprehensive policy are in place, and whether the policy is or is not explicitly labeled comprehensive family policy is more a cosmetic than a substantive matter. Financing may not be at a level proponents consider adequate, but it is axiomatic that in social pro-

---

8. Sheila B. Kamerman and Alfred J. Kahn, eds., *Family Policy: Government and Families in Fourteen Countries* (Columbia University Press, 1978), pp. 431–32.

9. Ibid., p. 475.

10. *Family Planning Services*, Hearing before the Subcommittee on Public Health and Welfare of the House Interstate and Foreign Commerce Committee, 91 Cong. 2 sess. (GPO, 1970), p. 357.

11. "A Statement in New Hampshire, August 3, 1976," *The Presidential Campaign, 1976*, vol. 1: *Jimmy Carter* (GPO, 1978), pt. 1, p. 463.

grams—as in national defense—financing is never at a level proponents consider adequate and is always at a level critics consider wasteful. Recognition of governmental responsibility for income support, health programs, and the like is not in dispute. The apparent objective of the proponents of comprehensive family policy is not a wholly new master plan in response to old questions, but a greater effort along accepted lines.

A September 1976 "Preliminary Report" by Joseph A. Califano, Jr., then Carter's special adviser, concluded that the most severe threat to family life stems from unemployment and lack of an adequate income. Three key steps, he said, should be taken promptly: (1) give parents the job opportunities they seek; (2) restore trust and confidence in families as a premise of federal programs; and (3) increase understanding of the ways in which public policies affect families.[12] Whether those steps were meant to flesh out a "strong pro-family" policy is not clear, since the package answered no questions about day care, about child support responsibility, about abortion and adolescent pregnancy, about health services for children, about neglect, or even about poor families without an employable adult member.

In the course of the presidential campaign, the candidate continued to speak out on the family unit and also to address the abortion issue. As for the family unit, Carter's collection of campaign promises included (1) securing welfare law provisions to encourage families to stay together; (2) requiring deserting fathers to support their children; (3) instituting transfer policies in the armed forces that would consider impact on families; (4) ending tax laws that discriminate against families; (5) retaining tax exemptions for dependent children; (6) supporting federally funded day care for working mothers; (7) discouraging building of freeways that displace families; (8) instituting a "family impact statement"; and (9) insuring that government actions be sensitive to the needs of families.[13] As for abortion, Carter promised government efforts and personal efforts—through moral suasion—to minimize abortion, opposed the use of federal money for abortion, and recognized that the president must comply with court decisions on the use

12. Joseph A. Califano, Jr., "American Families: Trends, Pressures and Recommendations: A Preliminary Report to Governor Jimmy Carter," in *White House Conference on Families, 1978*, Joint Hearings, pp. 285–99.

13. *New York Times*, March 19, 1977. The nine items constitute section C.5.a. of the compilation of Carter campaign promises.

of medicaid funds for abortions. He also stated a preference for a legislative approach that would minimize abortion and feature better family planning, adoption procedures, and contraceptives for those who believe in their use. Gathered together, the Carter campaign promises dealing with the family unit and abortion could make a family program. Apparently realizing that it was a program that would be challenged by many liberals, administration leaders did not formally adopt these promises as their national family policy.

A collection of ideas and initiatives that would define a coherent pro-family policy eludes formulation because the meaning of *pro-family* cannot be agreed upon. Within the bureaucracy, the search for agreement has been haphazard, leaderless, inept. "It is enormously difficult to translate 'pro-family' from slogan into program," Mary Jo Bane wrote in a 1977 paper prepared under HEW contract.[14] When an assistant secretary for planning twice proposed bringing Bane into the administration to work on that translation, he was twice rebuffed—on affirmative action grounds. "They were looking then for blacks, not women," he explains. As for the Administration for Children, Youth, and Families—no different an agency from when it was the Office of Child Development or just the Children's Bureau—its principal mandate is to distribute Head Start and child abuse program grants, not to become creative.

After six months in office Secretary Califano summarized administration family policy as welfare reform, an improved child health assessment program for medicaid-eligible children, and adoption–foster care improvements, all in all a desirable if less than novel approach.[15] Judged technically impractical, efforts to eliminate the income tax advantage enjoyed by some cohabiting couples over otherwise comparably situated married couples were abandoned. A federal child-care initiative for working mothers was not part of the program. The president and his HEW secretary—both firm opponents of abortion—went to war with the HEW bureaucracy on medicaid-financed abortion.

The litany of HEW in-house documents produced after January 1977

14. "Discussion Paper: HEW Policy Toward Children, Youth, and Families," prepared under order #SA-8139-77 for Office of the Assistant Secretary for Planning and Evaluation, p. 44.

15. Letter, Joseph A. Califano, Jr., to Vice-President Walter Mondale, July 25, 1977. *Congressional Record*, daily edition (July 26, 1977), p. S12822.

demonstrates that it is harder for those involved to know what should go into family policy than it is to understand why family policy became an appealing idea. Among readily available public documents alone, there has been a paper by the HEW Family Impact Task Group; a discussion paper for the Office of Assistant Secretary for Planning and Evaluation on HEW policy toward children, youth, and families; a decision memorandum on adolescent pregnancy and related issues; a paper on alternatives to abortion; and several speeches by the assistant secretary for human development services giving renewed assurances—without substantive details—of the administration's interest in families.

HEW's papers all provide evidence that defining a family policy turned out to be more trouble than the Carter administration ever anticipated. Indeed, as early as February 1978 the secretary of HEW began to sound like a man anxious to play down the whole question. "The Administration, to date, has established no formal overall 'family policy,' but a great deal of attention has been focused on the interaction of programs and proposed legislation with an impact on families."[16] The following year President Carter himself did no better in clarifying what his administration had in mind in the way of family policy: "Our major social initiatives and goals for this year will be undertaken with vigor and with a commitment to the security and enhancement of the American family structure."[17]

Ordinarily, bland and vague language buried in a supplementary State of the Union message signals that no more will be heard of the subject. But two campaign proposals—one for a system of family impact analysis and one for a White House conference—had acquired independent lives. Not readily terminated, they became nagging reminders of the Carter administration's family problem. "Later this year," the president reported early in 1980, "we will hold the White House Conference on Families which I initially proposed during my 1976 campaign. This conference, the culmination of three years of work, will help focus public attention on the problems affecting families and on the means needed to solve or avoid those problems."[18] In fact,

16. *Welfare Reform Proposals*, Hearings before the Subcommittee on Public Assistance of the Senate Committee on Finance, 95 Cong. 2 sess. (GPO, 1978), pt. 2, p. 213.

17. "State of the Union—Message from the President—PM19," *Congressional Record*, daily edition (January 25, 1979), p. S634.

18. "State of the Union—Message from the President—PM148," *Congressional Record*, daily edition (January 22, 1980), p. S103.

the experience of a quasi-official family impact seminar and the troubled, three-year pre-history of the conference on families had already focused public attention on some reasons why government is ill-suited to solve many family problems.

Process as Policy: Family Impact Seminar

In the early 1970s thinkers about families, exposed to the economists' concept of externalities, or spillover effects, came to wonder about the effects on families of public policies not intended to bear on families. The suggestion that there might be incidental—and presumably undesirable—consequences for families of government actions taken for some different purpose evoked instant agreement from such luminaries in the family field as Margaret Mead, the anthropologist, and Edward Zigler, the social psychologist who was first director of the federal Office of Child Development. For Zigler, indeed, a systematic measurement of externalities constitutes one of three components of what he called a coherent family policy:

A family policy would entail the continuous analyses of the impact of other governmental policies for their effects on family life, so that any cost-benefit analysis of these policies would include in its equations the factor of whether the policy in question helps or hurts American families.[19]

Margaret Mead and Senator Walter Mondale agreed, at that same time, on the model for analyzing spillover effects on families: "a family well-being impact statement, for instance, comparable to the environmental impact statements." Looking at every piece of major legislation, every program, in terms of what it does to the family, "makes a great deal of sense to me, yes," Mead announced.[20] As for Mondale, impressed with what the environmental impact statement had done, especially in connection with the dispute over a supersonic transport plane, he envisioned a similar system of family impact statements that, to use his example, in the case of a tax proposal would lead legislators to ask the Internal Revenue Service, "What is this going to do to the average family?"[21]

19. *American Families: Trends and Pressures, 1973*, Hearings before the Subcommittee on Children and Youth of the Senate Labor and Public Welfare Committee, 93 Cong. 1 sess. (GPO, 1974), p. 69.
20. Ibid., p. 124.
21. Ibid., p. 125.

As unstructured discussions of family impact statements continued, their planned dimensions expanded. Not only might such statements deal with possible spillover effects on families of legislative proposals dealing with other subjects, impact statements could also deal with the success or failure of public action—whether legislative or administrative—especially directed to families. Moreover, enthusiasts like Urie Bronfenbrenner urged family impact assessment "at every level of government," from federal to state and "down to the counties and the districts, so that in every one of those lawmaking and executive groups there is a subcommittee or a group that says: 'What will this decision mean for families?' "[22]

The family impact idea failed to capture the fancy of other federal officials as it captured Senator Mondale's. Nor did Mondale continue to push it subsequently as he led his subcommittee through extensive hearings in 1974 and again in 1975. Day care then replaced family impact as the point of departure. Neither Mondale's subcommittee staff nor other proponents of the proposed day-care legislation tried a family impact analysis of the bill that served as the subject of hearings. Opponents, however, emphasized "the value of the mother's presence in the home" and characterized the proposal as family-destructive.[23]

The manner in which self-identified defenders of traditional family roles stymied day-care–child development legislation provoked a revived interest in family impact analysis. In an exploratory inquiry published in the form of an occasional paper, Sheila Kamerman concluded that everything about family impact was uncertain: focus, sponsorship, model. But, she wrote, in the end a family impact statement—a form of policy analysis—would turn out to be a way of ordering knowledge, or, in the absence of knowledge, ordering prejudices as a prelude to counting votes:

Successful development of a family impact statement requires a systematic policy analysis in which consequences are made explicit. Alternative values would be identified, with an indication of how each could be realized or what

22. Ibid., p. 142.

23. See, for example, the views of Sidney Berman, M.D., past president of the American Academy of Child Psychiatry, in *Child and Family Services Act, 1975*, Joint Hearings before the Subcommittee on Children and Youth and the Subcommittee on Employment, Poverty, and Migratory Labor of the Senate Labor and Public Welfare Committee and the Subcommittee on Select Education of the House Committee on Education and Labor, 94 Cong. 1 sess. (GPO, 1976), pt. 8, p. 1690; and the views of Representative Gunn McKay, Democrat of Utah, in ibid., p. 1473.

the consequences of potential actions might be for varying sets of values. Where choices conflict, the final decision would have to be made in the political arena.[24]

Since Kamerman had discovered no hidden dangers, the Foundation for Child Development financed the creation in February 1976 of a seminar group to test the political, administrative, and substantive feasibility of developing a process to produce family impact statements on selected public policies. Over the next three years the Family Impact Seminar, which grew to twenty-one members, convened seven times. By the seventh meeting, the bloom was off: thirteen of the twenty-one members sent regrets. Participants in earlier meetings heard one another's research described and were brought up to date on the conferences, institutes, and seminars ("from Groves at Grossinger's to social workers in Chicago to parents and teachers at Disneyland") attended by A. Sidney Johnson III, the seminar's director. Johnson had been staff director of the Mondale Children and Youth Subcommittee throughout the original family impact discussions and the preceding and subsequent proposals for child and family services legislation. During the seminar's first year Johnson also served as part-time consultant to Joseph Califano in his role as adviser on families for Jimmy Carter's presidential campaign. Later, Johnson acted as part-time consultant on matters relating to the White House Conference on Families.

Without waiting for word from the seminar on any aspect of the feasibility of a family impact statement, Jimmy Carter's campaign paper resolved uncertainty about political feasibility and simultaneously put limits on an administrative system to conduct impact analyses:

> One idea that Senator Mondale has proposed is that each federal program present a family impact statement, to analyze how it would affect the family, much as federal programs now prepare environmental impact statements. We don't need a new bureaucracy, but the President and Congress should routinely conduct such an analysis when any major decision is made, and when I am President this will be done.[25]

A year or so later, the seminar published its preliminary findings on the similarities and differences between family-impact and environmental-impact analyses:

> Seminar work to date underscores the limits of any analogy to the environmental impact process. . . . Thus, the Seminar hopes to encourage much of

24. Sheila B. Kamerman, *Developing a Family Impact Statement*, An Occasional Paper from the Foundation for Child Development (New York: FCD, 1976), p. 17.
25. "A Statement in New Hampshire," *The Presidential Campaign*, p. 465.

the same kind of informed thinking, heightened consciousness, and public discussion that has been stimulated by the environmental impact concept without recommending the creation of a comparable federal bureaucracy with powers to require family impact statements on all proposed programs.[26]

Long before it produced its first actual family impact statement, the seminar arrived at two further judgments to list with its distaste for a new bureaucracy. One was that the diversity and pluralism of families—differences among families in income levels, in household composition, in stages in the life cycle, and in ethnic, racial, regional, and neighborhood factors—mean any single public policy may affect different families in quite different ways, and may affect members of the same family in quite different or conflicting ways. The other was that the "eloquent pleas" for "a comprehensive national family policy" were a mistake that might in the long run do more harm than good to families. All three judgments—one against new bureaucracy, one affirming pluralism and diversity, one discouraging a new comprehensive national policy—happened to accord with the prevailing political ethos. For practical purposes, no value attached to the Family Impact Seminar's philosophical judgments. If, however, the exercise could produce a genuine family impact statement that might serve as a prototype, the process and the sample product could be embraced as the long-sought family policy.

Three and one-half years and four foundation grants after it had been organized, the seminar published its first policy analysis. Carefully labeled "A Preliminary Report," *Teenage Pregnancy and Family Impact* mixes inconclusive cameos on families that have experienced teenage pregnancy, summaries of commissioned papers, a brief historical background of current policy, a statement of the seminar's "Value Assumptions and Guiding Principles," and a section called "Family Impact Analysis of New Legislation." The latter includes a review of legislative history and a family impact analysis of the grant program in adolescent pregnancy enacted in 1978. The analysis takes the form of a testing of the legislation's substance against seven family impact principles "identified as being fundamental to any policy concerned with teenage pregnancy which intended to have positive impact on all three families involved."[27]

26. *Family Impact Seminar: An Introduction* (Washington, D.C.: FIS, 1977), p. 11.
27. *Teenage Pregnancy and Family Impact: New Perspectives on Policy* (Washington, D.C.: FIS, 1979), p. 35. The "three families involved" are the mother's, the father's, and the new family resulting from the pregnancy.

Judged by its maiden effort at an impact analysis and statement, the Family Impact Seminar offers little promise for resolving the dilemmas that beset all efforts to strengthen families while acknowledging their diversity and pluralism. The seminar recommends putting more emphasis on the families, encouraging the involvement of teenage males in primary prevention, encouraging the collection of information about the family situations of teenage clients, and so on. Exhortation to "think family" turns out to be the message of family impact, but there is no informed prediction of the consequences of failing to do so. Yet informed prediction, not exhortation, was the hoped-for unique contribution to family policy of family impact statements.

Policy by White House Conference

Jimmy Carter's campaign statement on the American family, issued in August 1976, began by declaring that "the American family is in trouble," and ended by naming Joseph A. Califano, Jr., to serve as a special adviser on "how federal programs can aid and support the American family."[28] Encouraged by favorable reaction from the media and elsewhere, within a couple of weeks Califano contacted academics, religious leaders, labor and business leaders with special interest in the family, economists, women's groups, social workers, and others described as "knowledgeable people," asking that they share with him ideas and recommendations on the issue. "During the coming weeks," Califano informed them, "Governor Carter intends to discuss the American family and, as President, to use his office to help create an environment that will nourish and strengthen family life in America."[29]

Several hundred responses later, Califano filed with Carter a "preliminary" report—actually the only report—called "American Families: Trends, Pressures and Recommendations." The similarity of its title to that of the 1973 Senate Subcommittee on Children and Youth hearings, *American Families: Trends and Pressures*, should not have been a surprise, since A. Sidney Johnson III, staff director of the subcommittee in 1973, served as principal draftsman of the September 17, 1976, Califano report. This fifteen-page document reviewed changes

28. "A Statement in New Hampshire," *The Presidential Campaign*, pp. 462, 465.
29. Letter to the author from Joseph A. Califano, Jr., August 16, 1976.

in family structure, functions, and values; discussed economic, tax, welfare, housing, health, and other public policy bearing on families; deplored Nixon-Ford "indifference"; and concluded that although "a comprehensive understanding of the problems facing families and children will take time," some problems could be promptly confronted: more jobs, a curb on inflation, restoration of trust and confidence in families as the basic institution for meeting human needs, and a beginning review of the impact of federal programs on families.

The Califano report included no recommendation for a White House conference, and Johnson has said that none was made. Had there been such a recommendation, it would have been the only specific proposal for possible presidential action in a document that tended to be strong on castigating the Ford administration and weak on delineating a Carter program. Whatever purpose was served by the Califano report, it did not accomplish for Carter what, say, the Task Force on Public Welfare, organized by president-elect Richard Nixon in 1968, accomplished for him in addressing the welfare issue. The report by the task force was specific; it emphasized how a new administration could quickly make its mark in an important field; and it seemed to offer a lot for a little money. To be sure, the Califano report should be regarded as a campaign document rather than a policy document. Yet its thin section of conclusions and recommendations does deal vaguely with policy needs, though without suggesting any substantive or procedural move in connection with family issues that Carter could offer to make as president.

Two weeks after its completion, parts of the Califano report found their way into a Carter speech to an audience for which the subject was both interesting and timely—the National Conference of Catholic Charities. In 1976 the largest nationwide grassroots consultation ever sponsored by the Catholic Church in the United States—the Call to Action program—indicated that family-related issues were topmost among thousands of social and pastoral concerns identified by Catholics. Lay and ecclesiastical delegates to the Catholic Charities conference were delighted to be in attendance at Carter's unveiling of a projected public-private approach to the restoration of families:

One step I intend to take soon after becoming President is to convene a White House Conference on the American Family. My goal will be to bring together leaders of government, leaders of the private sector like yourselves, and ordinary citizens and parents to discuss specific ways we can better support and strengthen our families. That Conference can be an important first step toward restoring the public-private partnership in social services that has been so hampered by Republican neglect.[30]

For the time being, process could be a surrogate for substance: a White House conference on the American family could substitute for a national family policy. Under the best of circumstances, a conference might yield an agreed program that could become a family policy. The history of White House conferences lent no encouragement to that view, but there had never been a conference on the family. Under less happy circumstances, a conference might find itself unable to agree on a program. At a minimum, however, any conference could be counted on to be for jobs, against inflation, for tax reform, for quality education, and for comprehensive social services. Since Carter brought no more well developed plan with him, a conference that agreed only to these banalities would leave the new administration about where it began, but with a credit for careful consultation. What could not be foreseen was the very worst of all circumstances—that the administration would prove unable to convene a conference through virtually all of Carter's four-year term, and that the family policy idea would be more embarrassment than credit.

White House conferences on five disparate subjects ranging from handicapped individuals to wildlife conservation won either outright endorsement or sympathetic interest from Carter during his presidential campaign, but Carter initiated the idea of only one of them—the conference on the American family.[31] Of the others, one was in the planning stage, another was previously authorized, and the remaining two were suggested by questioners who could not reasonably interpret the candidate's polite response to constitute a commitment to proceed. Carter was clearly not White House conference–happy. His personal attachment to a White House conference on the American family appears a unique rather than a routine reaction. No such conference was proposed in connection with any of the other major themes of the Carter campaign—the tax system, health insurance, the economy, government organization, nor were White House conferences routinely endorsed after the Carter election.

To the contrary, in the second year of his presidency, Carter decided

30. "Speech to the National Conference of Catholic Charities, October 4, 1976," *The Presidential Campaign*, vol. 1, pt. 2, p. 904.
31. *The Presidential Campaign*, vol. 1, pt. 1, pp. 599, 614; pt. 2, pp. 896, 1066.

to veto a bill sponsored by John Brademas, House Democratic whip, authorizing $3 million for two White House conferences, one on the arts and one on the humanities. The president's veto plan had already been made known to Brademas when White House congressional liaison and domestic policy advisers intervened, arguing that a veto would seem petty. "They took him in relays to wear him down," it was explained at the time, and Carter finally did change his mind.[32] (Brademas, in turn, dutifully interprets approval as a demonstration of Carter's "serious commitment to strengthening the arts and humanities in American life" rather than as the expedient political decision made reluctantly and under pressure that it actually was.)[33]

Six weeks after Carter's inauguration, the White House conference—now a conference on families rather than on the American family, thanks to an unsolicited memorandum from the ad hoc HEW Family Impact Task Group, which urged acceptance of a "neutral" model rather than the traditional husband-wife-children model[34]—looked like a going concern but was already showing signs of trouble. By way of letting it be known that his role as Carter's adviser on federal programs for families accompanied him to HEW, Secretary Califano—rather than a White House staff member—sent individual letters to 400 members of the family constituency saying that the conference staff, when assembled, would develop an ongoing relationship with individuals and organizations concerned about families.[35] Among his few amendments to the previously submitted Ford budget, Carter included a $3 million item for a conference "which will take place in the spring of FY 1979"—two years later. From the budget justification, it appeared that sure-footed planners were in charge:

General Statement

The White House Conference on Families will explore the problems of the American family and will examine the impact of our institutions, public policies and laws, employment, media, and voluntary organizations on the capability

32. *New York Times*, May 4, 1978.

33. *Congressional Record*, daily edition (May 4, 1978), p. H3621.

34. Paper prepared by the HEW Family Impact Task Group, January 10, 1977. The group included personnel from the Office of the Assistant Secretary for Planning and Evaluation, the Social and Rehabilitation Service, the Social Security Administration, the Office of the Assistant Secretary for Education, the Office of the Assistant Secretary for Human Development, and the Office of the Assistant Secretary for Health. The paper "presents considerations of the relationships between this Department's programs and efforts to strengthen the stability of American families."

35. Letter to the author from Joseph A. Califano, Jr., March 4, 1977.

of families to meet basic needs and respond to changes and increased pressures produced by our society. The problems confronting the American family are of major concern to parents, community leaders, families, youth, and organizations throughout the country. Addressing these problems is a complex but urgent and necessary undertaking. While many American families are strong, healthy and viable, others are being adversely influenced by circumstances beyond their control. Therefore, it is mandatory that we move to explore ways to increase the resources and opportunities available to a significant number of American families. It has become increasingly clear that many families require assistance in preserving the family unit if the family structure is to be preserved as the foundation and back bone of our society.

Objectives for FY 1978:

In FY 1978 extensive plans will be made for a White House Conference which will take place in the spring of FY 1979. This Conference will attempt to identify problems and pressures created by our existing institutions and to develop the best methods and approaches for correcting and preventing those problems that tend to threaten the healthy development and maintenance of family life. The Conference will be designed to solicit input from representatives from the fields of government, education, social welfare, religion, labor and business, families, and special interest groups across the nation.

Staff will be composed of 15 permanent and 15 other than permanent two-year term positions at an estimated cost of $1.06 million for the two-year period.

Every effort will be made to tap resources from the private sector to provide additional support for the Conference.[36]

Testimony from Arabella Martinez, assistant secretary for human development, promptly dispelled the image of competence and direction suggested by Califano's letter and the budget statement. "Somewhat misleading as it is too specific," Martinez said of language in her own written testimony that borrowed from the budget justification. "We are barely in the preplanning stages and no decisions have been made about the theme, the timing, the location or any other facet of the proposed conference."[37] A year later, Martinez could have made the same assessment, but by six months after that, when decisions finally made had to be unmade, it would have been too rosy a characterization of a shambles. By the second anniversary of Carter's statement of intent, White House conference planning—normally a routine fusion of public relations and subject-matter specialization—or its absence

---

36. *Departments of Labor and Health, Education, and Welfare Appropriations for 1978,* Hearings before the Subcommittee on Labor and Health, Education, and Welfare of the House Committee on Appropriations, 95 Cong. 1 sess. (GPO, 1977), pt. 6, pp. 828–29.

37. Ibid., p. 691.

managed only to alienate or discourage social welfare, Catholic, black, and women's interest groups and to irritate sympathetic legislators.

Alienation of the Activists

Managers of high-visibility national commissions and public conferences should understand the importance of classifying relevant interest groups as activists and skeptics. In general, the activists tend to be the slightly underprogrammed groups, not quite fully occupied, not quite consumed by a predetermined goal or goals. Sometimes they are organized on an ad hoc basis in response to the conference opportunity. The skeptics—standoffish—are clear about what they want and confident about it. They are the Urban League, the Children's Defense Fund, the Child Welfare League, and the like, which have seen conferences and commissions come and go. The skeptics know that this conference will come and go and the issues will remain. They are not likely to get too involved, or too critical, especially if the conference avoids specificity. Conference activists, while usually not as skilled as the skeptics, are potentially far more troublesome—and more useful. The conference is of prime importance to the activists, a cause to be reported on to boards, to be discussed in newsletters, to be watched and built up to. As a tour operator in January welcomes charter enrollees who provide insurance that a planned July tour will have the requisite minimum number of subscribers, so conference planners should welcome and cultivate the conference activists. The latter—like charter enrollees—must be kept informed and enthusiastic over the long six months when details are being worked out. Anticipation is a significant part of the experience for activists, and a failure to satisfy their need for involvement in the pre-event period foredooms the chances for the success of the event itself. Properly cultivated, activists will ultimately be coopted by management. They—again like early subscribers—are the bread and butter of the conference.

Piqued by the initial downgrading to HEW level of what they believed was a promised *White House* conference, the activist interest groups nonetheless organized to make contact with and influence conference decisionmakers. Activist pique grew, however, as decisionmaking authority remained unsettled. For example, trouble with blacks developed when a newly organized coalition of nine national black organizations calling itself the HEW Coalition and claiming to "collectively represent the majority of Black families in the United States, either through direct or indirect services," agreed at its first meeting in April 1977 to make the White House Conference on Families its first concern. Having contacted Califano's erstwhile ghostwriter of the "American Families" report, Sidney Johnson, now part-time consultant on the White House conference, the coalition, correctly or not, found "very patronizing" a Johnson memorandum advising Califano not to meet with the coalition, but to include individual member organizations in the briefings scheduled with Assistant Secretary Martinez. Subsequent efforts to establish a dialogue with the appropriate officials resulted in referrals over the course of a year to seven different persons at HEW—from Martinez down. "To date," Theodore Taylor of the HEW Coalition explained in February 1978, "there has been no attempt by HEW to establish any significant linkages with Black organizations."[38] No black organizations were participating in the development of a philosophical orientation for the conference, in the identification of people to fill key positions, or in discussions about program content, structure, implementation, and possible outcomes of the conference. The failure of HEW staff to come to an accommodation with the HEW Coalition left this vocal black group frustrated and nettled, since a major reason for its organization was to take advantage of an apparent opportunity to claim a distinctive black contribution to family policy development. It was not an auspicious beginning for the conference.

But HEW incompetence appears to have been evenhanded in its dealings with activist groups in the family policy constituency. Shortly after the inauguration the Catholic Bishops Conference, proud that it was at the National Conference of Catholic Charities that Carter had announced his intention to convene a White House conference, established a committee to coordinate Catholic participation in the conference. Chaired by Msgr. Francis Lally, secretary of the United States Catholic Conference Department of Social Development and World Peace, the committee included, among other organizations, the Catholic Conference, the National Council of Catholic Women, the National Conference of Catholic Charities, and the National Catholic Education Association. This formidable group believed the White House conference to be, as Msgr. Lally later put it in a letter to Vice-President

38. *White House Conference on Families, 1978,* Joint Hearings, p. 19.

Mondale, "one of the more important domestic initiatives undertaken by President Carter's Administration."[39]

If there was any comparable sense of the importance of the conference in HEW, no evidence of it reached Msgr. Lally's committee. Like the black HEW Coalition, the Catholic committee complained that after almost a year had passed, its willingness to place its resources at the service of conference planners could hardly be implemented for want of identifiable planners:

Among those aspects of planning for the White House Conference which are causing concern to our membership are (1) The delay in the appointment of the national advisory body and staff for the White House Conference on Families, (2) A lack of information as to the preliminary goals and objectives of the Conference, (3) The absence of an identifiable planning process for the Conference and (4) A firmly established date for the White House Conference.[40]

Activist groups predictably took the White House conference far more seriously than it was taken in the White House or in HEW. Probably for the benefit of the White House political staff, Msgr. Lally's remarkable letter to the vice-president described family and family problems as of foremost concern to the Catholic community in America. "Catholic parishes, parochial schools, charitable institutions and social ministry programs are a testimony to a long tradition of service and commitment to American families."[41] Expressing admiration for the administration's proposal to assess family needs, Msgr. Lally seemed to plead for a chance to link the Carter conference to the organized Catholic network—to serve the interests of both groups while advancing a just cause.

Having been present at the creation, the Catholics took particular offense at the downgrading of responsibility for the conference from White House to HEW, all the more so since the administration failed to make a formal announcement or to offer an informal explanation to the interest-group leaders. Brother Joseph Berg, a sometime lobbyist for the National Conference of Catholic Charities who staffed the Catholic Coordinating Committee for the White House conference, bridled at an HEW report that Secretary Califano had moved planning activity into his own immediate office. Berg complained to Senator Alan Cranston that "it was my impression that the President had asked HEW for advice on how the Conference might be put together. The President

39. Letter, Msgr. Francis J. Lally to Vice-President Walter Mondale, December 15, 1977, in *White House Conference on Families, 1978,* Joint Hearings, pp. 79–80.
40. Ibid.
41. Ibid.

has never indicated that the Conference would be anything less than a WHITE HOUSE CONFERENCE. It is time to establish an office for the Conference in the White House. . . . We must let the country know that this is a President's Conference."[42]

It never was nor did it ever become a president's conference, nor even a secretary's conference. Understandably, the conference could hardly compete for the president's time and attention with a Mideast summit, say, or even with domestic economic concerns. And Secretary Califano, it was said within HEW, never really wanted to turn to it. Remaking a conference on the family into a conference on families required political and administrative skill. Instead, a leadership vacuum was allowed to develop. The closest that conference planning came to the centers of power was with the later appointment of the wife of the assistant to the president for domestic affairs, Stuart Eizenstat, as consultant responsible for outreach activities. Working part-time, Frances Eizenstat, a refugee from the disorganized and failing Day Care and Child Development Council of America, made things a little better.

First, however, things got much worse as blacks who organized as activists and Catholics who organized as activists were joined in disaffection by the social welfare–activist Coalition for the White House Conference on Families, a group of twenty-seven national organizations from the American Association of Marriage and Family Counselors to the Young Women's Christian Association National Board. They complained in common about ignored requests for meetings, perfunctory replies to questions about the conference planning process, and promised deadlines for action that were not met. "It was astonishing to me," Robert Rice of the Family Service Association of America, who served as convener of the coalition, has said, "that politicians could so miss the boat by not attending to the great interest in families. I'm not much for White House conferences generally, and I was not urging a series of Conferences on Families. I only wanted one, but rather than a group to put substance into an existing plan for a Conference, the Coalition had to back up and become an advocacy group for the idea of a White House Conference lest it be allowed to die of inattention."[43]

Yet none of these groups—blacks, Catholics, or national voluntary

42. Letter, Brother Joseph Berg, CSC, to the Honorable Alan Cranston, February 10, 1978, in *White House Conference on Families, 1978,* Joint Hearings, pp. 473–75.

43. Interview with the author, October 2, 1978.

and professional organizations—could dent the office of HEW's assistant secretary for human development. When, however, a joint congressional oversight hearing was scheduled to review plans for the White House conference, somebody had to produce a plan to review. The Office of Human Development was relieved of responsibility and the secretary's office took over. A presidential statement formally setting December 9–13, 1979, as the dates for the conference was released a couple of days before the hearing, thus making public the sum total of what was firm in HEW's conference plans.

Richard Warden, assistant secretary for legislation, who had close ties to the family and children's lobby dating back to his interest, while lobbyist for the AFL-CIO's United Automobile Workers, in child development legislation, offered assurances that things would move right along, although nominations were still being accepted for both chairperson of the advisory committee and executive director of the conference. After all, the commitments of both the secretary of HEW and the president were "very, very strong." Evidence for that, Warden suggested, could be seen in Carter's announcement that week of the dates for the conference and Califano's action in moving the conference office up to his personal office.[44] Representative John Brademas, a veteran of the child development legislation wars, seemed unimpressed with the whole record. "As a Democrat who thinks that even Democrats ought to be expected to make some serious effort to carry out their campaign promises," he said to his friend Kenneth Keniston, chairman of the Carnegie Council on Children, apropos of the administration's family policy activity, "there may not have been quite as vigorous an effort, as there at least by now should have been, to implement the promises of the candidate in the actions of his administration following his inauguration."[45]

Triumph of the Traditionalists

Ironically, as the effort turned vigorous, the results turned to ashes. After discarding endless lists of potential nominees to run the conference—"They call you and read you a list of names you want to hear, then they call me and read me a list I want to hear," a black children's

44. *White House Conference on Families, 1978*, Joint Hearings, p. 264.
45. Ibid., p. 284.

advocate said of the consulting process—Califano's personal staff assistants had a team in place, though one not publicly identified, two months after the congressional hearing. Wilbur Cohen, former secretary of HEW, who helped draft the Social Security Act in 1935 and qualified as a charter member of America's liberal-activist-intellectual social welfare fraternity, would be national chairman. To balance him, one of Califano's assistants, Patricia Fleming, would serve as executive director. Fleming was young, a working mother of three children, black, experienced on Capitol Hill and in the department. She was also divorced, a fact not likely to be pertinent to any federal-level job other than that of executive director of the White House Conference on Families.

Cohen approached the conference in businesslike fashion but without special enthusiasm. Made aware of the attitude of the black HEW Coalition, he expressed confidence that he could soften the outrage of its convener, once a Cohen assistant at HEW. "I agree with you," Cohen in his pacifying way told an acquaintance who argued that the conference would not be a forum at which to resolve serious problems, "they should not have a Conference, but since there is going to be one, why don't you help me plan an agenda." And before his appointment was announced, Cohen had outlined both an agenda and a plan. Under Cohen's chairmanship, the White House conference would quickly assume an orderly, conventional character. The various disaffected groups would be consulted and pacified.

Fleming apparently saw the conference as an event of importance and consulted with leaders of prominent national black organizations about whether she should agree to serve. Despite some negative advice, she had agreed to accept before the HEW Secretary's Office heard objections from within and outside the administration to the appointment of a divorced woman as executive director of a conference on families. These objections introduced troubles the secretary did not want. Califano either suggested or directed the appointment of a white, male, married, Catholic codirector. The predictions made by the blacks who had advised Fleming not to take the job turned out to be right, and Fleming resigned from the conference staff before her appointment as director was publicly announced.

Without making reference to Fleming's problems, Wilbur Cohen, who had said earlier, "I think I should have some say-so" in the designation of a conference director, and who could look ahead to trouble because of his belief in public intervention to prevent large families, announced that a health problem would preclude his continuing to serve as chairman. The conference family formed to produce a conference on families had dissolved in two months, thus beating by some years the national average for conventional family dissolution. A quick solution could not be achieved. At status quo ante—that is, lacking both a chairperson and a director—the conference that the president had said in October 1976 he would convene "soon after becoming President," and that he had finally announced in January 1978 would be convened in December 1979, was postponed in June 1978 until some unspecified date in 1981. Responding after a two-month delay to a "Dear Joe [Califano]" request from Senator Cranston for a thorough accounting and for answers to detailed questions about the circumstances surrounding Fleming's and Cohen's resignations, Under Secretary of HEW Hale Champion, in an eight-page letter, termed the postponement "a positive development over the long run."[46] Champion simply ignored the pointed questions Cranston had raised about whether Fleming's divorce was a factor in her withdrawal, whether she had been asked to accept a white, Catholic, married, male codirector, and whether pressure exerted on or within the administration figured in Fleming's withdrawal.

Running out of money and fearing to ask even for a congressional mandate, let alone more money, the planning staff, now joined by Frances Eizenstat, whose participation provided a channel to the White House, renewed the search for conference leaders. Exactly a year after Cohen had been named chairman, Jim Guy Tucker, a one-term former congressman from Arkansas, became Cohen's successor. And a year after the question had been raised of a codirector for Fleming, John Carr—white, male, married, and Catholic—became her successor as executive director. Senator Cranston's suggestion that consideration be given to placing the conference staff in the White House was rejected. After all, Hale Champion answered, the department's "expertise" in the White House conference business and "the interrelated nature of families issues to the Department's functions" made HEW best suited to manage the conference.

The happenings at what would formally be recorded as the first-ever White House Conference on Families—actually two regional confer-

46. Letter, Hale Champion to the Honorable Alan Cranston, September 29, 1978, in ibid., pp. 738–45. The "positive development"—postponement until 1981—would later be reconsidered and regional conferences in lieu of a Washington conference scheduled for June and July 1980.

ences in June 1980 and one in July 1980, all far from the White House—
are obscured by the prehistory of the conference. If, indeed, policies
can strengthen families, little or no reason ever existed to expect such
a conference to affect policies. After reviewing the records of all the
White House conferences on children from 1909 through 1970, I wrote
in 1976 that "the White House conference is a better technique for
bolstering the ego of many of its participants than for formulating a
workable policy program."[47] My assessment is shared by Stephen
Hess, national chairman of the 1970 Conference on Children and of the
1971 Conference on Youth, who doubts whether the nation benefits
enough from such conferences to justify the time and cost. "It is the
broad-based conference on an emotionally charged subject that deserves re-evaluation," Hess has written.[48] Some politicians also have
doubts about the value of the White House conference technique. The
record of White House children's conferences, Walter Mondale once
said, is that "they make strong, sweeping, perceptive reports which
ultimately do nothing but gather dust."[49] And Abraham Ribicoff, who
as congressman, governor, secretary of HEW, and senator has seen a
few White House conferences on social issues, wonders whether they
serve any useful purpose or are just a means to sweep problems under
the rug by a great deal of publicity.[50]

Even HEW staff too young or too new to public affairs to remember
earlier White House conferences can hardly be so naive as to expect
hundreds or thousands of people to assemble for three or four days of
meetings, either in scattered sites around the country or in a group of
Washington hotels, and produce useful conclusions on public policies
dealing with abortion, homosexual relationships, adolescent sexuality,
termination of parental rights, child support, or domestic violence.
Explicit and widely shared recommendations on such divisive issues
must be suspect, as being the product of a nonrepresentative assembly.
Given the subjects to be addressed, the best to be hoped for from a
White House conference is that it might keep up the spirits of its
constituent groups by affording them recognition from the top and a
forum for the expression of their beliefs and hopes. But that is not
achieved by the prolonged disregard of ethnic, religious, and profes-

47. *The Children's Cause* (Brookings Institution, 1976), p. 130.
48. "The White House Conference—White Elephant?" *Baltimore Sun,* July 24, 1978.
49. *Congressional Record* (December 9, 1970), p. 40507.
50. Ibid., p. 40505. See also Rochelle Beck, "The White House Conferences on
Children: An Historical Perspective," *Harvard Educational Review,* vol. 43 (November
1973), pp. 653–68.

sional groups organized in response to the conference idea. Nor is it achieved by the ultimate selection of conference leaders and subleaders representing only the most traditional family styles.

The inevitability of a conference "mess" should have been apparent from the moment the conference on families was conceived. Even in the care of a more able administrative team than HEW at first provided, trouble was unavoidable, because diversity of family styles and traditionalism in family style peacefully coexist only so long as neither one gains actual or symbolic advantage over the other. Planning for a White House conference ruptured the peace between the two. Although the President insisted that "this Conference will clearly recognize the pluralism of family life in America," merely a divorced director-designate turned out to be too severe a strain. Recognizing the pluralism of family life antagonizes those to whom that pluralism is anathema. Eventually a choice becomes necessary. When seven leadership slots— director, chairman, and five deputy chairmen—were finally filled, the inclusion of one widow was the extent to which the pluralism of family life in America was recognized.[51] Predictably, traditional issues like job-related pressures on families and the tax treatment of families dominated the collective recommendations of the three conferences.

A Self-Created Problem

The truth is the president, the vice-president, and the HEW secretary created a "family policy" problem for themselves. Jimmy Carter, Walter Mondale, and Joseph Califano embraced family policy before the implications of the concept were thought through. Neither a family impact seminar nor a White House conference is a way to design program specifics to fit the superficially attractive concept of family policy.

51. Deputy Chairperson Coretta Scott King was the widow. The other members of the leadership cadre were Executive Director John Carr, once coordinator for urban issues of the United States Catholic Conference; Chairman Jim Guy Tucker, congressman from Arkansas 1977–79 who had lost a Democratic primary race for the Senate nomination in 1978; and four other deputy chairpersons: Mario Cuomo, lieutenant-governor of New York; Guadelupe Gibson, associate professor of social work at the Worden School of Social Work, San Antonio, Texas; Maryann Mahaffey, president pro tem of the Detroit City Council and professor of social work at Wayne State University; Donald V. Seibert, chairman and chief executive officer of the J. C. Penney Company. For a roster of the forty-person National Advisory Committee, see White House Conference on Families, *Report from the White House Conference*, vol. 1, no. 1 (August 1979), pp. 10, 12.

The Family Impact Seminar, an outgrowth of Mondale's somewhat simplistic extension of environmental impact statements to family impact statements, would probably be a more useful enterprise if it were stripped of the intellectual pretentiousness that leads it to abstract discourses on "ecological perspectives" and "evolving frameworks for analysis." The seminar might then recognize that its model might better be the Children's Defense Fund, a private lobby dedicated to monitoring, reporting, negotiating, litigating, and exhorting. Without jollying up the products as impact analyses, the CDF reports carefully on selected issues involving children and suggests new policy directions or shows the consequences of existing policy. Like the CDF, the Family Impact Seminar is self-anointed and belongs to a class of public interest lobbies dependent for survival on selecting particular issues and emphases that appeal to individual and organized philanthropies. The seminar could be the conscience of the Congress or of the community on family-related issues. By taking on that role, as the CDF does in its area, the seminar would force itself to try to draft a family policy agenda with priorities, a job no group in or out of the federal government has addressed. The seminar might also find that its agenda and priorities so overlap the CDF's that the seminar need not be rescheduled for another semester. If it maintains the nonfocus of its first four years, however, the seminar only clutters the catalog and promises students more than it knows how to teach.

As for the White House Conference on Families, it need not be replicated. Though Carter committed himself to a White House conference that would bring together public and private leaders and ordinary citizens and parents "to discuss specific ways we can better support and strengthen our families," he never came to grips with the differences between "the family" and "the diversity of families" as norms for a program, and learned belatedly that exhortation and homily do not constitute a family policy. To hope that substance and order might emerge from any White House conference is to hope for an outcome always desired and never achieved. But the problems associated with staging the White House Conference on Families go beyond the confusion over logistics, the amateur leadership, and the excessive numbers of participants faced by all White House conferences. The problems of staging this particular conference involved symbols and substance as well, and are an indication of the problems that would arise in framing a national family policy.

PART TWO

Intractable Problems

CHAPTER THREE

Matters of Faith and Morals

Since its high-level unveiling in 1976, family policy has remained an abstraction, leaving out of consideration the detailed elements of the complex institution it is supposed to address. With political attention concentrated on rescuing a foundering conference, and the limited academic attention directed to an inchoate technique of family impact analysis and to international comparisons of social policy writ large, content has received less attention than wrapping. Meanwhile individual families confront the same problems that families confronted before the evolution of "family policy" as a political theme. Whether and how some of those problems can be eased by new public programs or changes in existing programs should merit the attention of any administration, particularly a professedly family-oriented one.

One challenge for social policy is found in family problems that all rational people recognize to be problems and that no rational person wishes to perpetuate—for example, adolescent suicide, a problem often mentioned by President Carter. But the hardest family problems for government to deal with are those that involve choices between incompatible goals or values each of which has merit, each of which commands responsible and consequential support. Such problems are unaffected by big appropriations, big research programs, and the eventual discovery and universal application of a vaccine or miracle cure. Among the most intractable of these problems are those posed by unwanted pregnancies, adolescent pregnancies, public relief for needy families, nonsupport of children, separation of children and parents, and domestic violence.

Years of effort to make birth control a respectable subject for public discussion and an allowable item of public expenditure culminated in 1970 in the enactment of the Family Planning Services and Population Research Act, known in public health and legislative circles as Title X (of the Public Health Service Act). Its sponsors hoped that Title X would

49

make family planning services available to all those who want but cannot afford them, and would improve knowledge of human reproduction so that "each individual family could determine its size by choice rather than by force of circumstances."[1]

From the first discussions of a federal initiative, three issues have been in dispute: whether priority for receipt of services should be accorded low-income women; whether services should be available to sexually active adolescents on a routine basis; and whether family planning and birth control should extend to abortion. A low-income priority is ostensibly intended to preclude services from being monopolized by a well-informed middle class shifting from fee-for-service arrangements and thereby squeezing out the poor. But as Grace Olivarez complained in 1973, "That [low-income priority] language smacks of 'Stop those welfare women from overbreeding.'"[2] A means test was not imposed, though HEW briefly tried to do so in 1972. Instead, the location of services in low-income neighborhoods, an apparent middle-class reluctance to look for bargains in family planning services, and federal officials' near unanimous interest in avoiding the abortion question by financing family planning services combined to wipe out the suspicion of a plot against procreation by the poor.

As for adolescent sexuality and abortion, there are no more readily accepted solutions to the moral dilemmas they pose than there were when Title X made its way through an uneasy Congress in 1970. Public policy now permits all women who want to abort a pregnancy at an early stage, and can pay for the procedure, to do so. Such tolerance of abortion is morally unacceptable to a large segment of the population. But a different segment finds it morally unacceptable for Congress and the administration to be unwilling to use federal funds to finance elective abortions. Public policy concentrates attention on the sexually active adolescent after she has become pregnant, a concentration regarded as pragmatically unacceptable by some, yet defended by others as morally preferable to routine acceptance of teenage sexual activity. These widely divergent moral judgments are as likely to resist resolution through explicit family policy as they have resisted resolution in its absence.

1. *Family Planning Services and Population Research Amendments of 1973*, Hearings before the Special Subcommittee on Human Resources of the Senate Labor and Public Welfare Committee, 93 Cong. 1 sess. (Government Printing Office, 1973), p. 1.

2. Ibid., p. 176. President Carter appointed Olivarez director of the Community Services Administration in 1977.

Abortion

Abortion policy is unambiguous, balanced—and unsatisfactory to both sides. Each side finds enough wins in the record to encourage it to sustain the fight. Some of the techniques used, however, are depressing to a democratic society. Congress, concluding that the abortion issue is not susceptible to the usual political trade-offs, appears willing to institutionalize the balance and minimize discussion. Administration leaders who profess interest in family policy avoid defining abortion as a family problem. But if the pursuit of family policy turns from generalities to specifics, abortion is a subject from which there is no escape.

Protagonists of each side of the abortion-policy controversy shy away from being labeled as for or against abortion, preferring to describe themselves as pro-choice or pro-life—but in either case as pro-family. For pro-choice forces, restrictions on the right to abortion that lead to the birth of an unwanted child ignore the primary goal of family policy—to facilitate or enhance caring, supportive relationships between members of a strong family. Since an unwanted birth, the argument continues, results only in a new family or a larger family, not in a stronger family, those who are truly pro-family must be pro-choice.

For pro-life forces, on the other hand, abortion of a fetus is abortion of the family itself—to support abortion is to support a cavalier disregard for the unity of the family. "As long as the human family has only woman naturally equipped to bring forth its own kind," says Dr. Mildred Jefferson, president of the National Right to Life Committee, "it must not grant her the privilege of throwing the offspring away."[3] Similarly, Amitai Etzioni, the sociologist, says of the fetus that "it is a potential child, which both wife and husband have a title to, and it is the last stronghold of the family bond."[4] In this view, pro-life and pro-family—whether Jefferson's human family or Etzioni's nuclear family—are inseparable concepts.

Abortion is the most intractable and most prominent of family policy issues. Unlike ambiguous public policy responses to some other family-

3. *Proposed Constitutional Amendments on Abortion*, Hearings before the Subcommittee on Civil and Constitutional Rights of the House Committee on the Judiciary, 94 Cong. 2 sess. (GPO, 1976), pt. 1, p. 452.

4. "The Fetus: Whose Property?" *Commonweal* (September 21, 1973); reprinted in *Proposed Constitutional Amendments on Abortion*, Hearings, pt. 2, p. 1088.

related questions, however, abortion policy is clear, its legitimacy established by the recent explicit, highly publicized judicial and legislative decisions that have spawned a dual approach. One element, resulting from the Supreme Court's *Roe* v. *Wade* decision of January 1973, is validation of early abortion as a constitutionally protected exercise of the right to privacy—total decriminalization of abortion procedures during the first trimester of pregnancy and limited decriminalization thereafter.[5] Three and one-half years later, the Court upheld Connecticut's prohibition on use of medicaid funds for abortions.[6] With what amounted to prior assurance of constitutional validity, Congress in 1977 adopted a second element of abortion policy: severe restrictions on federal financing of abortion procedures in the federal-state program of aid to the medically indigent (medicaid).[7] Although abortion policy is clear, neither element—freedom of choice in early months of pregnancy or denial of federal medicaid benefits— is acceptable to both sides in the controversy. But neither element is in jeopardy because present arrangements come as close as public policy can come to satisfying entirely different perceptions of what is pro-family policy.

Differences about abortion, unlike some other disputes that have their origins in religious and moral diversity, cannot be laid to rest— without being settled—by an agreement to disagree. It is one thing to "live and let live," figuratively, over an issue like liquor sales on Sunday or compulsory school attendance for children of Amish parents or aid to parochial schools, another thing if the issue itself is perceived as "live and let live," literally. When faith and morals lead to a conviction

5. *Roe* v. *Wade*, 410 U.S. 113, 164 (1973):
 1. A state criminal abortion statute . . . that excepts from criminality only a *life saving* procedure on behalf of the mother, without regard to pregnancy state and without recognition of the other interests involved, is violative of the Due Process Clause of the Fourteenth Amendment.
 (a) For the stage prior to approximately the end of the first trimester, the abortion decision and its effectuation must be left to the medical judgment of the pregnant woman's attending physician.
 (b) For the stage subsequent to approximately the end of the first trimester, the State, in promoting its interest in the health of the mother, may, if it chooses, regulate the abortion procedure in ways that are reasonably related to maternal health.
 (c) For the stage subsequent to viability the State, in promoting its interest in the potentiality of human life, may, if it chooses, regulate, and even proscribe, abortion except where it is necessary, in appropriate medical judgment, for the preservation of the life or health of the mother.
6. *Maher* v. *Roe*, 432 U.S. 464 (1977).
7. *Congressional Record*, daily edition (December 7, 1977), pp. H12829–31, S19439–45.

that life exists from the instant of fertilization, abortion is no less than impermissible homicide. When faith and morals permit a conviction that life begins only at some later time, abortion can be a matter of free choice before that time. When faith and morals lead to uncertainty, abortion may be either acceptable or unacceptable personally. Even those for whom abortion is unacceptable personally, however, may have no objection to public policy permitting freedom of choice. These people, uncomfortable with abortion but not intolerant of it, are fair game for both prohibitionists and free-choice proponents. Prohibitionists hope to convince them that nothing less than life is involved; free-choice proponents hope to convince them that all economic and procedural barriers that discourage access to early abortion should be eliminated.

If there were as well-accepted scientific indicators pinpointing the beginning of life as pinpointing its end (even with all the controversy surrounding the latter), a large part of the abortion policy argument would cease to be relevant. Neither politicians nor ethicists evince support for public policy that tolerates—let alone pays for—abortion of a human life. But scientific judgments disagree on when human life begins, and conclude that it is a religious and moral question "unanswerable by scientists."[8] A consensus on what abortion does and hence on what public policy regarding it should be depends on a prior consensus on religion and morality. Since the United States is far from any such consensus—indeed, takes pride in protecting an increasing diversity of religious and moral views—no end to the dispute over abortion policy can be foreseen. But this dispute is different from most political disputes: neither its perpetuation nor the degree of its intensity will affect national policy.

Federal abortion policy is less consistent than either side would like. On the one hand, no money appropriated under Title X may be used in programs where abortion is a method of family planning. Abortion, therefore, is not included in the armamentarium of HEW's family planning services programs, planning, training, and public information activities, and population research. Nor will federal dollars routinely finance abortion for those who otherwise qualify for federally subsidized health services. On the other hand, no woman is legally

8. The conclusion is that of Gerald Edelman, Nobel laureate in medicine. *Abortion*, Hearings before the Subcommittee on Constitutional Amendments of the Senate Judiciary Committee, 93 Cong. 2 sess. (GPO, 1974), pt. 2, p. 249.

forbidden to abort at any early stage of pregnancy. In practice, more-over, relatively few women are debarred by the medicaid cutoff. If federal money is not available for abortion, the procedure itself is not proscribed. In early 1980, one-fifth of the states were paying all abortion costs for their medicaid populations. Some poor women will succeed in raising private money, aided, perhaps, by the responsible man. Some others will be served at a greatly reduced fee, or for no fee, by a sympathetic abortion facility. Still others will find that a sectarian social service agency—Protestant or Jewish—though ostensibly not in the business of providing cash relief, is nonetheless willing to pay for an abortion because it is a nonrecurring cost. Or a competent social service agency will have an established relationship with a gynecologist willing to donate professional services from time to time at the agency's request. The present restriction may preclude federal financing of 200,000 abortions annually, but the actual number of abortions for-gone is surely a good deal smaller. Nor has persuasive evidence been advanced that there has been a growth in the incidence of nonprofessional abortions.

Irreconcilable Rights

One and one-third million abortions—as against 3.3 million live births—take place annually in the United States, the overwhelming majority of them private, fee-for-service transactions between physician and patient.[9] Since the Supreme Court has thrown a blanket of constitutional protection over those transactions, continued provision of the fee-for-service arrangement is assured barring only constitutional change or a decision by the Court to overrule itself. The former is as unlikely as the latter. It is not unknown for the Court to overrule an earlier judgment—*Plessy* v. *Ferguson*, which sustained the separate-but-equal doctrine and was overruled fifty-eight years later in *Brown* v. *Board of Education*, is the leading example—but even ardent right-to-life supporters see no way of effecting a change in the Court's opinion beyond the implicit accommodation to the opposition made in the medicaid decision. No changed social circumstances can be claimed; the biological case for dating the beginning of life at one stage of fetal

9. Jacqueline Darroch Forrest, Ellen Sullivan, and Christopher Tietze, "Abortion in the United States, 1977–1978," *Family Planning Perspectives*, vol. 11 (November–December 1979), p. 329.

development rather than another is no better or worse; the dangers of infection have been reduced by continuing developments in chemistry and pharmacology; new evidence has shown that women who have legal abortions do not harm their chances of bearing normal, healthy children in subsequent pregnancies. Perhaps the only ground on which the Court might overrule itself coincides with the only circumstance likely to spur a constitutional prohibition—experimental evidence dating the viability of the fetus to a much earlier time than has up to now been established. Since it is inconceivable that experimentation with human subjects can be pursued in adequate numbers to make that case, the status quo seems assured.

Before the mid-1960s abortion policy had long been a nonissue. A pattern of state statutory law that made abortion a criminal act emerged around 1830, replacing the more liberal common law attitude to abortion that characterized early nineteenth century America.[10] Whether abortion restrictions were due to changed moral sensibilities, to an intent to deny women independence, or to a desire to protect women from the danger of infection resulting from the abortion procedure is a matter of some dispute. Restrictions on elective abortion, in any event, were largely unchallenged, and even little discussed, for more than a hundred years after their enactment. The literature of abortion then was largely a professional and technical literature, and proponents of legal abortion were both scarce and likely to be thought of as suffering from character defects. Women's hesitancy to organize on behalf of women's causes and the understood danger of infection attendant on any surgical procedure further reinforced statutory prohibitions.

After World War II the development of penicillin all but wiped out whatever validity there had been to the concern about infection, but an attack on abortion restrictions came only after women organized to fight for equal status. State legislatures moved slowly to repeal or reform, often reluctant to take action that might be popular with some women, but would be unpopular with many important organized religious groups and would open the pioneering state or states to the charge of being indifferent to the protection of the unborn. (Indifference to a woman's right to control over her body did not yet provoke political action.) In the half-dozen years preceding *Roe* v. *Wade*, during which some states reconsidered their abortion laws, individual freedom to

10. James C. Mohr, *Abortion in America: The Origins and Evolution of National Policy* (Oxford University Press, 1978).

decide for abortion became an accident of residence. Before the Supreme Court decision of 1973, fewer than half the states had followed Colorado's lead and liberalized their statutes.

In the long period during which abortion was judged an illegal operation in every state, challenges were simply not sufficiently numerous and persistent to endanger the widespread prohibition on abortion, which stemmed in large part from the amalgamation of an ambiguous concept—the beginning of human life—and an anachronistic one—the danger of abortion. Both ambiguous and anachronistic, and thus failing two tests of legitimacy, much of the underpinning of abortion policy became fair game for challenge. The results of the challenge could not be and surely are not universally accepted, but they are legitimate. Legitimacy does not imply the absence of opposition.

The liberalization of abortion might also have been served by a different strategy. Judith Blake has argued the case for independent state action rather than the use of federal judicial pressure.[11] Additional states would inevitably have moved toward abortion liberalization just as they moved toward the liberalization of divorce. Resentment of federal intervention could not have served as an opposition rallying point. On the other hand, efforts to enact a constitutional prohibition would have been no less intense once liberalization became more common than exceptional. Those intense efforts can be expected to persist, because proponents are motivated by moral and ethical beliefs not subject to compromise. The intensity of their beliefs, however, does not produce the kind of broad support necessary to achieve constitutional change.

Since the safety of the abortion procedure is not now in dispute and fostering population growth is not a public issue, opposition to freedom of choice in abortion as a matter of public policy is effectively concentrated among those who hold to a particular view of when life begins, namely, at the moment of fertilization or when the embryo attaches to the maternal uterine wall five or six days later. ("What comes into existence at the moment of conception," John Cardinal Krol says, "is nothing less than a human being in the earliest stages of development."[12]) For people who so believe, saving the life of the mother

11. Judith Blake, "The Supreme Court's Abortion Decisions and Public Opinion in the United States," *Congressional Record*, daily edition (September 27, 1978), p. S16332.

12. *Documentation on the Right to Life and Abortion, National Conference of Catholic Bishops* (Washington, D.C.: U.S. Catholic Conference, 1974), p. 37.

becomes the sole possible ground on which to tolerate a public policy that abides abortion. And even here there is a pro-life presumption: where maternal survival is involved, no destructive procedure is done against the fetus at all. Fetal loss results unavoidably from a positive procedure undertaken to avoid the mother's death. In certain circumstances, if the surgeon does not follow a positive procedure, a specialist in reproductive medicine once explained to a congressional inquirer, the mother dies. "So you have no choice. The fetus dies, but you have not killed him. You have saved the mother."[13] That situation aside, a belief in what has been termed the "humanity of the fetus in utero" precludes any further tolerance of abortion.

To the contrary, any public policy restricting the abortion decision is unacceptable to those who insist that the fetus is an integral part of the mother's body and that the sole issue is a woman's right to unrestricted control over her own body. That position implicitly denies that the fetus constitutes life, thus avoiding what would otherwise be a fight certain to be lost if waged on behalf of a woman's property right over control of her body against a fetus's right to life. As a practical matter, since nearly 90 percent of elective abortions occur within the first twelve weeks of pregnancy, pro-choice forces find it unnecessary to consider the existence of life after quickening—the first motion of the fetus in the uterus—although some proponents of freedom of choice would surely not accept quickening as the moment at which a woman's rights over her body cease.

Among those who in no way equate a fetus with life and who are unconcerned about religious and moral questions of the rights of the fetus and its humanity, there is no agonizing over what is viewed as a way to rectify a mistake that would otherwise weaken the family. Among the far larger numbers whose religious or moral views create uncertainty about the rights of the fetus, the choice is a troublesome one that weighs anxiety about the effect of an unwanted child on family stability against anxiety about the ethics of destroying an entity that may or may not be life, but is surely in what Archibald Cox has called "the penumbra of life."[14] Two of the major Protestant denominations that have addressed the issue—the United Church of Christ and the United Methodist Church—come to a defense of freedom of choice by

13. *Abortion*, Hearings, pt. 2, p. 238.

14. *The Role of the Supreme Court in American Government* (Oxford University Press, 1976), p. 53.

opting for the rights of the family against what one denominational group describes simply as "the fetus" and the other describes variously as "unborn human life" and as "new life just forming."

The implication is that factors other than its [the fetus's] existence may appropriately be given equal or greater weight at this time—the welfare of the whole family, its economic condition, the age of the parents, their view of the optimum number of children consonant with their resources and the pressures of population, their vocational and social objectives, for example.[15]

Because human life is distorted when it is unwanted and unloved, parents seriously violate their responsibility when they bring into the world children for whom they cannot provide love. . . . A profound regard for unborn human life must be weighed alongside an equally profound regard for fully formed personhood, particularly when the physical, mental and emotional health of the pregnant woman and her family show reason to be seriously threatened by the new life just forming.[16]

If the issue is joined, it is impossible to design policy to satisfy both the extreme pro-life and the pro-choice positions. Obviously, the latter—without acknowledging life—can accommodate the former, but the former cannot accommodate the latter, since life cannot be made subject to free choice. Roger Wertheimer, writing two years before the Supreme Court's abortion ruling, defined the problem precisely, although neither Catholics nor Protestants are either unanimous or alone in holding to their assigned position:

The liberal's proposal is predicated on abortion being a crime without a victim, like homosexuality or the use of contraceptives, but in the Catholic view the fetus is a full-scale victim and is so independent of the liberal's recognition of that fact. Catholics can no more think it wrong for themselves but permissible for Protestants to destroy a fetus than liberals can think it wrong for themselves but permissible for racists to victimize blacks.[17]

The Inevitability of the Status Quo

Neither constitutional change nor additional legislation concerning abortion is politically feasible, not because either side lacks the neces-

15. "Freedom of Choice Concerning Abortion," adopted by the General Synod of the United Church of Christ, June 29, 1971; cited by Theresa Hoover of the Religious Coalition for Abortion Rights, in *Proposed Constitutional Amendments on Abortion*, Hearings, pt. 1, p. 319.

16. "Resolution on Responsible Parenthood," adopted by the 1972 General Conference of the United Methodist Church; cited by Theresa Hoover in ibid., p. 320.

17. "Understanding the Abortion Argument," *Philosophy and Public Affairs*, vol. 1 (Fall 1971), p. 73.

sary intensity of feeling to make the required effort, but exactly because the issue is so divisive that politicians shy away from the consequences of winning. "If I have a girl 12 or 13 years old, I do not want the U.S. Senate to have to make a decision," former Senator Warren G. Magnuson, Democrat of Washington, said in 1977. "If that young child became pregnant, I just do not think we are competent [to decide whether to permit abortion]."[18] Others fear that the legitimacy of policy will be jeopardized by the suspicion of untoward influence exerted by one or another religious group, a claim specifically made at the federal district court level by the National Abortion Rights Action League in its 1978 challenge to the constitutionality of the Hyde amendment that prohibited the use of federal medicaid funds to finance abortions. Still others anticipate a high probability either of disobedience to law or of efforts to obstruct lawful behavior. The passage of a constitutional prohibition on abortion "would merely restore the practice of millions of illegal abortions," former Senator Edward W. Brooke, Republican of Massachusetts, who for several years led the freedom of choice forces in the Senate, once told his colleagues. The Constitution, he added, "was not meant to be the repository of every proposed solution to every social ill."[19]

That view of constitutional change is as likely to be advanced by opponents of abortion as by its supporters. Former HEW Secretary Califano, for example, an antiabortion leader, opposes any amendment to overturn the Court's position. "My own position, as far as the constitutional amendment is concerned, is that it does not make any sense that we run to the Constitution on abortion, we run there to stop busing, we run to the Constitution on prayers in schools. We have to stop running to the Constitution to solve all of our problems."[20] And Representative Robert H. Michel, Republican of Illinois, who argues the antiabortion case in the House HEW Appropriations Subcommittee, uses language much the same as Califano's: "I personally happen to be one of those individuals who does not like to see our Constitution cluttered up with amendments for busing, for abortion, for booze, or anything else of that nature."[21]

18. *Congressional Record*, daily edition (August 4, 1977), p. S13675.

19. *Abortion*, Hearings, pt. 1, p. 447.

20. *Nominations of Joseph A. Califano, Jr. and Laurence N. Woodworth*, Hearing before the Senate Committee on Finance, 95 Cong. 1 sess. (GPO, 1977), p. 25.

21. *Departments of Labor and Health, Education, and Welfare Appropriations for 1979*, Hearings before a Subcommittee of the House Committee on Appropriations, 95 Cong. 2 sess. (GPO, 1978), pt. 2, pp. 77–78.

Others find the booze and busing comparisons singularly inapposite. Senator Thomas F. Eagleton, Democrat of Missouri, a liberal who is Catholic, describes it as his "profound moral conviction that life is a continuum, from first beginnings in the womb to the final gasp of the dying, and that the first function of society, the primary responsibility of government, is to protect life."[22] Consequently, Eagleton considers abortion unacceptable except where the life of the mother is endangered and "for this reason" votes for restrictions on abortion. Representative Stephen L. Neal, a Democrat and an Episcopalian from North Carolina, rejects the postulate that life begins at the moment of conception, but acknowledges that if he did accept it, "I, too, would feel compelled to work to end abortion—whenever and however possible."[23]

Veteran members of Congress not given to hyperbole have described the abortion issue as being harder than any other decision they have faced. Magnuson, for example, calls it "probably the most sensitive subject today in the United States."[24] Ex-Senator Birch Bayh, Democrat of Indiana, who opposes restrictions on abortion, characterizes the question of whether to permit even the private practice of abortion as "the most deeply felt philosophical, religious, and moral issue I have ever confronted."[25] Senator Bob Packwood of Oregon, a liberal Republican, says flatly that "abortion is the most divisive basic issue I have run across in my experience. It far outweighs, in terms of its supporters and its opponents, gun registration, fluoridation, or any other issue of temporary or permanent significance."[26] John Brademas calls abortion "an infinitely more complicated issue than others," and one that cannot be viewed "in terms of the leadership's ability to resolve a matter."[27]

Both sides use the concept of family stability to defend their positions. Although he opposes the liberalization of restrictions on medicaid financing of abortions, Senator John C. Stennis, Democrat of Mississippi, does not consider himself inhumane or calloused. Rather, as he once said, freedom of choice is an assault on the family and therefore on the American system:

22. *Congressional Record*, daily edition (December 7, 1977), p. S19444.
23. Ibid. (November 3, 1977), p. H12174.
24. Ibid. (August 4, 1977), p. S13671.
25. Ibid. (November 3, 1977), p. S18582.
26. Ibid. (June 29, 1977), p. S11030.
27. *National Journal* (December 10, 1977), p. 1932.

I believe that on this matter of abortion, abortion at will or by choice, whatever it may be called, by and large, as it is carried on and practiced now with private funds, or public funds, or anything else, it is an attack on the family.

That is the main issue; it is an attack on the human family. . . .

Very respectfully, I believe that whatever is an attack on the human family is an attack even on our form of government, because the human family is a major institution in the bedrock and foundation of our system of self-government.[28]

Pro-choice proponents relate their goal to the family cause by stressing the unhappy consequences almost certain to be visited on a family by the addition of an unwanted child. "Some of these people," Representative Millicent Fenwick, Republican of New Jersey, points out, "are mothers trying to protect their children. They are young married women with three or four children, the husband not making much money, or any money, and they are trying to work out some kind of a solution to a difficult life."[29]

A policymaker's region, religion, sex, political liberalism, or constituency is not a reliable predictor of his or her position on abortion. For example, Bob Packwood, a non-Catholic from a heavily Protestant state, may be the Senate's most unyielding supporter of pro-choice, but his Oregon colleague, Mark Hatfield, also a non-Catholic and a liberal Republican, has become a leader in support of a constitutional prohibition deemed "a priority of the highest order" by the National Conference of Catholic Bishops. "The purpose of this amendment," Hatfield says of a proposed constitutional prohibition, "is to restore an essential unity to what the law recognizes as a person, and what we know from science, observation, and conviction to constitute a human being. Our task is to insure that rights endowed by God are not denied by the State."[30] Hatfield denies the validity of pro-choice, reaching the conclusion Wertheimer had assigned to "Catholics." "I do not, after all," Hatfield says, "believe merely in my right to be; I believe in the right of all life to be. It would be hypocritical cowardice to hold such a conviction, but not to propose, as a legislator, that society embrace this view."[31] Paradoxically, however, former Representative Robert F. Dri-

28. *Congressional Record*, daily edition (December 7, 1977), p. S19446.
29. Ibid. (November 3, 1977), p. H12171.
30. *Abortion*, Hearings, pt. 1, p. 7.
31. *Congressional Record* (May 31, 1973), p. 17557.

nan, Democrat of Massachusetts, who is a Catholic priest not given to "hypocritical cowardice," voted against pro-life restrictions.

Other members of Congress reject Hatfield's "hypocritical coward-ice" argument, insisting that abortion restrictions represent efforts to impose a code of morality or a religious conviction on those who would exercise their right to freedom of religion. According to Representative William Clay, Democrat of Missouri, a black Catholic who believes neither in abortion nor in legislating against it, "It's the concept of the holy wars all over again." "The heathens must be conquered and convicted. That's what's wrong with this amendment. I oppose the amendment strictly on the basis that it flies in the face of the first amendment—and sets a dangerous precedent for Federal legisla-tion."[32] But whereas William Clay is scornful of "holy wars" against abortion and argues the absolute primacy of the first amendment, Henry J. Hyde, Republican of Illinois and Congress's most effective proponent of restrictions on abortion, asks whether the abolitionists who fought slavery were illegally trying to impose their theology on the nation. As for the first amendment, Hyde finds it no bar to moral principle:

Aren't moral perceptions contained in our country's founding documents? ". . . All men are created equal, and are endowed by their Creator with certain inalienable rights. . . ." Does this language violate the wall of separation between church and state?[33]

What the Constitution gives, it may, in any event, take away. Even if proponents were to acknowledge—as they do not—that an abortion restriction represented preference for the precepts of a particular reli-gion, a constitutional prohibition on abortion would have to be con-strued as an implied exception. Despite the stated goal of right-to-life leaders to bring an amendment through Congress in the early 1980s, there is scant prospect that a constitutional prohibition on abortion will actually come to the states for ratification.

Achieving the required two-thirds majority of each house is always hard, and especially so for proposals to use the Constitution to regulate human behavior. The complexity of the question, moreover, gives right-to-life forces trouble in coming to agreement on just what is to be forbidden. The opposition tends to emphasize the scientific impossi-

32. Ibid., daily edition (April 27, 1978), p. H3312.
33. Letter (April 25, 1978) to the editor from Henry Hyde, *New York Times*, May 3, 1978.

bility of defining the time at which life begins and the practical impossibility of writing precise constitutional language. A few years ago, for example, the late Senator Dewey Bartlett, Republican of Oklahoma, in the course of a lucid plea for an antiabortion amendment, argued that life begins with conception. Bartlett then had to respond to a question about the meanings of "conception." Did he intend it to suggest fertilization or implantation? First responding that "perhaps you could say it begins at conception and is reenforced at implantation," then deciding that "I will amend slightly what I said. I will say life begins with conception, fertilization," Bartlett finally found himself dodging as "a lot of legalistic specifics" the question of whether anything that prohibits birth after fertilization would be an aborting effort.[34] No chairman of a constitutional amendment subcommittee could let such an opening pass, and Birch Bayh professed wonder at "how you could look at members of the Constitutional Amendment Subcommittee dealing with one of the most complicated, controversial issues and tell us that we are not supposed to get involved in legal specifics when we just have to know how far this proposal is going to go."[35] Before his questioners let loose, Bartlett was in the curious position of asserting that life begins with fertilization and simultaneously denying that removal of a fertilized egg by scraping the womb constituted abortion. "I grant," he acknowledged, "that that is an area of disagreement, and an area of confusion."[36]

Specifying just what a constitutional prohibition on abortion is to prohibit is not made easier by the diversity of popular views on when human life begins. Judith Blake has reported the results of Gallup surveys of January 1973 and April 1975 in which respondents were asked their views on whether human life begins at conception ("when sperm and egg first meet"), at quickening ("when the woman first feels movement inside her"), at viability ("when the unborn baby could probably survive if it were born prematurely"), or at birth. In both surveys men saw life as beginning at a later time than women, and Catholics saw life as beginning at an earlier time than non-Catholics. In the second survey half the respondents said that life began at conception, up from the 43 percent who had so responded the week of the *Roe* v. *Wade* decision in 1973. But even so, in the more conservative

34. *Abortion,* Hearings, pt. 1, p. 424.
35. Ibid., p. 425.
36. Ibid., p. 426.

response (which Blake suggested might be the result of right-to-life propaganda on this issue) half the respondents viewed life as beginning at quickening or later.[37] That view apparently does not carry over to the acceptance of abortion before quickening. In a 1976 Gallup survey 45 percent of the respondents expressed support for a constitutional amendment prohibiting abortions except when the pregnant woman's life is in danger.[38] Other survey evidence, however, indicates that rape and fetal deformity are also accepted as grounds for abortion.[39]

In the period during which all these surveys were taken, only the right-to-life groups were on the offensive. Since *Roe* v. *Wade* was the law, and constitutional change a right-to-life pipe dream, it was unnecessary for free-choice proponents to mobilize support for their position. As the pipe dream turns into a bona fide cause, free-choice supporters can be expected to raise exactly the kind of legal specifics with which Birch Bayh and his constitutional amendment subcommittee colleagues unnerved Dewey Bartlett. Is saving the life of the mother to be the sole permissible exception? If so, a substantial bloc of potential supporters—those who regard post-quickening or post-viability abortion as destructive of human life but earlier abortion as a private matter—are lost. So are the substantial blocs that tolerate the abortion of a deformed fetus or of a fetus resulting from rape or incest. Yet a constitutional prohibition that does not prohibit early-stage abortion will have little bearing on the reality of abortion practice. And a proposed amendment that allows the abortion of a deformed fetus asks its supporters to limit their regard for right-to-life to perfectly formed human life, a position with which many cannot agree.

A cause that only loses strength as it moves from abstract slogan to legal specifics, right-to-life cannot be accomplished without legal specificity. But a consensus broad enough to make constitutional change possible cannot agree on legal specifics beyond prohibiting abortion in the third trimester of pregnancy except to save the life of the mother. On the pro-choice side, that lowest common denominator is likely to be fought only by those who hold most tenaciously to the view that the principle of woman's control of her own body can allow no exception. For pro-life groups, however, a third-trimester prohibition, though a desirable objective, is far too limited to be acceptable as constitutional

37. Blake, "The Supreme Court's Abortion Decisions," p. S16330.
38. Ibid., p. S16332.
39. Ibid.

language. So is a prohibition after the first trimester even if those terms were acceptable to the free-choice side—and they are not acceptable.

Constricted Policy Choices

The politics of abortion has two distinct elements—electoral and policy. The electoral element can make a substantial, perhaps decisive, contribution to the outcome of a legislative campaign. For example, Dick Clark may have been defeated for reelection to the Senate in 1978 because Iowa voters believed he was too involved in African affairs and not enough in Iowa affairs or because the political arm of Iowans for Life, its Pro-Life Action Council, campaigned against him. But in any case abortion politics clearly played an important role in effecting the outcome. A compelling issue matters, and most elections produce one winner, one loser, not a compromise composite or a deferral of the outcome to a later time. Pro-life groups are therefore organizing to make their friends winners and their opponents losers.

The politics of abortion policy offers more limited rewards. With the Hyde amendment firmly in place, fighting occurs only over marginal exceptions to its prohibition on the expenditure of federal medicaid money for abortions. The stakes are small—federal participation in the financing of a few hundred abortions annually. Because policymakers who try to respond to the public anxiety about abortion are stymied by insoluble questions of theology and philosophy and by practical considerations of constitutional law and constitutional restraint, they end up by arguing about what meaning to give a handful of words. Abortion policy questions in Congress and in HEW now involve interpreting such nontheological terms as "medical procedures," "promptly," and "long-lasting." And however the interpretations go, whether federal money is available or withheld, most of the abortions will be performed.

Although abortion will be an important issue in individual elections for the indefinite future, the ability of pro-life forces to legislate their views peaked with the medicaid limitation adopted in the late 1970s. Despite that success, and despite earlier statements of support provided to the antiabortion cause by President Carter and Secretary Califano, pro-life is at a federal policy dead end. By giving pro-choice constitutional protection, the Court has made the views of federal officials irrelevant unless they are willing to embrace constitutional changes. That dangerous course is approached but not pursued. Consider, for example, candidate Jimmy Carter's statement on abortion in an interview with the National Catholic News Service on August 9, 1976:

I think abortion is wrong and I think that government ought not ever do anything to encourage abortion. . . .

I think that the government—and it will under my administration—should do everything possible to minimize abortions under whatever ruling the court might have in effect at that particular time. . . .

I would do everything I could through moral persuasion and through my own actions as President, under the laws which I will be sworn to enforce, to minimize a need for abortion. . . . It's obvious to me that human life should be protected. . . .

I have come out openly in opposition, throughout the campaign, against the use of federal money to finance abortions.[40]

Califano, at his confirmation hearing, was just as unequivocal:

Governor Carter and I come from quite different religious, cultural and social backgrounds, yet our views on this subject are identical. My views are as follows:

First, I personally believe that abortion is wrong.

Second, I believe that Federal funds should not be used for the purpose of providing abortions.

Third, I believe that it is imperative that the alternatives available to abortion be made available as widely as possible. . . .

My view would be exactly what Governor Carter's would be, a view which he repeatedly stated during the campaign. We would recommend that Federal funds not be used to provide abortions. . . .

Federal funds are not appropriate for it, to use Federal funds for an abortion, for women rich or poor.[41]

For a cabinet nominee addressing as controversial an issue as abortion, Califano's answers were unusually explicit—enough so to have cost him the vote of Bob Packwood, whose liberal Republican views on social policy overlap Califano's. Packwood has explained that he was disaffected by Califano's intransigence on the abortion issue in contrast to his willingness to temporize on other hard questions of social policy. "Anytime he wanted to avoid a question, he did," said Packwood. "Anytime he was not prepared to answer, he did not. But when it came to the issue of abortion, he was waiting to answer, willing to answer, wanting to answer."[42] Packwood's reading of what he termed Califano's "vivid description of his innermost feelings" led the senator to

40. The Presidential Campaign, 1976, vol. 1: Jimmy Carter (GPO, 1978), pt. 1, pp. 455–57.
41. Nominations of Joseph A. Califano, Jr. and Laurence N. Woodworth, Hearing, p. 5.
42. Congressional Record, daily edition (January 24, 1977), p. S1172.

predict that within whatever discretion the law allowed Califano would use the weight of his office, the weight of his personality, and the weight of President Carter's prestige to limit abortions in any way possible. Though the senator's prediction was accurate, it underemphasized the importance of the qualification "within whatever discretion the law allowed" and of Califano's sensitivity to a defensible legal position.

Within a few months, the Court had upheld the Connecticut limit on medicaid abortions, Congress had adopted the first Hyde amendment, and the way had been cleared for HEW to carry out the stated goal of the president and his HEW secretary—to "do everything possible to minimize abortions under whatever ruling the court might have in effect at that particular time."

When regulatory authority is delegated to a cabinet officer and his position on a disputed subject is known, and known to accord perfectly with that of the president, rational persons must expect him to resolve deliberately ambiguous questions in favor of the position he has espoused. Califano's clearly stated opposition to abortion entitled him to tilt in the direction of a restrictive abortion rider. In fact, however, rather than doing "everything possible to minimize abortions," regulations adopted to implement the version of the Hyde amendment enacted in 1977 tilted—within admittedly narrow limits—in the direction of maximizing the abortion possibility.[43]

Henry Hyde found the regulations "outrageous . . . the weakest regulations possible," whereas the Religious Coalition for Abortion Rights, in a reaction typical of freedom-of-choice groups, described them as "compassionate and fair."[44] Widely divergent reactions to HEW's clarification of deliberately ambiguous legislative language were inevitable, but given the stated predilections of the president and of the HEW secretary, pro-choice groups had expected to find the regulations "outrageous" and right-to-life people had expected to find them "fair." Instead, HEW's decisions about the meaning of "medical procedures" and of "promptly" provoked a role reversal.

There was no way that the secretary's regulations could satisfy spokesmen for the Senate majority, who insisted that " 'medical pro-

---

43. *Federal Register*, vol. 43 (February 2, 1978), pt. 3, pp. 4570–82. For Hyde's detailed critique of the regulations and the HEW response, see *Departments of Labor and Health, Education, and Welfare Appropriations for 1979*, Hearings, pt. 2, pp. 174–81.

44. *Congressional Record*, daily edition (January 30, 1978), p. E230.

cedures' necessary for the victims of rape or incest" included abortion, and could also satisfy spokesmen for the House majority, who insisted that such "procedures" excluded abortion. So, in a joint letter to Califano, Senators Magnuson and Brooke, chairman and ranking minority member of the Senate Labor-HEW Appropriations subcommittee, told the secretary:

It is clearly spelled out in the legislative history that "medical procedures" for rape and incest include abortions. That was made abundantly clear in a colloquy on the Senate floor on December 7 when Senator Brooke asked Senator Magnuson, "Am I correct about our intent that medical procedures do include abortion? Is that the Chairman's understanding?" Senator Magnuson replied:

"That is correct. I think we should make it clear to the Secretary, Mr. Califano, that we mean that a woman who is a victim of rape or incest may have an abortion as long as she reports the incident, and he (the Secretary) should issue regulations . . . that will carry out that intent."[45]

On the other hand, Representative Hyde insisted that "if the term 'abortion' were meant to apply to treatment following rape, the amendment would have said so. 'Medical procedure' is clearly treatment of a far less drastic nature than abortion and a reasonable reading of the amendment in question requires this distinction."[46] But the term "medical procedures" was deliberately left undefined. Every member voting for the term could in good conscience believe himself to be voting for a narrow or a broad exception to financing abortions after rape or incest. No more specific provision could be agreed to because majorities in each house were unyielding in their contrary positions, and the business of government demanded the enactment of the appropriations bill.

Not only did the House give plenty of warning that it was leaving a policy decision to the secretary of HEW, but George Mahon, chairman of the Appropriations Committee, claimed that the ambiguity of the language was to its advantage: "That language [medical procedures] it seems to me is a little bit fuzzy and at the same time not too bad. . . . It could possibly include abortions, but the regulations would have to be promulgated and rigorously enforced by the HEW."[47] David Obey, Democrat of Wisconsin, who has thought about the abortion

45. Letter, Edward W. Brooke and Warren G. Magnuson to the Honorable Joseph A. Califano, December 22, 1977.

46. *Congressional Record*, daily edition (January 30, 1978), p. E231.

47. Ibid. (November 3, 1977), p. H12169.

dilemma as much as any member of the House, and who proposed twenty-seven different versions of compromise language to the conference committee, agrees that in "medical procedures" the House was buying a pig in a poke. Does "medical procedures" mean abortion? "There is no one here who can honestly answer that question," Obey told House colleagues. "The fact is what that language means, in the end specifically what it means will be determined by the regulations which are established by HEW, and they will determine whether or not there will or will not be abortions under that language."[48] Eventually, the House did adopt the "medical procedures" language, its meaning left for Califano to determine.

Initial signals indicating that the secretary would act in a way consistent with his stated antiabortion beliefs provoked legislative and editorial lobbying for a different outcome. There was a different outcome, a "liberal" one that surprised at least those who had assumed that an antiabortion secretary of HEW working for an antiabortion president would resolve any statutory ambiguity as narrowly as possible. But Califano took the high legalistic road, citing an opinion by Attorney General Griffin Bell that "medical procedures" for victims of rape or incest who report the incident "promptly" must indeed include abortions. "My personal views," Califano insisted, "are of no relevance to the legal duty of interpreting what Congress intended and writing regulations that embody that intent."[49] On that issue, Obey's view was that if Secretary Califano could determine what congressional intent was on abortion, he was "a whale of a lot smarter man than I am." Since the secretary's personal views were well-known to a Congress that steadfastly avoided clarifying its intent and insisted on throwing the decision to him, Califano's "liberal" regulations disappointed antiabortion legislators who had hoped to achieve indirectly what they had been unable to achieve directly. That Califano accompanied his lawyerlike interpretation of congressional intent with a personal plea for a much tighter law disarmed both sides. Pro-life forces could not challenge a secretary who insisted that his legal responsibility overrode his personal preferences. And pro-choice forces could not complain about a secretary who was outspoken in opposing abortion but on their side in interpreting ambiguity in the law. The game was not worth the

48. Ibid.
49. *New York Times*, January 27, 1978.

candle. The "medical procedures" exception served to justify payment for only sixty-one abortions during the last eleven months of 1978.[50]

Pro-choice won most of the important abortion policy fights of the seventies, but pro-life clearly won the federal medicaid battle. A fight that had begun over whether to impose any restriction on federal financing of abortion under medicaid became a fight over whether to allow any federal financing of abortion under medicaid. Without even bothering to discount for a high rate of error that inflates the count, it can be said that the federal financing of medicaid abortion has virtually ended.

Application of the Hyde amendment, despite regulations that Hyde termed "total emasculation" of the amendment, has reduced federally financed medicaid abortions by 99 percent. Where HEW estimates ran to 200,000 annually before the amendment, the department reported only 2,421 from February 14, 1978, to December 31, 1978, including an inflated total of 811—one-third the reported national total—from Ohio, where the Department of Public Welfare would record and report as four separate abortions the claims for the same abortion separately filed by a physician, an anesthesiologist, a hospital or clinic, and a laboratory.[51] For pro-life groups, this huge reduction is heady stuff, inspiring a continuing drive for a flat constitutional prohibition.

Viewed from a nonmedicaid perspective, the balance tilts in the other direction—an estimated total of under 23,000 legal abortions nationally in 1969 is dwarfed even by the conservative estimate of 616,000 in 1973, the year of the Supreme Court decision altering legal abortion policy. Surveys of hospitals, clinics, and physicians providing abortion services show that total to have reached 1.25 million five years later. Nevertheless, for the National Abortion Federation, a pro-choice group of about 160 abortion facilities plus other advocacy organizations and individuals, the pro-choice success indicated by the increased number of abortions is marred by the limitation on medicaid financing.

Interest groups and causes need victories or reasonable hopes of victories to keep the troops enthusiastic and to sustain themselves. In

50. *Departments of Labor and Health, Education, and Welfare Appropriations for 1980,* Hearings before a Subcommittee of the House Committee on Appropriations, 96 Cong. 1 sess. (GPO, 1979), p. 146.

51. "Medicaid Abortions in Ohio," memorandum, Terry Thomas, Ohio Legislative Budget Committee and Office, to Senator Harry Meshel, August 29, 1979. I am indebted to William J. Shkurti, special assistant to the attorney general of Ohio, for pursuing my inquiry into the Ohio report.

the abortion fight, both sides can claim victories, both have dedicated troops, and both are well-positioned to sustain the fight. Abortion can be counted on to be the dominant family-related public problem for the indefinite future, and the one the policy process is least likely to resolve, because neither side is comfortable with less than total victory, each side views its cause as sacred, and both are right.

Adolescent Pregnancy

Some kinds of families should never be formed. More than fifty years ago, Justice Holmes's celebrated explanation, "Three generations of imbeciles are enough," upheld for the Supreme Court a Virginia statute providing for compulsory sterilization of severely retarded persons confined in public institutions.[52] If one can be confident of the diagnosis—a confidence that was probably not warranted in the case under review[53]—Holmes's conclusion is hardly unreasonable. But freedom to choose is the controlling ethic, since there are few circumstances in which past and current events make it possible to predict with a high degree of certainty the future social costs of family formation—to say nothing of future physical, emotional, and economic disadvantages likely to be suffered by the members of a family. Consequently, prior restraint on family formation is almost unknown in democratic society, although public and private efforts to discourage family formation are countenanced for various reasons. For example, geneticists discourage first pregnancies in women over thirty-five because of the high risk of fetal defects. Neo-Malthusians, worried that population growth will depress living standards, espouse small family size, or urge couples who are not determined to have children to avoid forming families entirely. Others concerned about the ability of particular classes of people to furnish a child the varieties of supports thought necessary for a decent life will especially discourage family formation or family additions by very poor people or emotionally disturbed people. For obvious reasons, almost everyone discourages children from having children.

On the other hand, unmarried single persons, long discouraged on moral and psychological grounds from forming parent-child families,

52. *Buck v. Bell*, 274 U.S. 200, 207 (1927).
53. Clement E. Vose, *Constitutional Change* (Heath, 1972), pp. 13–17.

are now less likely to be discouraged in efforts to adopt and are more likely to keep a biological child than to give it up. Single-parent adoptions, if not routine, have belatedly come to be accepted as usually preferable to indefinite foster care of a child and invariably preferable to institutional care. Family formation through artificial insemination by either known or anonymous donors is an identifiable practice, and for a known donor may carry paternal custodial and visitation rights.

The Policy Problem

Because science advances and judgments change, the moral and ethical issues—and some practical problems—that arise from efforts to influence who should be encouraged, who discouraged, from family formation do not lend themselves to easy resolution. All that can be agreed to, perhaps, is that a prospective parent who lacks a combination of physical, economic, and emotional resources for pregnancy and child care should be discouraged, and that persons under eighteen almost invariably fall into that class. The policy problem is to find an acceptable way to institutionalize discouragement. Though no objection is heard to the continued pursuit of an entirely safe vaccine that might provide adolescent men and women long-term, say septennial, protection against procreation, that ideal does not qualify as an immediately helpful response to a perceived demand for prompt action of some sort.

At its peak in the 1950s, the adolescent birthrate was a silent crisis. Physicians and lawyers quietly arranged for pregnant adolescents to be "cared for" financially during late pregnancy and delivery, then relieved of their infants so that infertile wives, usually from another jurisdiction, might adopt infants they could not themselves conceive. Silence was perceived to be a benefit to all the actors: the adolescent could be spared stigmatization as an unwed mother, and spared the burden of caring for a child she was ill-equipped to care for; adoptive parents could satisfy their desire for a child or children; cooperating professionals could feel that the service was benefiting the biological mother as well as the adoptive parents; all the participants could feel that the arrangements would benefit the infant. A court, giving perfunctory approval to arrangements of this sort, also could regard the outcome as better for the child than either institutionalization or prolonged foster care while he or she awaited adoption. As long as it was unthinkable for a visible, unwed adolescent to keep her child, neither prevention nor long-run services to mother and child got much attention even from the most compassionate of policymakers.

Now that keeping the baby of a teenage mother within the biological family is routine, attention focuses on the statistics. Whether adolescent pregnancy is perceived as a growing or declining problem depends on one's disposition to emphasize rates or absolute numbers. The cheerful interpretation notes that despite the new sexual permissiveness, the birthrate for eighteen- and nineteen-year-old women has been declining or steady since the mid-1960s, marred only by a deviation in 1970 (table 3-1).

The rate for fifteen-, sixteen-, and seventeen-year-olds—down about 20 percent between the 1950s and the mid-1970s—was about the same in the late 1970s as in the late 1960s. Only among the youngest group— children ten through fourteen—where the whole numbers remain small, was the birthrate higher in the 1970s than in the 1950s and 1960s. A more depressing reading that focuses on whole numbers notes that despite a steady decline since 1973, the number of live births to women under eighteen in 1978 still exceeded the number in any of the years between 1966 and 1969.

Table 3-1. Procreation among Females under Twenty, by Age Group, 1966–78

	Number of live births			Birthrate [a]		
Year	10–14	15–17	18–19	10–14	15–17	18–19
1966	8,128	186,704	434,722	0.8	35.7	120.3
1967	8,593	188,234	408,211	0.9	35.3	116.7
1968	9,504	192,970	398,342	1.0	35.1	113.5
1969	10,468	201,770	402,884	1.0	35.7	112.4
1970	11,752	223,590	421,118	1.2	38.8	114.7
1971	11,578	226,298	401,644	1.1	38.3	105.6
1972	12,082	236,641	379,639	1.2	39.2	97.3
1973	12,861	238,403	365,693	1.3	38.9	91.8
1974	12,529	234,177	361,272	1.2	37.7	89.3
1975	12,642	227,270	354,968	1.3	36.6	85.7
1976	11,928	215,493	343,251	1.2	34.6	81.3
1977	11,455	213,788	345,366	1.2	34.5	81.9
1978	10,772	202,661	340,746	1.2	32.9	81.0

Sources: Data for 1978 and 1977 are from U.S. Department of Health, Education, and Welfare, National Center for Health Statistics, *Final Natality Statistics, 1978*, DHEW (PHS) 80-1120 (HEW, 1980), and *Final Natality Statistics, 1977*, DHEW (PHS) 79-1120 (HEW, 1979); data for 1966–76 are from DHEW, *Health—United States, 1978*, DHEW (PHS) 78-1232 (HEW, 1978).

a. Live births per 1,000 females.

Even total numbers are susceptible to different interpretations. Consider that about 1 million teenage women became pregnant each year of the mid-1970s. In one year, 1974, about 41 percent of those pregnancies terminated in abortion or miscarriage and 28 percent resulted in births conceived after marriage—mostly to the eighteen- and nineteen-year-old group. Two-thirds of the remaining 31 percent resulted in out-of-wedlock births, and one-third in births to couples who married after conceiving a child.[54] One observer will be struck by the magic total of 1 million pregnancies, another by the 270,000 abortions, close to 30 percent of all abortions. Still another will narrow in on other numbers—the 210,000 births to unmarried teenage mothers, including the 12,500 births to children between ten and fourteen—and conclude that these represent the worst of it, that 210,000 is not 1 million, that things are not as grim as they are said to be.

Since the dimensions of the problem can be read so differently, disagreement is likely over the proper balance of public program activity between prevention of pregnancy and services to teenagers during pregnancy and after childbirth. Disagreement is also likely over how to pursue a prevention strategy. Sex education, ready access to contraceptive materials, moral suasion, and abortion, each alone and in various combinations, are preventive techniques supported by different groups that agree only on one thing: that adolescent parenthood is not as a rule desirable. Deploring adolescent parenthood is not a question of politics, race, religion, or attitude to the welfare state. No social theorist makes a case for children as parents, nor is there one to be made.

Although a report on one study of 9,000 births at a Copenhagen hospital concludes that the late teens are the best time for a woman, if provided with proper care, to give birth,[55] the physiological, economic,

54. Alan Guttmacher Institute of Planned Parenthood Federation of America, *11 Million Teenagers: What Can Be Done About the Epidemic of Adolescent Pregnancies in the United States* (New York: Guttmacher Institute, 1976), p. 10. U.S. Department of Health, Education, and Welfare, National Center for Health Statistics, *Teenage Childbearing: United States, 1966–75,* Monthly Vital Statistics Report, vol. 26, no. 5, supplement, DHEW (HRA)77-1120 (HEW, 1977). Memorandum to the Secretary of Health, Education, and Welfare from the Deputy Assistant Secretary for Planning and Evaluation, "Initiative to Address Adolescent Pregnancy and Related Issues—DECISION MEMORANDUM," August 4, 1977. Wendy H. Baldwin, "Adolescent Pregnancy and Childbearing—Growing Concern for Americans," *Population Bulletin,* vol. 31, no. 2 (Washington, D.C.: Population Reference Bureau, 1976), esp. pp. 35–36.

55. Marie Rebenkoff, "Study Shows Teen Years Are Easiest for Childbirth," *New York Times,* April 4, 1979.

and emotional arguments taken together point to the advantages of delaying family formation to the post-teen years. Research reported in *11 Million Teenagers* shows that the risks of infant death, of low infant birth weight, and of both fatal and nonfatal complications during pregnancy, labor, and childbirth are all measurably greater for teenage mothers than for mothers in the so-called prime childbearing years of twenty through twenty-four. Any biological advantages young mothers may have in childbirth are likely to be lost by the absence of proper care, and the probability of lifetime educational and economic disadvantage as well as of marital dissolution is apparent. "Whatever other value judgments" may be made about the data, Daniel Callahan has put it, "I doubt that anyone would want to say that it is a good thing that teenagers get pregnant. On that much, agreement can be assumed."[56]

Adolescent sexuality and its consequences burst upon the consciousness of federal administrators in the 1970s. Even if the problem was relatively no more severe then than it had been ten or twenty years earlier, it only recently became an open problem, an acceptable target for public policy. Identified, measured, and universally condemned before the Carter administration took office, adolescent pregnancy invited a policy response. When HEW Secretary Califano told a House subcommittee "Something has to be done about that problem," nobody quarreled.[57] But just what thing was to be done?

To comfort or to preclude represented the policy options. The family planning lobby, cheered by what it believed to be demonstrable success in reducing birthrates among older adolescents by providing easy access to contraceptive information and materials, had initiated a major drive for expanded federal support. Programs supported by philanthropic foundations to offer a variety of services—psychological, medical, contraceptive—to sexually active and pregnant teenagers suggested another model for federal action. Should a public program undertake to cushion the consequences of adolescent parenthood and to counsel against repetition, or should it seek to maximize the opportunities for preventing and for terminating adolescent pregnancy? Could it do both? Neither one alone would be undesirable or wasteful. To move in one direction would not preclude moving in the other as

56. Alan Guttmacher Institute, *11 Million Teenagers,* pp. 22–23, 57.

57. *Departments of Labor and Health, Education, and Welfare Appropriations for 1978,* Hearings before a Subcommittee of the House Committee on Appropriations, 95 Cong. 1 sess. (GPO, 1977), pt. 2, p. 22.

well. But if public policy shies away from prevention and termination, it does less than it is capable of doing to minimize the formation of weak families. If policy shies away from ex post facto services, it does less than it is capable of doing to shore up weak families.

Children having children makes for weak families, but policymakers have done better deploring the phenomenon than facing adolescent sexuality realistically and acting in accord with the limited ways in which public policy can respond to it. Someday continence, which is, as Sargent Shriver reminded a House committee in 1978, "the most cost-effective, safe, and certain family planning technique available to men as well as to women"[58] may be widely adopted by sexually driven and sexually curious adolescents. As best we know, however, a majority of men and almost 40 percent of women between fifteen and nineteen do not practice continence.[59] For public policy to ignore them, given the possible social and economic consequences, would make policy more irresponsible than the subjects. Responsible policy can help them to avoid pregnancy, to terminate unwanted pregnancy, or to secure prenatal and postnatal supporting services when pregnancy occurs and is carried to term. Politicians' views on ethics and morality as well as evaluations of actual experience with each strategy result in shifting emphases. Present policy downplays termination—at least at public expense—although politicians simultaneously dedicated to reducing adolescent pregnancy and to opposing abortion face a particularly awkward reality: despite the easier availability of contraceptive services, the recent decline in births to adolescents reflects an increase in the number of reported legal abortions performed on women under twenty.[60]

If ethical and moral principles also preclude accepting adolescent sexuality as a fact of life, rather than as a pathology, the policy options are effectively reduced to one—that of services to pregnant adolescents before and after delivery. But what services are most likely to overcome

58. *Fertility and Contraception in America: Adolescent and Pre-Adolescent Pregnancy*, Hearings before the House Select Committee on Population, 95 Cong. 2 sess. (GPO, 1978), vol. 2, p. 623.

59. "Testimony of Joseph A. Califano, Jr.," *Adolescent Health, Services, and Pregnancy Prevention and Care Act of 1978*, Hearings before the Senate Committee on Human Resources, 95 Cong. 2 sess. (GPO, 1978), p. 28.

60. Maurice J. Moore and Martin O'Connell, *Perspectives on American Fertility*, U.S. Bureau of the Census, Current Population Reports, Special Studies, series P-23, no. 70 (GPO, 1978), p. 51; L. R. Berger, "Abortions in America: The Effects of Restrictive Funding," *New England Journal of Medicine*, vol. 298 (June 1978), pp. 1474–77.

the myriad weaknesses that accompany family formation at too young an age, and to discourage further pregnancies? In some cases the appropriate services may be educational, in others nutritional, in still others psychological. Nor can "all the above" be ruled out in many instances. Consequently the answer is that the services made available must be comprehensive. Stated differently, if abortion is barred and the existence of adolescent sex is not recognized until pregnancy occurs, family-strengthening proponents have no alternative other than to offer a variety of services and to hope their availability will make a bad situation better, that is, will strengthen weak families formed by adolescent parents and will discourage repeaters. "We would define many of those services," Dr. Julius Richmond, assistant secretary of HEW for health, has explained, "if not as primary, as secondary prevention."[61]

From one point of view, the comprehensive services strategy is squarely in accord with a commitment to pursue public policies that strengthen families. It is inconceivable, after all, that providing services to pregnant adolescents and, later, to these same women and their infants can have anything other than a family-strengthening effect. No logical case can be made that health services, counseling, training in maternal development, job counseling, and day care will further weaken these families. The most depressing outcome that can be envisaged is that all the services together are inadequate to overcome the several family weaknesses inherent in adolescent parenthood. Even then, the effort at least will have been made, the commitment to a family-strengthening program discharged.

The general strategy had its heyday in the sixties, but subsequently came to be disparaged as "throwing money at problems." It was distinctly unfashionable by 1978 to "throw money at problems." That unflattering description of earlier efforts—especially those made during the Great Society era to meet the health, educational, and welfare needs of the poor and of minority groups—readily became part of the accepted philosophy of the Carter administration. But when it came time to act on Secretary Califano's dictum that "something has to be done" about the problem of adolescent pregnancy, throwing comprehensive services at pregnant teenagers proved to be the only "something" compatible with the administration's opposition to abortion and

61. *Fertility and Contraception in America*, Hearings, vol. 2, p. 196.

its discomfort with Planned Parenthood's nonconservative approaches to contraception.

The Choice of Life Support over Primary Prevention

The enactment in 1967 of token family planning amendments to welfare titles of the Social Security Act and to the Economic Opportunity Act, followed in 1970 by general family planning legislation, formally moved birth control services from the roster of politically forbidden activities to the roster of important social problems that Congress considers the public's business. The sponsors of these initial acts claimed that their public benefits would be universal, though class-related: direct services to the poor and near-poor, indirect services to the non-poor through research into safe and foolproof methods of contraception. At first, adolescent sexuality was part of but not central to these family planning discussions. Later, however, the need to give specific content to the amorphous idea of family policy spotlighted adolescent pregnancy on the legislative agenda even as birthrates among young mothers declined without legislation particularly addressed to that group.

The sponsors of the 1970 act were pleased enough to skirt references to teenagers. Had there been more attention to that subject, the legislation would most likely have been burdened with restrictions on services to unemancipated minors. Consider, for example, a comment by Representative Peter Kyros, Democrat of Maine and an active member of the House Public Health and Welfare Subcommittee, on testimony from the late Alan Guttmacher, then president of Planned Parenthood. "We cannot indiscriminately provide family planning services to all youngsters from the age of 12 and beyond," said Kyros. "I just do not see how anyone could suggest that." Guttmacher had not suggested it, but he might have. Even then, Planned Parenthood sometimes dealt with adolescent sexuality by starting children on "contraception before the initial sex experience."[62] That exchange remains typical of the difference between those who argue that to protect adolescents from pregnancy is a public responsibility and those who insist that any program must be sensitive to likely public reaction.

62. *Family Planning Services*, Hearing before the Subcommittee on Public Health and Welfare of the House Interstate and Foreign Commerce Committee, 91 Cong. 2 sess. (GPO, 1970), pp. 286, 288.

Family planning legislation did provide a channel through which increased awareness of adolescent fertility has been pushed on policymakers. For example, the March 1973 report on population and family planning activities to the House Appropriations Committee from the deputy assistant secretary for population affairs—a position established by the 1970 act—summarized first findings from a pioneering study of sexual behavior, contraceptive practices, fertility, and nuptiality of females aged fifteen to nineteen, based on a sample of 1,479 black and 3,132 white women. Those findings indicated that in the early seventies 46 percent of all unmarried females had had intercourse by age nineteen, that more than half of sexually active teenagers did not use contraceptives, and that 82 percent of the blacks and 46 percent of the whites incorrectly answered multiple-choice questions relating to the time of the menstrual cycle when the greatest risk of pregnancy occurs.[63] A companion report from the state of Georgia underscored the issue by noting that adolescent pregnancy accounted for 23 percent of total births in 1970, and for more than one of every five deliveries in the state since 1960.[64]

With the same or comparable data appearing year after year, interest grew in creating a special program to help school-age mothers. That interest increased sharply in 1973 after the Supreme Court decision to throw a constitutional protection around abortion. Reacting to that decision, Representative (later Governor of Minnesota) Albert H. Quie and others introduced the School Age Mother and Child Health Act, which Quie described as a way "to redirect the focus of our social services programs to promote the preservation of life, elevate the well-being of the pregnant woman who wishes to give birth, and assist her and her infant in establishing themselves in society." The proposal, said Quie, would provide "life support" services to teenage girls and their children.[65] Comparable bills, sponsored by Senators Edward Kennedy and Birch Bayh in 1975, had the same "life support" rationale, but time ran out on the Ford administration before it was ready to endorse a program.

63. *Departments of Labor and Health, Education, and Welfare Appropriations for 1974,* Hearings before a Subcommittee of the House Committee on Appropriations, 93 Cong. 1 sess. (GPO, 1973), pt. 1, p. 363.

64. Ibid., pp. 334–35.

65. H.R. 10878, 94 Cong. 1 sess. (GPO, 1975); *Proposed Constitutional Amendments on Abortion,* Hearings before the Subcommittee on Civil and Constitutional Rights of the House Judiciary Committee, 94 Cong. 2 sess. (GPO, 1976), p. 656.

In the inevitable fashion of a new administration, President Carter and Secretary Califano went hunting for a distinctive solution, a hunt that took on special intensity when, a few weeks after he assured Congress of his concern, Califano was shown numbers that added up to more than a million teenage pregnancies a year. "When Joe saw those numbers," one of his special assistants has said, "they just dazzled him." One effect was a directive to HEW planning officials to convene an interagency team to develop legislative proposals addressing the issue. The interagency "team" that it was thought necessary to assemble—according to its chairman's later report to the secretary, "because of the complexity and multi-faceted nature" of the issues, and according to others involved, because of the complexity and multifaceted nature of HEW—fit the ordinary definition of *crowd* better than that of *team*. About 50 people were in the work group, which consisted of representatives from each of the department's principal operating components, all assistant secretaries, and the general counsel. In turn, in the course of its deliberations, this inside group solicited opinions from a diverse mixture of 150 outside persons and groups, from the American Association of Sex Educators, Counselors and Therapists to the National Conference of Catholic Bishops. More than half the outside groups participated in the deliberations of the inside group.[66]

Early in August 1977 a package of trouble in the form of a decision memorandum was transmitted to the secretary by his interagency team. At a disingenuous briefing two weeks later, Califano reported only that the administration was considering a coordinated family and youth program to prevent unwanted pregnancies. The program might include, he said, better adolescent family planning clinics, greater incentives to states to encourage sex education in the classroom, and incentives to encourage schools to allow teenage mothers to enroll. For the next four months department officials continued to characterize the memorandum as an "internal document" while trying to decide the politic way to deal with two critical recommendations not discussed at Califano's briefing. Each of these proposed a public policy that was certain to outrage more people than any president and secretary of HEW would ever want to outrage. After thirteen pages of facts, find-

66. Memorandum to the HEW Secretary, "Initiative to Address Adolescent Pregnancy and Related Issues."

ings, assumptions, options, and explanation of a set of packages that would permit "you to accomplish" (not "the Department to recommend") "both *prevention* and *significant support for pregnant adolescents*," the memorandum took up the subjects of abortion and of contraceptive services for minors without parental consent. Neither recommendation appeared compatible with either President Carter's or Secretary Califano's stated views:

Abortions—Information, Referrals and Services. While the options do not address the provision of abortion per se, the Task Force considers abortion information, counseling, services and research essential to reduce the numbers of high-risk adolescent births, particularly for younger adolescents.

Recommendation: Even if Federal funding is not available for pregnancy termination, we recommend that *health and service providers make available abortion information and counseling,* and where appropriate, *referrals to and from abortion services,* to permit the adolescent a full range of choice, and to assist those who do choose to terminate their pregnancy to receive adequate and safe abortion services. . . .

Parental consent and the provision of contraceptive and health services to minors. Between 30 and 40 States now permit adolescents to obtain medical contraceptive services without parental consent. Approximately 800,000 sexually active adolescent women live in States where legal barriers may be a significant impediment to obtaining contraceptive services. . . .

Recommendation: HEW should encourage State policies permitting adolescents to receive contraceptives without requiring parental consent. The adolescent must bear most of the risks and consequences of an unintended pregnancy and should be permitted to avoid the pregnancy. HEW officials should work closely with State political and community leaders, including religious organizations, to seek modification of laws, where necessary, and at the same time, encourage contraceptive service providers to be sensitive to the desirability of family involvement, particularly for young adolescents. [Emphasis in original.][67]

Califano's dilemma was real. Personal conviction steered him away from public support of abortion. Separating "pregnancy termination" from abortion information and counseling, and from referrals to and from abortion services, must be construed as an artificial separation. The political pressure to develop a real alternative to abortion made attractive the recommendation to encourage state policies permitting adolescents unrestricted access to contraceptives without parental consent. Such a proposal, however, would scarcely become an administration dedicated to strengthening families. Yet it would be irresponsible to ignore teenage pregnancy.

67. Ibid., pp. 13, 14.

The dilemma was resolved by falling back on a plan that had been available from the beginning—comprehensive centers providing specialized care for pregnant teenagers. Spelled out in a legacy from Sargent Shriver's brief presidential campaign and submitted to Califano by a so-called Special Task Force months before the HEW interagency team was even organized, the comprehensive center approach clearly favors emphasizing life support over pregnancy prevention. The "Family Development Program" recommended by the task force would among other things, according to its report, "provide practical, ethical and politically viable alternatives to abortion," and would lead "to verifiable improvements in family life."[68]

The origins of the teenage pregnancy program finally decided on by the Carter administration can be traced to an attempt by the Department of Obstetrics at the Johns Hopkins Medical School to upgrade services for adolescents, a group difficult to manage as obstetrical patients. Beginning with an effort to give pregnant adolescents the training and support they needed to understand and cope with labor, and to teach them about reproduction, maternal health, parenting, and family planning, that program added educational and vocational counseling and other services for the mothers, as well as postnatal services for both adolescent mothers and their infants. This comprehensive services center—sustained by financial support and other help from the Kennedy Foundation—had enrolled about 1,500 young women from ages eleven to seventeen between late 1973 and early 1978. Its leaders say that most enrollees in the prenatal program go through labor and delivery smoothly, that their complication rate for toxemia and anemia as well as the prematurity rate has been significantly reduced, and that fewer than 5 percent of the women who go through a follow-up program experience repeat pregnancies within a year, and only 11 percent of them—less than half the national average—become repeaters within eighteen months. Nearly nine out of ten women in the follow-up program were said to be either back in school or employed. "Our whole program," explains the center's prenatal director, "is oriented toward prevention, even though the adolescents are already pregnant. This takes the form of prevention of repeat pregnancy."[69]

The Hopkins people, understandably pleased with their model,

68. "Family Development Program," submitted to the Secretary of HEW by a Special Task Force, March 17, 1977, *Fertility and Contraception in America*, Hearings, vol. 2, p. 656.
69. *Fertility and Contraception in America*, Hearings, vol. 2, p. 208.

regard it as a prototype for a national program. And with some modifications, which put greater emphasis on access to services by sexually active nonpregnant adolescents—an approach used in a voluntary program outside a medical setting called The Door, established in New York City in 1972—the Hopkins "life support" model did become the Carter administration's adolescent pregnancy initiative. The Door's important contribution is its emphasis on privacy and confidentiality plus its old-style settlement house–community center services (photography, theater, weaving) to accompany counseling, family planning, contraception, prenatal care, abortion referral, early child care, postnatal services, and treatment for venereal diseases. Where Hopkins uses pregnancy as the basic point of departure for services, The Door's leaders view adolescent sexuality within what they call "the whole range of problems and challenges that come with this time of life, with awareness of the complexities of being a teenager in today's society, and with the recognition that exploring sexuality is a normal, healthy part of being a teenager."[70]

Picking up precisely on this last point—the belief that exploring sexuality is "a normal, healthy part of being a teenager"—proponents of a different federal approach have insisted that accepting adolescent sexuality as normal behavior rather than as an illness to be treated is the key to overcoming adolescent parenthood. The most eloquent—and most effectively organized—spokesmen for this view represent Planned Parenthood, the country's oldest and largest voluntary family planning organization. Planned Parenthood leaders insist the evidence is clear: make family planning services readily available and teenagers will come after them. During the 1978 legislative hearings on teenage parenthood, Frederick Jaffe, late president of Planned Parenthood's Guttmacher Institute, said publicly and privately that private physicians are unable or unwilling to meet the contraceptive needs of teenagers. He cited as evidence survey findings that of all teenagers who had ever used oral contraceptives, 44 percent of whites and 58 percent of blacks obtained their first prescription from a family planning clinic, although fewer than one-fifth of teenagers depend on clinics for other health services. The number of teenagers served by family planning clinics increased 600 percent between 1969 and 1976, Jaffe said, an

70. *Family Planning Services and Population Research Act Extension of 1978*, Hearing before the Subcommittee on Child and Human Development of the Senate Committee on Human Resources, 95 Cong. 2 sess. (GPO, 1978), p. 327.

increase that demonstrates the ability of such clinics to reach and serve teenagers and help them avoid first pregnancies. And in a not altogether unfair, though politically injudicious, comparison between Secretary Califano's pet cause and his own, Jaffe suggested that "if 500,000 teenagers were enrolling in the anti-smoking campaign each year, the Secretary would have come here this morning, not the Assistant Secretary for Health."[71]

It is absurd to assume all sexually active teenagers to be troubled or sick, the Planned Parenthood argument continues. To the extent that policymakers make that assumption, however, to that extent will they turn away from a straightforward emphasis on delivery of contraceptives through specialized family planning clinics. The idea that contraception alone will not reduce the incidence of teenage pregnancy is termed a "myth" by Planned Parenthood people who deny the validity of HEW's persistent contention that contraceptive services must be accompanied by other services in a comprehensive program like that at Hopkins or The Door.

The HEW position is troubled by internal inconsistencies that have left both congressional health specialists and some agency bureaucrats uncomfortable. Indeed, picking his words carefully, Assistant Secretary Julius Richmond has explained that the department's initiative "is built around certain premises which reflect both Secretary Califano's and the President's concerns. These are, first, that the problems of adolescent pregnancy require a range of comprehensive services." Since Dr. Richmond also has acknowledged that "we do not know precisely how many adolescents only need access to family planning information and how many need a more intensive program which includes a comprehensive set of services, including counseling,"[72] the premises reflecting Secretary Califano's and the president's concerns must have been based either on hunch or faith that a major fraction of the target group of adolescents did need comprehensive services, not just delivery of contraceptive services. Comprehensive services comparable to those provided at the Hopkins Center, specifically identified by Califano as a model for HEW's proposal, cost around $2,000 a year per client. At the originally requested first-year authorization level of $60 million (later scaled down to $50 million), comprehensive services could be provided to a maximum of 30,000 adolescents.

71. *Fertility and Contraception in America*, Hearings, vol. 2, p. 200.
72. Ibid., p. 181.

Within a week after Califano formally transmitted a draft bill to the House, the chairman of the Health Subcommittee, Paul Rogers, Democrat of Florida, was said to have asked the secretary whether he "really wanted" the teenage pregnancy bill and to have been told in response that the president wanted it.[73] Rogers apparently could not bring himself to push it in the House, a reluctance already evident when he introduced the bill with the notation "by request." At the end of the session, Edward Kennedy grafted it to health services amendments in the Senate. With two-thirds of the House absent, 110 members approved a conference committee version of the health services amendments that incorporated an administration-endorsed adolescent pregnancy title espousing "coordination," "linkages," "integration," and "comprehensive services." Mandating "primary emphasis on services to adolescents who are 17 years of age and under and are pregnant or who are parents," the act emphasizes life support, downplays primary prevention, forbids use of grants to pay for abortions, and is ambiguous about abortion counseling.

Administrative Location as Policy Signal

Supporters of the adolescent pregnancy program compensated with vigorous activity for the program's restricted substance. A cabinet officer can gear up for speedy implementation of a program in which he believes, or can play by the book and wait for signs of congressional willingness to enact authorizing legislation and appropriations. With adolescent pregnancy, the secretary of HEW geared up for speedy implementation. The administration's adolescent pregnancy bill, which incorporated the Special Task Force's "Family Development Program," had hardly been introduced, but already was in trouble, when Secretary Califano named Lulu Mae Nix to "orchestrate all HEW adolescent pregnancy activities" as director-presumptive of a planned Office of Adolescent Pregnancy Programs. A member of the Special Task Force, Nix, as state administrative director of the Delaware Adolescent Program, ran the only existing statewide counterpart of the planned national effort.

Critics of the proposed legislation's narrow approach tried to salvage what they could of a prevention emphasis by attending to the details

73. John Iglehart, "Health Report: Congress Has a Feeling of Malaise About Health Care Issues," *National Journal* (May 20, 1978), p. 808.

of administrative organization. Working through Alan Cranston, chairman of the Senate Subcommittee on Child and Human Development, proponents of prevention sought to push Califano into an administrative arrangement that would subordinate Nix's Adolescent Pregnancy Office to the Office of Population Affairs, the federal focal point for family planning activity. In a "Dear Joe" letter, Cranston indicated that he thought the deputy assistant secretary for population affairs should have far more than the planned advisory role in the development and implementation of programs under the adolescent pregnancy legislation: "It would seem to me to be a most efficient use of Department resources if Dr. Nix were to coordinate these programs in close consultation with an advisory group . . . and report to the Deputy Assistant Secretary for Population Affairs. . . . I believe the direct involvement of the DASPA in the direction of the adolescent pregnancy initiative will be crucial to its success."[74]

Cranston's and Califano's views of what would constitute success did not necessarily mesh. Control by the Office of Population Affairs would have signaled a relatively low priority for the various comprehensive services to already pregnant teenagers envisioned by the "Family Development Program." A freestanding initiative reporting directly to the assistant secretary for health, on the other hand, would signal a health emphasis and an explicit rejection of emphasis on contraceptive services to nonpregnant, sexually active teenagers. Under Secretary Hale Champion's reply to Cranston's letter indicated that Califano's choice was the freestanding initiative, although he hoped the obvious implication of that choice would not be drawn:

With the advice of a number of people both within and outside the Department, I elected at least at the outset to place it as a freestanding initiative reporting directly to the Assistant Secretary for Health (ASH). Making that decision was quite difficult because I think it is important that the Department administratively signal that the location of the Office in ASH does not indicate an exclusive or even primary health emphasis.[75]

An ambiguous signal rather than a clear one comes out of all this. A program that the secretary insisted did not carry even a primary emphasis on health and that could have been located anywhere in the

74. Letter, Senator Alan Cranston to the Honorable Joseph A. Califano, Jr., July 18, 1978, in *Adolescent Health, Services, and Pregnancy Prevention and Care Act of 1978*, Hearings, pp. 104–06.

75. Letter, Hale Champion for Joseph A. Califano, Jr., to the Honorable Alan Cranston, August 23, 1978, in ibid., p. 107.

department was in fact located in the Office of the Assistant Secretary for Health. Invited by an important and friendly congressman to signal an emphasis on contraception and family planning by locating the program in the Office of Population Affairs, the secretary declined. Locating it in the Administration for Children, Youth, and Families, which would have signaled an emphasis on services to the adolescent, her child, and the families involved, might have been logical in view of the legislation's preoccupation with comprehensive services, but logic was not a major consideration. Somehow, Lulu Mae Nix had been offered and had accepted a job to run a program Congress was then a long way from enacting and HEW was a long way from defining clearly.

Earlier characterized by Planned Parenthood leaders as representing "a high point of confusion," the administration's position continued to be confusing. Administration support made it possible for a bill passed by the Senate to be accepted by House conferees and adopted just before adjournment of the session in October 1978. The only explanation of the bill provided to members gave no clue that the issue was at all troublesome: "There are about 1 million adolescent pregnancies every year—and this legislation is intended to help this particular population which needs assistance in obtaining appropriate care."[76] At the first possible moment after passage, Nix was formally installed, and let the child welfare world know that her office was ready to accept grant proposals for review so that money could flow to approved projects as soon as appropriated. It was not good public relations, because applicants inevitably would face either disappointment or postponement. The manner by which adolescent pregnancy legislation had been slipped through the House made it nobody's baby, and nobody now felt particularly responsible for its support. Even its reluctant House sponsors, Representatives Paul Rogers and Tim Lee Carter, were not now available for help. Rogers retired in 1979, and Carter, ill, was frequently absent. Accordingly, the House's Labor-HEW Appropriations Subcommittee felt no pressure on behalf of adolescent pregnancy, and the House voted no funds for it. After Senate action, the 1979 supplemental appropriation finally earmarked $1 million for adolescent pregnancy. Of the $65 million authorized for 1980, the House voted $15 million, the Senate $20 million, and the conference version provided $17.5 million. Not only did the $115

76. *Congressional Record*, daily edition (October 14, 1978), p. H13562.

million authorized for two years shrink to an actual appropriation of $18.5 million, Congress subsequently received the president's request to rescind $10 million of the $18.5 million. While waiting for the money, those who responded to HEW's premature request for proposals had plenty of time to lose their enthusiasm, and Lulu Mae Nix had plenty of time to learn why some HEW veterans thought her naive for accepting her job before there was a job.

There is nothing inherently wrong with the adolescent parenthood legislation enacted in 1978. If its appropriation any year came up even to the initial year's authorization of $50 million, and the whole appropriation was spent on adolescent services, the federal match—limited to 70 percent—would cover the costs of a Hopkins-type program for about 36,000 cases. At least 36,000 teenage mothers are unquestionably in need of comprehensive services. But an adolescent parenthood policy is not an adolescent pregnancy policy. The former undertakes to restructure the lives of adolescent mothers and mothers-to-be and to provide health and other services for them and for their children. By doing so, providers hope to discourage another pregnancy, at least during adolescence. An adolescent pregnancy policy may include adolescent parenthood services as part of its effort, but directs no less attention to preventing adolescent pregnancy and to terminating pregnancy.

Neither freely distributed contraception nor routinely accepted adolescent sex evokes widespread support. Planned Parenthood's view of sexually active teenagers as healthy persons who would respond in growing numbers to an offer of family planning clinic services that cost about $70 per client per year has been set aside rather than explicitly rejected. If that view were adopted as a matter of national policy, it would mean accepting adolescent sexual activity as normal behavior and rejecting adolescent parenthood by making preventive services available everywhere. Instead, while doing less than it might to prevent family formation by adolescent parents, whatever national policy there is does serve to shore up a few of those families that should never have been formed.

CHAPTER FOUR

The Care and Support of Children

ACCORDING to President Carter's formulation of the trade-off between government action and family strength, "government steps in by necessity when families have failed."[1] To fail, in this context, means to be welfare dependent or to be functionally dependent, that is, to require care or protection outside the family circle. Dependent families are provided cash assistance, food relief, and social services for which they pay the price of government intervention in many aspects of family life. Nondependent families presumably take nothing and abide no intervention. Accordingly, a good deal of what is discussed as family policy actually refers to ways of precluding dependency and to ways of making dependent families more like nondependent families.

Since public assistance status is often used by politicians to define a family as "failed," welfare policy, when it focuses on ways to move clients off welfare or to blur the distinction between welfare and nonwelfare status, takes on a family policy cast. If relief clients can be restored to self-sufficiency or if their dependency status can be obscured, government no longer plays a special role in regard to these families as opposed to families generally. Eliminating government intervention in the affairs of dependent families can come about then either from shoring up a family's ability to make its own way or from substituting a routine benefit for a discretionary one. (Universal, free child care, for example, might substitute for discretionary day-care support, and thereby end the dependency of some low-income parents.) The objective common to both approaches is to avoid having a family labeled as inadequate or failed, but the approaches differ according to the disposition of the policymaker to resist or just to obscure the idea of prolonged dependency. The former disposition leads to an emphasis on self-help, the latter to an emphasis on universal benefits.

1. "A Statement in New Hampshire, August 3, 1976," *The Presidential Campaign, 1976*, vol. 1: *Jimmy Carter* (Government Printing Office, 1978), pt. 1, p. 463.

In the United States, policy tilts toward self-help and away from universal benefits.

If there were no indigent families, or at least no indigent families dependent on public assistance, a large part of the interest in family policy would disappear. This is not to say that the problems of troubled families whose troubles are basically noneconomic cannot independently command public policy attention. It does suggest that the appellation *family policy* is a convenient handle for attending to two expensive public problems: families dependent on public assistance and families that invite public intervention by such indicators of dysfunction (not necessarily accompanied by public assistance status) as abusive behavior, adolescent pregnancy, and child neglect. In urging the development of a body of family policy for the United States, proponents inevitably depend for their rationale on one or both of these issues of inadequate income and dysfunctional behavior. This chapter considers the status of public policy on some matters of special importance to low-income families with children: child care, public relief, and child support enforcement.

Child Care

Whatever else comprehensive family policy may involve, both its opponents and proponents regard child care and child development—especially of preschool children of the poor—as important to the family policy debate. Increased federal activity in child care and development has been an enduring issue since the invention in 1964 of Head Start, a popular program for disadvantaged children. Through most of the 1970s, both conservatives who opposed it and liberals who favored it understood child care legislation to be the sine qua non of family policy.

The tide is running with the opposition. On three occasions—at the beginning, in the middle, and at the end of the seventies—self-styled pro-family groups destroyed proposals that would have extended the federal role in providing a variety of child and family services modeled on the Head Start experience. President Nixon vetoed one bill. President Ford never had to confront a second. President Carter withheld his support for a third.

Nixon's veto of the Economic Opportunity Amendments in 1971 played on the family-weakening theme: "For the Federal Government to plunge headlong financially into supporting child development would commit the vast moral authority of the National Government to the side of communal approaches to child rearing over against the family-centered approach."[2] At least one Nixon associate believes the president to have been less concerned about the presumed family-weakening effects of child development programs than about his credibility with the Republican right wing. Elliot Richardson, Nixon's secretary of health, education, and welfare, has suggested that the ringing denunciation of intervention in family affairs was designed to disarm conservatives critical of Nixon's surprising move to recognize Communist China.[3] That one of those conservative critics in the Congress termed the veto "a signal that a lot of people have been looking for" lends credence to a judgment about which Richardson is "morally certain."[4] In any event, Nixon's veto caused no uprising among the moderates, and his choice of language delighted the extreme conservatives.

The techniques that these conservatives used in 1975 to oppose a direct descendant of the 1971 legislation dissuaded many congressional sponsors from further involvement. One anonymous flyer vaguely credited to the *Congressional Record* a statement that under the proposed Child and Family Services Act of 1975 "as a matter of the child's right, the government shall exert control over the family."[5] Originating in Indiana, the flyer generated spin-off versions distributed widely enough to stimulate opposition to the bill in every part of the country. John Brademas, the bill's principal House sponsor, felt especially aggrieved because a major television station in South Bend, his hometown, attributed the statement that "government shall exert control over the family" to the bill's authors, used such characterizations as "stupid" and "incredibly naive," and declared that "buried in the

2. "Veto of the Economic Opportunity Amendments of 1971," *Public Papers of the Presidents: Richard Nixon, 1971* (GPO, 1972), p. 1174.

3. See Gilbert Y. Steiner, *The Children's Cause* (Brookings Institution, 1976), chap. 5, for a detailed account of the congressional passage and presidential veto of the 1971 child development bill.

4. Ibid., p. 115. See also Elliot Richardson, *The Creative Balance* (Holt, Rinehart and Winston, 1976), p. 133.

5. "Raising Children—Government's or Parent's Right?" in *Background Materials Concerning Child and Family Services Act, 1975*, H.R. 2966, Committee Print, Subcommittee on Select Education for the House Committee on Education and Labor, 94 Cong. 2 sess. (GPO, 1976), p. 77. Different versions of the original flyer are reproduced on pp. 211–15.

measure are proposals that we feel threaten the family structure itself."[6] When the station eventually offered a retraction, the apology treated the original source much more gently than the editorial had first treated Brademas: "The information which formed the basis for our original editorial came from material put together by vigorous opponents of the bill . . . a group that Congressman Brademas claims is out to smear him through a campaign of political dirty tricks."[7] Brademas's own language was less circumscribed. "Never in my 17 years as a representative in Congress have I seen a more systematic, willful attempt to smear both me and my work in the House of Representatives," he said.[8]

Systematic the effort surely was. As many as 5,000 letters a week addressed to the president piled up in HEW's Office of Child Development (now the Administration for Children, Youth, and Families). At one stage, Walter Mondale, a prime sponsor and Senate subcommittee chairman, was reported to be receiving up to 7,000 letters a day.[9] This was no routine spate of opposition to a controversial proposal. Nor was congressional reaction routine. Brademas put out a fact sheet and actively pushed for corrections and retractions of media statements. A memorandum to all minority (Republican) members of the House Education Committee from the minority's senior staff member warned that the letters opposing the bill being received by members of Congress were "the result of fear, innuendo, and deception and represent the ultimate in the BIG LIE."[10] The Democrats brought up a very big gun to boom a response to the flyers and the letters they stimulated. Representative Thomas P. O'Neill, majority leader and Speaker-presumptive, took the floor to protest the "growing erosion of confidence

6. "WSBT–AM/FM/TV . . . Editorial," broadcast over WSBT-TV on October 25, 26, and 27, 1975, and over WSBT radio on October 27, 1975. *Background Materials,* Committee Print, p. 126.

7. Broadcast over WSBT-TV on November 8, 9, and 10, 1975, and over WSBT radio on November 10, 1975. *Background Materials,* Committee Print, p. 127.

8. Jack Colwell, "Brademas Victim of Political 'Dirty Trick,' " *South Bend Tribune,* November 2, 1975.

9. John H. Meier, "Current Status and Future Prospects for the Nation's Children and Their Families," speech at the Annual Convention of the National Association for the Education of Young Children, Anaheim, California, November 13, 1976, p. 11. At the time, Meier was director of the U.S. Office of Child Development and chief of the Children's Bureau.

10. Memorandum, Martin L. La Vor to All Minority Members, "The Child and Family Services Act of 1975," November 26, 1975.

by Americans in their public officials . . . when that confidence is destroyed as a result of tactics of smear and deception, the tactics of Watergate, unwittingly aided by a lackadaisical press."[11]

Never a good prospect for congressional passage, the bill would not have moved even had there been no opposition flyers. Whereas in 1971 child development legislation passed both houses, in 1975 Mondale himself admitted he had no serious expectation of comparable progress. Those anticipating a new Democratic administration in 1977 believed child development could become one of its achievements. In 1975, however, a bill that was not going to be enacted into law did create a serious disturbance, and it left some fallout. Both Democratic and Republican legislators discovered that merely the suggestion that proposed legislation might intrude on traditional styles of family governance could produce a politically frightening outpouring of protest. Congressional personnel and high officials in the Office of Child Development remembered the closetsful of mail long after the fact. Democratic politicians worried about being tagged as supporters of what the columnist James J. Kilpatrick called in 1975, as he had in 1971, a scheme "for the essential Sovietization of the American family."[12] Academics, intellectuals, and social altruists who continued to be enamored of the child development cause reviewed the destructive consequences to that cause inflicted by four or five versions of an amateurish throwaway and reached the same conclusion many politicians reached. Before any further child development business could be transacted in Congress, a new foundation would have to be laid that would reassure people suspicious of planned intervention in family life.

For the sponsors of legislation on child development, child care, and family services, the situation at the end of the seventies was worse than at the beginning. In 1971 Congress had at least passed a child development bill, so that Nixon's veto served to outrage supporters rather than depress them. Even the nasty defeat in 1975 left many proponents of child care legislation disposed to fight back at a propitious time. That time seemed to have come in 1979. An administration committed to the use of government on behalf of family-strengthening activity was a likely bet to support the efforts that had begun in 1971 with the Mondale-Brademas bill. Senator Alan Cranston, Mondale's successor

11. *Congressional Record* (December 1, 1975), p. 37891.
12. James J. Kilpatrick, *Washington Star*, October 14, 1975.

as chairman of what is now known as the Child and Human Development Subcommittee, made that logical assumption. But after Cranston started moving a bill, he found himself publicly abandoned by the administration at the hearing stage. On the House side, the process was less spectacular, but only because the weak House sponsor, recently reprimanded by his colleagues for improper behavior, lacked enough influence even to get his bill a hearing.

After eight years of indignation over Nixon's veto message—coupled in four of them with outrage over tactics used by the opposition—child care supporters in and out of Congress did not anticipate that one of their own, Arabella Martinez, HEW assistant secretary for human development services, would be sent to recapitulate existing federal child care support and would conclude, "Given the size and nature of this commitment, we do not believe that another categorical program for child care is warranted at this time."[13] Even more troublesome than the we-can't-afford-it reaction was the admission in Martinez's statement that maybe federal child-care legislation is not such a good idea at all, that the value problem is complex and divisive:

Serious questions remain, for example, as to what constitutes the best way to achieve quality child care, and what the federal role and responsibility should be. The hearings which this Subcommittee is conducting may bring us closer to some consensus on these matters, but none exists just now. On some very fundamental issues, wide differences remain. To cite just one example, there are those who believe that we are helping families with the funds we have committed to the care of children whose parents must work. But there are others who would argue just the reverse. They believe that providing public support for child care places government in the role of supplanting an important parental responsibility, namely the care of young children. On even so basic a question as that, there are differences; in the face of such wide divergence it is understandable that there is still no single national policy with regard to child care.[14]

Cranston could choose between carrying on a fight that would embarrass him and the administration before the bill was lost and cutting it off quickly, to minimize trouble. Looking ahead to his own reelection problems in 1980, he had no disposition to play the martyr. When, after Martinez's performance, Cranston found that part of the child development coalition was fussing over perceived inadequacies

13. Arabella Martinez, "Statement before the Senate Subcommittee on Child and Human Development," February 21, 1979, p. 8.
14. Ibid., p. 2.

in the bill's mandated child care services, and also found that the anti-interventionist (pro-family) Liberty Lobby was planning to testify at the next scheduled hearing, the senator decided to get out. Cranston canceled subsequent hearings, explaining that he did not think it likely that the bill could pass the Senate in timely fashion. Cranston refers to his bill as "a victim of these austere times," yet promises to continue efforts on behalf of unattended, vulnerable, helpless children.

United States senators have their pride, too, and in defending his, Alan Cranston has been surprisingly explicit about his feelings of betrayal. Cranston attributes the fiasco of 1979 to three factors: the negative mood of Congress and the American public toward proposals for new federal programs regardless of social need; disagreements over scope among the diverse groups that supported the bill; and the administration's position. On this last count, Cranston offers no apologies for either Carter or Mondale:

The Carter administration has withheld its support for S.4 even though Vice President Mondale was the Senate's leading advocate of child-care and child development programs during his years in the Senate, and the President, during his campaign, had expressed his support for the concept of child care and pledged his active cooperation in developing legislation.[15]

Cranston also goes out of his way to have it understood that his bill should not be thought of as essentially the same bill as Mondale's ill-fated 1971 bill:

The truth is that it is not. Nor is it the same bill as eventually modified by Mr. Mondale, which also met widespread criticism. S.4 is, instead, a fundamentally different bill, designed to meet some of the valid objections raised against its predecessors.[16]

The point is well taken. Among other differences, Cranston's bill operates through the states, which were deliberately bypassed in the earlier proposals; it deletes previously mandated family services, including social, medical, and prenatal care; it is marked by stinting frugality, limiting first-year appropriations to $90 million and actual first-year spending to 35 million 1980 dollars, as against the earlier bill's proposed first-year authorization of $1.2 billion.

None of this really mattered. However inoffensive Cranston's bill might be on money, intergovernmental, or social service grounds, there is no way that it could overcome a critical disability: the taint of

15. *Congressional Record*, daily edition (March 15, 1979), p. S2928.
16. Alan Cranston, "Letter to the Editor," *Washington Star*, March 15, 1979.

intervention in family prerogatives. The Carter administration used softer language than others had used previously, but adopted the position of the Nixon and Ford administrations when faced with even a modest proposal to extend public responsibility in child care, obviously still regarded by a large segment of the population as purely family business. As Arabella Martinez put it, "On some very fundamental issues, wide differences remain."

Public Assistance and Family Stability

The causes of family stability are more mysterious than self-evident. Not money or its absence, or religion or its absence, or children or their absence, or intelligence or its absence, is a sure indicator of family stability. No one knows what effect the American welfare system has on family stability, but logic and imagination have produced a variety of beliefs. Some choose to believe that families are destroyed by a system that in every state recognizes child dependency resulting from the absence of a parent from the home but in only half the states recognizes child dependency resulting from parental unemployment. Logic is on the side of those who so believe. The facts, however, are less self-evident. Desertion as a cause of eligibility for aid to families with dependent children (AFDC, originally ADC) is no less consequential in states with an unemployed-parent component than in states without such a component. Illegitimacy accounted in the seventies for the eligibility of nearly one-third of all welfare-dependent children.[17] Would the fathers and the mothers involved marry and establish stable family relationships if the welfare rules were different? Who knows? In many cases, the father is unknown; in others, there may already be a family relationship despite the unmarried status of the parents. Changing the rules to make poor married people with children eligible for AFDC might or might not increase the stability of the family. Money may divide as well as cement families.

Nonetheless, of all the specific criticisms leveled against the federal-state public assistance system since World War II, the most persistently

17. U.S. Department of Health, Education, and Welfare, Social Security Administration, *Aid to Families with Dependent Children: 1975 Recipient Characteristics Study*, DHEW(SSA)77-1177 (HEW, 1977), pt. 1, p. 31; Social and Rehabilitation Service, *Findings of the 1973 AFDC Study*, DHEW(SRS)74-03764 (HEW, 1974), pt. 1, p. 37.

voiced is the allegation that it fosters family instability. No such allegation was heard in earlier years. The program to aid dependent children was largely ignored during its early years because it seemed to fit so well the family-stabilizing model envisioned by its sponsors: permanent or long-term loss of a father by death, disability, or institutionalization leaves a mother unable to maintain a family; public support at a level suitable for her particular circumstances sustains the family.[18]

The welfare system was created to keep families together when economic adversity seems to leave no alternative to cash assistance to parents. An inventive mind can suggest other ways of providing assistance, inhumane ways that do not try to keep families together. Institutional care of dependent children is one. Limiting relief benefits to children who are made available for adoption is another. For obvious humanitarian and practical reasons, these are not the choices for which society has opted. The philosophical goal of the AFDC system was the same in 1980 as it was when it was invented in 1935: to help the miner's widow or her industrial equivalent care for her children.

Since social insurance and union pensions have taken over much of the protection of miners' orphaned children, most welfare cases now involve children outside the protection of social insurance. Their dependency does not stem from an act of God but from calculated action by one or both parents. Whereas public assistance once compensated for irreversible, involuntary, tragic dependency, that situation ceased to fit most of the customers by the early 1950s, when only one in five ADC cases involved death of the father. By the early 1960s the figure had dropped to one in fourteen, by 1973 to one in twenty, and by 1975 to one in twenty-seven.[19] The program was clearly supporting a large number of women and children who were not widows and orphans of West Virginia miners or of anybody else. Many of the women were not married to the fathers of the children. Many others had been deserted by their husbands.

In the years just after World War II, public dependency attributable to desertion became the main object of welfare reform. No attention appeared to be directed then to the idea, subsequently popular, that a deserting father might leave his family as an act of love, that is, in order

18. Jane M. Hoey, "Aid to Families with Dependent Children," *The Annals*, vol. 202 (March 1939), pp. 74–81. Hoey was director of the Bureau of Public Assistance.

19. *1975 Recipient Characteristics Study*, pt. 1, p. 31.

to qualify the family for assistance that would raise its standard of living above that provided by his earnings. To the contrary, all deserting fathers were taken to be evil men, indifferent to the fate of their families. Though later reform proposals heavily emphasized income guarantees to intact families, this earlier movement assumed that an absent father was always an irresponsible father who willingly victimized both his family and the state. In cases of desertion, income support was a controversial substitute for somehow compelling a father to meet his family responsibilities—an unwarranted substitute in the judgment of many governors and state legislators, a humane substitute in the judgment of many social workers.

Social welfare leaders have always been of two minds about how to respond to demands from politicians that deserters be pursued. On the one hand, it is hard to countenance a purely selfish act of desertion. On the other hand, to involve a deserted family in the pursuit of the deserter adds to the trauma already suffered by the family. In a compromise, welfare specialists agreed to legislation, enacted in 1950, that made it mandatory for welfare workers to give notice to law enforcement officials (NOLEO) when a child of a deserting parent received public assistance. To pursue or not to pursue the father was left to the local prosecutor—who usually lacked the resources and often lacked the inclination to chase the deserter.

The dispute over the NOLEO amendment turned as much on federal-state relations as on whether service to a deserted family should preclude pursuit of the deserter. Federal prosecution of deserting parents who cross state lines was gathering support when the more limited NOLEO arrangement emphasizing local discretion and eliminating the federal criminal aspect was worked out. The legislation did not infringe on states' rights, change the basic features of the program for aid to dependent children, or broaden the area of federal control over family matters.

It was another decade before Congress reacted again to the steadily growing numbers of ADC cases attributable to absence of the father, the euphemism for dependency caused by desertion, separation, and unmarried motherhood. The first glimmerings of interest in publicly financed sex education and birth control techniques as a possible way to attack ADC illegitimacy were preceded by an interest in paying an unemployed father to stay home with his family until he is again employed, that is, paying an intact family to stay intact. Desertion of a father is always destructive of family stability. The cause of desertion is clear in only a few situations, but working on the commonsense assumption that some cases of desertion stem from a father's unemployment and subsequent loss of confidence as family breadwinner, Congress made available to the states, first as a temporary measure, then on a permanent basis, an unemployed-father component of aid to dependent children (ADC-U, later AFDC-U). This represented the first national effort to tie family stability to an income guarantee to two-parent families. To be sure, AFDC-U has been something less than an actual guarantee, since half the states have never chosen to participate and the eligibility conditions imposed by many participating states keep the number of qualified families limited. The program, however, is not just peanuts. In a peak month, March 1977, it benefited 750,000 recipients, or about 6.6 percent of the total number of AFDC beneficiaries.[20]

Whether the unemployed-father option actually has any effect on family stability is far from clear. If it was never true that unemployed fathers left home to qualify their families for assistance, making intact families with an unemployed father eligible for benefits may have been a humanitarian measure without being a family-stabilizing one.[21] In 1961, the year ADC-U was enacted, 18.6 percent of ADC dependency could be attributed to desertion; six years later the comparable percentage was 18.1; in 1969 it was 15.9. When HEW reported the characteristics of its AFDC population in 1973, it no longer differentiated between "separation without court decree" and "desertion." Therefore, the reported combined percentages of 25.7 in 1973 and 25.0 in 1975 cannot be directly compared with the figures from the earlier years

20. U.S. Department of Health, Education, and Welfare, Social Security Administration, *Public Assistance Statistics, March 1977*, DHEW(SSA)77-11917 (HEW, 1977), p. 6.

21. In recommending that the ADC-U program be made permanent, the HEW secretary's ad hoc committee, at least, seemed more interested in role models and adequacy of support than in the presumed pressure on a low-income father to desert. "Excluding federal participation for payments covering the father in ADC if he is in the home makes the assistance grant inadequate to meet the needs of the entire family. . . . Excluding [unemployed fathers] from the grant weakens their position as head of the family. The best current knowledge of human behavior and child development strongly supports the importance of the father's role as family head in helping the children develop to sound adulthood." Report of Ad Hoc Committee on Public Welfare to the Secretary of Health, Education, and Welfare, September 1961, in *Public Welfare Amendments of 1962*, Hearings before the House Committee on Ways and Means, 87 Cong. 2 sess. (GPO, 1962), p. 83.

for desertion alone. But it is worth noting that the combined total was 26.8 percent in 1961, 27.7 percent in 1967, and 26.8 percent in 1969.[22] There is no reason to believe that the approximately 2-to-1 ratio of desertion to separation without decree changed much in 1973 and 1975. A reasonable hypothesis is that the percentage of family dependency attributable to desertion has stayed relatively constant around 16 to 18 percent and has been affected only marginally by payments to unemployed fathers.

AFDC as Antifamily Policy

Although the complex relationship between desertion and welfare has never been made clear, the conventional political wisdom that was heard throughout the years of effort to establish a guaranteed income says AFDC has perverse effects: invented to keep families together, it could be held responsible for breaking up families. Some who held this view believed that men in non–AFDC-U states deserted in order to qualify their families for benefits; others believed that men in both AFDC-U and non–AFDC-U states deserted secure in the knowledge that their families would be publicly assisted; and still others believed that desertion was frequently a sham, that low-income fathers would only seem to desert, thereby qualifying the family for benefits while secretly continuing to maintain ties to the family and even continuing to provide occasional financial assistance.

These would all seem to be rational behavior patterns for low-income or no-income fathers to follow, and it is appropriate for analysts to question whether actual behavior mirrors these patterns. But as yet there is no firm evidence one way or another. Even so, the suggestion that AFDC encourages desertion came to appear in official statements with increasing frequency as the debate over welfare reform went on. Thus HEW Secretary Robert Finch, asserting that "the family stability problem is reaching a critical stage," brought to the Senate Finance Committee Hearings on the Family Assistance Act of 1970 a chart

22. For 1961, *Child Support: Data and Materials*, Committee Print, Senate Committee on Finance, 94 Cong. 1 sess. (GPO, 1975), p. 154; for 1967, *Social Security and Welfare Proposals*, Hearings before the House Committee on Ways and Means, 91 Cong. 1 sess. (GPO, 1969), pt. 1, p. 486; for 1969, *Social Security Amendments of 1971*, Hearings before the Senate Committee on Finance, 92 Cong. 1 sess. (GPO, 1972), pt. 1, p. 91; for 1973, *Findings of the 1973 AFDC Study*, pt. 1, p. 38; for 1975, *1975 Recipient Characteristics Study*, pt. 1, p. 31.

headed "Incentives Under AFDC Break Up the Family." The secretary and his associates explained "how the present system provides a father with an incentive to leave his home. . . . The family is better off if the father is not at home. . . . There is a financial reward built into the present system for the family to break up."[23] Finch called it "vicious and irrational." Finch's successor, Elliot Richardson, first acknowledged that "we do not understand all the intricacies of family dissolution, nor do we have data that show a definite cause-and-effect relationship between welfare and family instability," then observed that "we do know that over 70 percent of the fathers of families currently on AFDC are 'absent from the home,' and that the present welfare system provides a prima facie incentive for breakup."[24]

Jimmy Carter's position paper on welfare reform gave a comparable message: "In [some cases], the system encourages fathers to leave the home so the wife and children will receive increased benefits."[25] And his message to Congress proposing welfare reform legislation flatly referred to the existing system as "anti-family," whereas the proposed new system with its income guarantees "strengthens the family."[26] At hearings before the Public Assistance Subcommittee in the spring of 1978, Senator Daniel P. Moynihan, who, after one of his earlier incarnations as a presidential adviser, had noted the skimpy research evidence linking desertion to AFDC ("There are not five cents worth of research findings"), summed up the record of Senate hearings: "Every Secretary of HEW for the last 15 years has come up and routinely intoned in this committee room that AFDC breaks up families."[27]

Moynihan was provoked by Secretary Joseph Califano's routine intonation of the AFDC-family breakup proposition. "The present system," Califano said, "is anti-family . . . contains substantial family-splitting incentives. In many cases, the family is better off if the father leaves the home."[28] To Moynihan's "How do you know?" Califano answered that both data and common sense supported his position.

23. *Family Assistance Act of 1970*, Hearings before the Senate Committee on Finance, 91 Cong. 2 sess. (GPO, 1970), pt. 1, p. 194.

24. Ibid., p. 409.

25. *The Presidential Campaign, 1976*, vol. 1, pt. 1, p. 607.

26. "Welfare Reform Message to the Congress," *Public Papers of the Presidents: Jimmy Carter, 1977* (GPO, 1978), vol. 2, p. 1451.

27. *Welfare Reform Proposals*, Hearings before the Subcommittee on Public Assistance of the Senate Finance Committee, 95 Cong. 2 sess. (GPO, 1978), pt. 3, p. 818.

28. Ibid., pt. 1, p. 3.

But by using a vulnerable reference, Califano exposed the evidential weakness of the conventional argument that AFDC destroys families. "Where unemployment is high and where income is low, in the hearings that Senator Mondale has run when he was chairing the subcommittee in his hearings on the family, the Human Resources Committee, there was substantial testimony and evidence—Walter Reuther was among the people who testified—to the effect that there was an increase in family breakup, in child abuse, in domestic violence within the family," said Califano.[29] Moynihan was kinder to the memory of Walter Reuther than to Califano's invocation of it: "You are asking us to use 1 percent of the gross national product [for income guarantees] because you think this will take care of family-splitting incentives. I ask you for evidence and, sir, you cite Walter Reuther. Now, Walter Reuther was, God rest his soul, a fine man. A social scientist he wasn't."[30]

Subsequently, the economist then serving as the administration's chief planner for welfare reform returned to the commonsense argument by telling Moynihan the burden of proof should "rest on those who deny that such a patently sensible change . . . will improve, over the long haul, the behavior and the prospects for family stability."[31] The last word was Moynihan's. "There is such a thing as evidence," he said.

Actually, the welfare reform movement did not grow out of a concern for family stability. Rather, it grew out of scholars' concerns for equity, adequacy, and simplicity in a public support program. Benefiting nonworking, single-parent families while refusing to benefit two-parent families with low-earning fathers invites questions of equity; allowing states to set benefit levels without regard to what is known about the income necessary to overcome poverty status invites questions of adequacy; administering a system that permits discretionary judgments to be made about eligibility and benefits invites questions of simplicity. The welfare reformers found these self-evident considerations compelling and convinced President Nixon that to describe the system was to expose the presence of inequity, inadequacy, and overcomplexity.

29. Ibid., p. 24.

30. Ibid., p. 25. Califano's reference to Reuther was in error. Mondale's Subcommittee on Children and Youth was formed in 1971. Its hearings on the family were held in 1973. No labor spokesman testified—least of all Walter Reuther, who died in May 1970.

31. Ibid., p. 27.

Whether the system could also be faulted for generating family dissolution, especially desertion, was less certain, because such a judgment required analysis of client behavior. Did fathers desert in order to qualify families for benefits or was desertion related to other things in the family situation? Does AFDC induce desertion or is AFDC a consequence of desertion? Whereas social scientists tended to pick their way carefully through these questions, politicians seized on the "prima facie incentive for breakup" provided by the AFDC rules and turned probable cause into likely guilt. By so doing, they both added strength to the case for reform and assumed an additional burden. The added strength came from the condemnation of the existing system as immoral for fostering family dissolution. The additional burden was to show, if possible, that the proposed program would safeguard family stability and that it was therefore more in accord with traditional American values.

Since family dissolution is not a prerequisite for AFDC-U eligibility, the assumption that families break up to qualify for AFDC becomes tenable if marital stability is greater in AFDC-U states than in other states. Little evidence can be found that an AFDC-U program reduces marital instability. Because there are no AFDC-U states in the South, it is difficult to separate regional from program effects. HEW reports that, for whites, the incidence of female-headed families is considerably lower in AFDC-U states; for blacks—controlling for region—an AFDC-U program appears to have no effect on family dissolution.[32] One older review found that most separated families on the New York City welfare rolls had been on the rolls before they reportedly separated, that is, families did not break up to qualify for benefits.[33] Since families could qualify in New York without breaking up, other factors produced a high desertion rate. Another review of desertion in nineteen states with AFDC-U programs showed that nine states had a higher percentage of AFDC cases caused by desertion years after the program was in place than before AFDC-U was permissible.[34] In the remaining ten states there was a decrease in the percentage of cases attributable to desertion. In other words, removing the need to desert in order to qualify a family effected no consistent change in stability patterns. The

32. Ibid., pt. 2, p. 206.

33. Lawrence Podell, *Families on Welfare in New York City*, Preliminary Report 1 (City University of New York, Center for Social Research, 1967), page v.

34. Gilbert Y. Steiner, *The State of Welfare* (Brookings Institution, 1971), pp. 82–84.

presumed connection between welfare rules and family instability must be viewed as not proved. It can be said that allowing intact families with unemployed fathers to qualify for AFDC did not discourage desertion. Beyond that, no practical way can be found of determining just why low-income deserting fathers desert.

For dedicated welfare reformers, AFDC suffers from so many other deficiencies that it would be enough to show that an alternative income transfer program has no family-destabilizing effects. A guaranteed income plan need not stabilize families. Even if it is acknowledged that AFDC's presumed destabilizing effect may not be demonstrable, neither is a stabilizing effect. As far as family stability is concerned, a guaranteed-income substitute for AFDC is in trouble only if the substitute proves to be more destabilizing than the status quo.

Social Experiments: Counterintuitive Findings

That this depressing possibility might actually be the way things are hardly dawned on the designers of the country's first social experiment—the Graduated Work Incentive Experiment, conducted by the Office of Economic Opportunity (OEO) on a sample of 1,160 husband-wife households in New Jersey and in Scranton, Pennsylvania, between 1968 and 1972.[35] For the designers, the critical questions to be addressed in a negative income tax experiment dealt with the effect of payments on work effort. Would income guarantees reduce effort? What level of guarantee is associated with what reduction, if any? What are the consequent costs? Do responses differ according to ethnic groups? So-called psychological and sociological responses were not to be ignored in the investigation, but those issues—health, self-esteem, social integration, perceived quality of life, family composition, marital stability, fertility rates—were to be second-level concerns. If useful data were forthcoming, fine, but interest in such data could not be allowed to interfere with the main inquiry. Many of the designers and managers of the experiment guessed that the sociological and psychological findings would be inconclusive or that they would show negligible effects. Work effort and costs were the research issues to be

35. The experiment and its operations are described in nontechnical terms in David Kershaw and Jerilyn Fair, *The New Jersey Income-Maintenance Experiment*, vol. 1: *Operations, Surveys, and Administration* (Academic Press, 1976).

explored, the areas where payoff was certain, and consequently the aspects of the experiment around which the sampling design was built.

When a preliminary report on the experiment was submitted—somewhat reluctantly—to the Senate Finance Committee in February 1970, it held that there was no evidence that work effort declined among those receiving income support payments. On the contrary, it indicated that the work effort of participants receiving payments increased relative to the work effort of those not receiving payments.[36]

That same report presaged trouble over the issue of family stability. Senator Russell B. Long, Democrat of Louisiana, was among the first to show an interest in that aspect of the experimental findings. Long called attention both to an indication in the 1970 report that families getting grants under the experiment tended to break up more than those not getting grants, and to an OEO caveat on "this single occasion" concerning the "extremely tentative" nature of the data. Why, he asked, were the data on family stability more tentative than the data on the work effort and income? The OEO's explanation was that the size of the sample drawn for the experiment's focus was too small to justify conclusions about family stability. "If we had designed the experiment to get at family stability, we would have probably had 10 times as large an experiment as actually conducted. . . . With only 35 families or 40 families or 50 families, that is not sufficient data."[37]

The New Jersey data were not sufficient to permit a firm set of observations on family stability, but they were more than sufficient to assure that the family stability issue was included in the design of subsequent income maintenance experiments. Long's questioning made it clear that a guaranteed-income program meeting all the criteria deemed critical by economists—efficiency, economy, comprehensiveness, simplicity—could founder on the family stability issue if the effects of income guarantees on family stability were not known. Fortunately, continued analysis of the data from the New Jersey experiment plus several later negative income tax experiments provided the required opportunities for a definitive examination of the effect, in experimental settings, of income guarantees on marital dissolution. By mid-1978, findings available from a large-scale (approximately 5,000

36. *Family Assistance Act of 1970*, Hearings, pt. 2, pp. 907–18. Harold Watts, director of the Institute for Research on Poverty at the University of Wisconsin, the prime contractor, thought the report premature. Ibid., pp. 955, 957.

37. Ibid., p. 967.

families) urban experiment begun in 1970–71 in Seattle and in 1971–72 in Denver could be added to those from New Jersey as well as to those from a rural experiment conducted on a sample of 616 families in North Carolina and Iowa.

While the findings on marital dissolution from each of the experiments may be set aside as unpersuasive in view of the small numbers involved and the complexity of the marital relationship, the consistency of the results gives them special significance. Each experiment seemed to show significantly higher dissolution rates in families that were given low or medium doses of income support than in families not provided the guarantee.

The Seattle-Denver income maintenance experiment tested eleven variations of negative income tax programs involving support guarantees ranging from 90 to 140 percent of the poverty level and phase-in tax rates ranging from 30 to 80 percent of earned income. The experiment provided training subsidies to many of the families, but it included neither a work requirement nor a job opportunity. Contrary to the expectations of the project's academic overseers, both the black and the white experimental families had significantly higher rates of marital dissolution than did comparable families not subject to the negative income tax treatment.[38] No such finding obtained for Chicanos. Among experimental white families, the dissolution rate exceeded that for control families by 61 percent. Among experimental black families, the dissolution rate exceeded that for control families by 58 percent. For both whites and blacks, the difference in the marital dissolution rate between the test group and the control group was substantially greater at low and medium income-support levels than at high levels—greater, that is, at levels around 75 percent of the poverty threshold and at that threshold itself than at levels above it.[39] Since there is no expectation of a public program to provide support above the poverty level, and most proposals, including President Carter's Better Jobs and Income Program, involve support payments at levels that maximized family dissolution rates in the test group, the Seattle-Denver findings could not have been more troublesome to those who for years had insisted that a system of assured income is essential for family stability.

Although not within acceptable limits of statistical significance, the North Carolina–Iowa experimental findings added to the gloom be-

38. *Welfare Reform Proposals*, Hearings, pt. 3, p. 842.
39. Ibid., pp. 820–21, 841–42.

cause income guarantees in that project apparently produced a rate of marital dissolution among experimental families one-third higher than among control families.[40] The small size of the sample and other statistical apologies would be more welcome as escape routes, however, had it not been that the rural pattern showed higher rates of family dissolution at lower levels of support than at higher levels— findings squarely in accord with those of the urban experiments.

No relief comes from adding the final results of the analyses and reanalyses of the New Jersey data. Experimental families at high support levels, it was found, are just about as likely to have dissolved after three years as control families, but experimental families at medium support levels showed a 30 percent higher rate of dissolution than control families, and those at low support levels showed a 90 percent higher rate of dissolution than control families.[41]

The Triumph of Independence over Income

The nagging consistency of these unanticipated results has stimulated efforts to explain rather than to dismiss them. Unlike labor supply effects, which are calculable and require no ex post facto rationalization, the findings about family dissolution do not speak for themselves. They are counterintuitive and are not what most politicians would like to encourage. "If it turns out that a negative income tax does induce a higher rate of family separation, is that good or bad?" Professor Robert Lampman, an early and thoughtful supporter of income guarantees, has asked. In political terms the question answers itself: a member of the House of Representatives or of the Senate could hardly urge his colleagues to support a welfare reform plan that carries with it experimental evidence that the plan nearly doubled marital dissolution rates among participants.

How can the results of the experiments on marital dissolution be explained, and does even a most persuasive explanation help the prospects for a negative income tax? Robert Spiegelman, project leader on the Seattle-Denver experiment, reports some hypotheses "that, in

40. Ibid., p. 821, 841. Michael T. Hanan, "Noneconomic Outcomes," in John L. Palmer and Joseph A. Pechman, eds., *Welfare in Rural Areas: The North Carolina-Iowa Income Maintenance Experiment* (Brookings Institution, 1978), pp. 190–91.

41. *Welfare Reform Proposals*, Hearings, pt. 3, pp. 819–22, 841–42.

retrospect, do appear to be reasonable and have been, in fact, accepted by others in the profession":

The hypotheses implied that the negative income tax creates two opposing forces acting on a family. One force encourages the members to stay together—we call that an income effect. Another encourages dissolution—we call that the independence effect.

The income effect decreases marital dissolution rates by increasing the family's well-being. This is the money they receive from the program, or the support that they receive from it directly.

At the same time, the independence effect increases the dissolution rate by reducing the financial dependence on the marriage of the more dependent partner, usually the wife. This is a result of the income she can receive outside of the marriage.

We also found that the existing welfare systems in Washington and Colorado do not provide an acceptable alternative to marriage as [does] the NIT program, the negative income tax program.

Because of the stigma that is attached to the receipt of such welfare benefits and the apparent uncertainty with regard to the ability to obtain these benefits, these benefits are essentially discounted by their potential recipients relative to those available from a negative income tax program with the same support level.

Our model of income and independence effects with the welfare discount accounts for the pattern of impacts by support level that we have observed. For low support levels, the destabilizing independence effect dominates the income effect. At the high support levels, the income effect is stronger and offsets this effect.[42]

The explanation is not without its flaws. Weigh, for example, the suggestion that welfare families discount benefits from existing programs—because of the stigma attached and the apparent uncertainty about their ability to get those benefits—so that AFDC-U and food stamps do not exert an independence effect comparable to that of the low-support negative tax plan. There is no evidence on whether AFDC clients feel stigmatized, but the sharp growth of the food stamp program, at least, and its use by students and low-income young working people must have reduced whatever stigma effect that welfare benefit produced in its first years. Even more difficult to accept is the suggestion that the "apparent uncertainty with regard to ability to obtain those [welfare] benefits" limited the independence effect. The uncertainty is presumably not a factor in the case of the negative tax with its income guarantee. But that hypothesis ignores the known temporary nature

42. Ibid., pt. 4, p. 1052.

of each of the experiments. Each participant was aware of the character of the program and therefore could not believe that a permanent new era of income stability was at hand. If staying on the AFDC rolls was deemed an uncertainty, AFDC at least had a thirty-five-year history. The experiment had many of the elements of queen-for-a-day. It had positive assurances of impermanence. How, then, could beneficiaries who did not restyle their lives because they discounted AFDC as "uncertain" be thought to restyle their lives on the basis of a temporary alternative to AFDC that would almost surely end within a known time span?

Spiegelman's explanation is not as full as that offered by some other students of the subject who accept the hypothesis that independence and income are countervailing forces. For example, John Bishop of the University of Wisconsin's Poverty Institute suggests that in addition relief payments cause a decline in the morale of the family "head," a perception shared by Russell Long. Citing work done forty years ago by E. Wight Bakke on the impact of relief, Bishop ties marital dissolution to the inability of a father to abide the "failure" tag implicit in the receipt of a low-level negative tax payment without a corresponding work requirement or requirement that he be seeking work. At higher levels of support, there is presumably enough money coming in to compensate for that blow to self-respect. At low levels, the independence of the mother and the father's sense of failure are thought to magnify each other, thus creating an environment most likely to foster marital dissolution. Bishop insists that the only way in which income support can be made compatible with marital stability is to provide such support to two-parent families "in a way that is not perceived as charity and that requires no contact with the welfare bureaucracy. If possible the family should be unaware it is being aided. Aid should arrive as part of the paychecks of the family's working members."[43]

Since Bishop's prescription is untested, no one knows whether subtle infusions of income support will overcome the apparently destructive effect on marital stability of low-level and medium-level income-support payments. Nor are we likely to find out, because there is no driving passion in Congress or in the administration to sponsor a kind of anonymous-donor support program. The earned-income tax credit, which provides negative tax benefits to low-income families

43. Ibid., pt. 3, p. 850.

with children, has been liberalized and benefits are paid through reverse withholding, but the bonus benefit so paid seems little different from the bonus benefit to the working poor associated with the purchase of food stamps—one of the existing programs that the negative tax scheme is designed to eliminate.

In sum, the findings on family stability of the income-support experiments have made it easier to lay to rest the negative income tax idea offered by President Nixon in 1969 as a family assistance plan, once renewed by him, and then reformulated by President Carter as the Better Jobs and Income Program. The cost of these proposals has always been high, but to oppose a seemingly fair and useful reform purely on grounds of cost leaves some policymakers uncomfortable. Now an unanticipated consequence has provided a new reason for hesitation.

Senator Moynihan quickly called hearings of the Senate Finance Committee's Public Assistance Subcommittee to hear accounts of the Seattle-Denver activity. Press comments took the attitude that "nothing works." HEW's welfare reform planners, however, shrugged off the findings on family stability and continued to support their guaranteed-income proposal. Moynihan subsequently contemplated asking those academic economists who in 1968 had called for adoption "this year [of] a national system of income guarantees and supplements" how they would proceed in 1979 in view of the experimental findings. Back to square one, perhaps?

Toward Renewed Emphasis on Children

With the experimental findings on the table, the welfare reform debate turns into a nasty fight between those who think family stability is the purpose of welfare and those who think a guaranteed-income plan is the only true welfare reform. Since the Seattle-Denver evidence has persuaded key politicians that a guaranteed-income plan at levels the leaders of the country think it can afford is incompatible with maximizing family stability in the affected population, it seems that old hopes for achieving both (desirable) objectives can no longer be entertained. Yet the choice between perpetuating the present system intact and contributing to family breakups is a dreadful choice to contemplate.

The emphasis on the family dissolution aspects of an income-guarantee program is a mistake, because it diverts attention from the main purpose of welfare policy—to provide for dependent children's needs. Whether those needs are invariably better met in a two-parent household than in a single-parent household has been in dispute for years, and it is not clear that a definitive answer is around the corner—or even in Seattle or Denver. Policymakers should be content to let an improved and more equitable system provide income support to children—and only children—without regard to whether their parents stay together or split.

The point is not that society should be indifferent to the question of family stability, but only that society does not know how to ensure it, obviously cannot buy it, and really cannot even know when marital stability is worth trying to preserve and when dissolution is a better course for everyone involved, including the children in the family. While those mysteries are being examined, children continue to be in need. The sensible course is to focus on a system that ties benefits to children in need and to turn away from the presumed effect of the system on marital stability. If family stability and children's needs cannot readily be accommodated, meeting children's needs should be the preferred goal.

Child Support Enforcement

When money troubles resulting from illegitimacy or desertion impel a woman to apply for public assistance, the bureaucratic response to her can be unquestioning, or punitive, or probing. The response chosen is more likely determined by the relative maturity of the relief program than by the behavior of the individual applicant.

According to the controlling ethic of the earlier years of the AFDC program, for example, when a father cares so little (or so much) for his family that he is willing to absent himself and leave family support to public assistance, society should accept the decision and respond in an unquestioning way to the financial and related needs of the abandoned family. Though no longer the dominant ethic, unquestioning acceptance of public responsibility remains the response preferred by some veterans in the welfare business. Those who believe compassion should drive relief policy argue that emotional costs to a deserted mother far outweigh the possible benefits in child support payments that might result from the pursuit of a deserting father. As for costs, it is difficult enough, the argument goes, for a deserted mother to sustain a family without having to worry about the father's angry reactions to pursuit. And since child support, paid under compulsion, is nearly always inadequate and invariably late, erratic, or otherwise undependable, its benefits are said to be marginal in any event. Accordingly, an unquestioning response would take the act of abandonment as a given and work with the victims to plan realistically for the future.

In general, however, compassion gives way to outrage as program dimensions come to exceed their sponsors' modest predictions. Applicants are viewed as causes of problems, not victims. A punitive response is probably inevitable when there are unanticipated beneficiaries who by manipulating the system qualify for program benefits and preclude shrinkage of costs. As the public assistance system matured and the number of recipients grew, responses turned punitive. In the case of desertion as cause for eligibility, demands for crackdowns first replaced expressions of pity in the 1950s and reached a peak in 1967. That year the House of Representatives actually initiated a freeze on federal cost-sharing if AFDC dependency was caused by desertion or illegitimacy and sustained the freeze in conference committee. Although Presidents Johnson and Nixon each delayed the effective date of the freeze before it was quietly repealed, the congressional message was clear. But it was an ineffective message, delivered in frustration and basically inconsistent with the AFDC statute that made the absence of the father and financial need grounds for entitlement to assistance.

After a while the punitive response fades and is replaced by a more selective one. Thus the cost-sharing freeze on dependency caused by illegitimacy or desertion has been replaced by a probing response: how did this dependency come to pass, and how can it be overcome? In AFDC the development of a system to enforce child support is one manifestation of the probing response given to applicants in recent years.

Privacy versus Responsibility

Family dissolution need not make mothers and children dependent on public welfare if private resources are stretched to sustain the various households that emerge from the dissolution, the principals agree on how those resources are distributed, and the agreement is honored. Yet family dissolution, particularly where young children are involved, usually brings money troubles in its wake. Sometimes the only practical resolution of those troubles is public dependency, an outcome that demeans dependents and dismays donors. When dissolution does lead to welfare dependency, it may be because there is not enough money to go around, but it may also be because there is no will: some fathers who could meet support obligations, preferring to spend their money in other ways, simply choose not to pay. An occasional voice can be heard explaining such behavior in terms of the "practical social climate," but the common disposition is to blame the father. "Where a father abandons his own family and is capable of paying toward their support, but runs away, or ignores a court order, it seems to me that that phenomenon is intolerable," Walter Mondale has said. "I know of nothing that offends Americans more than that."[44]

The offensive aspect of desertion most likely to produce a policy response is the high cost of such behavior to the public. Before AFDC recipient totals began a three-year decline that brought them to 10.4 million in April 1979, they grew from 3.5 million in 1961 to peak just under 11.5 million in March 1976.[45] Since divorce, legal separation, desertion, or illegitimacy account for the dependency of four out of five welfare-dependent children, the public costs of dissolution can be reduced if government coerces child support from "potential obligors": irresponsible, reluctant, or delinquent fathers. Savings are calculated both from existing cases and from the discouraging effect on potential cases—those fathers who might otherwise decide to ignore child support responsibility on the assumption that AFDC would automatically substitute for parental support. In short, to the extent that a system can be devised that deters fathers from shifting the burden of child support from themselves to public assistance, family dissolution declines as a public issue.

Child support by coercion or, in statutory language, child support enforcement takes on positive appeal when set in a family policy framework. This theme has been played on by the Senate Finance Committee: "The immediate result will be a lower welfare cost to the

44. *Congressional Record* (December 17, 1974), p. 40323. The phrase "practical social climate" is that of Elizabeth Wickenden on behalf of the National Assembly for Social Policy and Development.

45. *Public Assistance Statistics*, appropriate monthly reports as cited in note 20 above.

taxpayer but, more importantly, as an effective support collection system is established fathers will be deterred from deserting their families to welfare and children will be spared the effects of family breakup."[46] Thus it can be said of child support enforcement that it uses the good offices of government to compel some fathers to behave like most fathers and that it also can shift any particular family from dependency to independence. Unfortunately, however, the mechanics of child support enforcement demand a trade-off: an efficient program makes government a visible and omnipresent force in domestic relations, an arrangement hardly consistent with family privacy; but a program that minimizes government presence also minimizes compliance with the principle of paternal responsibility.

Unlike most income tax delinquents, who know they are likely to face action by the Internal Revenue Service, wage garnishment, and the threat of prosecution, child support delinquents for a long time could be reasonably confident that welfare agencies would make no more than a halfhearted attempt to effect compliance. Before 1975 the limited effort was justified by a combination of practical, political, civil libertarian, and intergovernmental considerations. As a practical matter, child support payments are often likened to the product of efforts to squeeze water from a stone. Nonsupporting fathers, it is said, either work irregularly or support a second family that would become dependent if the father's income were diverted to his first family. Politically, child support enforcement had few advantages for a local prosecutor, since the direct beneficiaries were likely to be residents of another jurisdiction and probably of another state, and a local second family could be adversely affected. Moreover, local appreciation for such an endeavor would rank well below appreciation for the prosecution of violent crime, perhaps even below appreciation for the enforcement of zoning ordinances. Civil libertarian concerns are legitimate in that locating child support delinquents could require access to confidential records not generally available because of the danger of misuse.

Finally, intergovernmental barriers often made enforcement frustrating. A complainant in Texas might or might not find authorities in Indiana willing to proceed under the terms of an interstate compact bearing the formidable name Uniform Reciprocal Enforcement of Sup-

46. *Child Support: Data and Materials*, Background Information Prepared by the Staff for the Use of the Senate Committee on Finance, 94 Cong. 1 sess. (GPO, 1975), p. 3.

port Agreement (URESA), subscribed to by every state and indifferently honored by every subscriber. If Indiana officials were disposed to act on behalf of the Texas complainant, the father involved might just relocate in Illinois or Ohio, and introduce a complication that could be repeated several times and be counted on eventually to wear down the complainant. Speaking from his experiences as a county attorney in a small Kansas county, Senator Robert J. Dole, Republican of Kansas, has explained that "the easiest thing to do when the father left a family and moved to some other state was to send the mother down to the welfare office. I am certain that was done in many other areas before the Uniform Support Act became law. We have tried to enforce support under this act and through our offices, but never with much success."[47]

To move beyond just notice to law enforcement officials of welfare status caused by desertion, and beyond URESA, which only slightly improved the chances for collection, requires the creation of a child support equivalent of the Internal Revenue Service, with comparable authority. But until the explosion of the AFDC rolls, the benefits of such an enterprise seemed relatively petty—certainly not substantial enough to merit setting aside big principles like protecting privacy and opposing federal encroachment. Liberals could not be expected to abide the idea of a giant parent-locator network having access to the presumably confidential social security identification system. Nor could they be expected to agree to the harassment that might be necessary to determine paternity, as a step toward establishing responsibility for child support. Conservatives, by the same token, would most likely shy away from adding this aspect of domestic relations to federal government jurisdiction and would also shy away from creating a new federal bureaucracy. To federalize child support enforcement meant forging a coalition of liberals who could be persuaded to set aside their anxiety about harassment and conservatives who could be persuaded to set aside their anxiety about enlarging the federal bureaucracy.

Senator Russell Long, a pragmatist without doctrinaire views about either protecting privacy or minimizing federal functions, began battling in 1967 to put the necessary coalition together. The formation and development of federal policy on child support enforcement since then demonstrates the ability of a particularly well placed legislator to move

47. *Child Support and the Work Bonus*, Hearing before the Senate Committee on Finance, 93 Cong. 1 sess. (GPO, 1973), p. 116.

to national policy a theory born of early experience and personal conviction. Long theorizes that failure to pursue nonsupporting fathers encourages disregard for family planning and leads to a proliferation of desertions. Untroubled by other people's philosophical musings over whether a bad marriage should be sustained or dissolved, Long is convinced that a father has an absolute responsibility to provide for his children. If that responsibility is enforced, Long believes, it has a chilling effect on voluntary dissolutions that cause public dependency. Thus the probable result of child support enforcement is to reduce the costs of public assistance, and the hoped-for bonus is to inhibit desertions and out-of-wedlock conceptions. "Wouldn't it seem," Long has asked, "that we might be able to make a father come home in some of these cases by the ability to go out and reach him and make him pay?"[48] Long's line of thought—like Dole's—flows from his experience as a young lawyer, which he frequently recalls during discussions of the child support question:

When I first started practicing law I wasn't in a large firm, I hung out my shingle as some fellows have been known to do, and I had mothers come to me from time to time. I found we could have pretty good success with this procedure if a father wouldn't pay for the support of his children. Either make him pay or put him in jail. And as long as you had him within the State, you had a fair chance to get something out of him.[49]

Reaching across state boundaries poses problems, however, and Long is persuaded that the answer is to "make all of the potential of the Federal Government available" on behalf of support enforcement. While HEW officials initially responded to the increase in illegitimacy as a cause of dependency by insisting that state plans include provisions for determining paternity and for using reciprocal arrangements for child support enforcement, Long was thinking about the superior and geographically unrestricted authority of the federal government:

But it seems to me the one big item we are leaving out is that father. He has a responsibility to those children. I believe that all of us in this room can agree that a man who sires a lot of children has the responsibility to pay and support those children, and it occurs to me that maybe you are right, that is placing too

48. *Family Assistance Act of 1970*, Hearings, pt. 2, p. 468.
49. Ibid. Senator Long's early experience as a lawyer for deserted mothers made a deep impression on him. Long referred to it again when his committee was considering President Carter's welfare reform proposal: "My impression was that if a lawyer back there at that time was hungry enough to go out and pursue a fellow, you could find him and make him pay something. You could drive those fathers out of their mind or out of the state, one way or the other." *Welfare Reform Proposals*, Hearings, pt. 3, p. 785.

great a burden on that mother to try to track that father down across this Nation. But this Federal Government can find him. He has a social security number, does he not, and when he goes to work, it occurs to me, if nobody else can find him to collect something for support of those children, maybe we ought to undertake to find him. We have a nationwide responsibility.[50]

For twenty-five years, preference was accorded ambiguity over clarity in establishing child support policy. Under the 1950 local discretion plan, and even with the 1967 amendments, federal policy amounted to little more than a polite request to states that they request deserting fathers to make child support payments. Was it federal policy to hold fathers responsible for support of their families? Sort of. Was it federal policy to provide public assistance to deserted mothers and children without coercing them to help squeeze support from the fathers? Again, sort of.

Yet ambiguity has its advantages. Unlike ambiguity, any kind of clarity in child support policy results in a paradox. A clear policy of no intervention in domestic relations emphasizes personal privacy rights, but also maximizes the likelihood of public dependency, with its inevitable intrusions on privacy. A clear policy of extensive intervention in domestic relations to avoid or reduce public dependency must maximize intrusions on privacy to accomplish the goal. In concrete terms, if a deserted mother can qualify for AFDC by a simple declaration, both mother and father can keep private the details of that failed marriage or nonmarriage. The state becomes a nonjudgmental provider of needed financial assistance. In so doing, however, the state now intrudes on many aspects of the mother's life and of the dependent children's lives. Front-end privacy reduces the chances for independence later.

On the other hand, if a deserted mother's public assistance is made contingent on her identification of the father, on her assistance in locating him, and on her willingness to assign her support rights to the state, government intrudes on a relationship that under other conditions would be private. The state has made a judgment that the father should provide and that other agencies of government and the mother should both be parties to ensuring that he does provide. The alleged benefits are that many fathers will pay, that some will not leave in the first place, that some will return, and that some dependent families

50. *Social Security Amendments of 1967*, Hearings before the Senate Finance Committee, 90 Cong. 1 sess. (GPO, 1967), pt. 1, p. 410.

will be freed of the state intrusion that accompanies public assistance. Enforcing paternal responsibility may deny front-end privacy, but in the long run it increases the chances for family independence.

Whether all the potential of the federal government should include the use of income tax data and of social security numbers as instruments for locating fathers guilty or suspected of child support delinquency varies according to perceptions of the relative importance of privacy versus responsibility and independence. Russell Long, unwavering about child support enforcement, has found it useful to espouse responsibility. There is more to the social policy world than the Senate Finance Committee, however, and there are other views of an appropriate federal role in family matters than one that focuses on a father's financial responsibility for his children. One of those other views is that neither the federal courts nor the Internal Revenue Service should be intruding on domestic relations. Another is that the establishment of a federal parent-locator service with access to all federal records raises serious privacy and administrative issues. A third is that deserted mothers may put themselves in jeopardy by identifying fathers who have deserted. Those who hold to these other views have not hesitated to make them known, once enlisting clear support from President Ford, as well as from other conservatives not usually thought of as welfare-oriented.

Until Secretary Califano overruled them early in the Carter administration, these anti-intervention views dominated the belief and behavior of HEW. Before Califano joined Long, a succession of department leaders took exception to a firm enforcement program without explicitly opposing it. Monitoring and enforcing state activity in paternity determination and support collection lacked appeal for HEW, where it was well known that in any overt federal-state clash the state more likely than not would win; where there was no federal apparatus or capacity for tracking down fathers; and where—properly enough—facilitating public assistance, not policing, was perceived to be the mission of the department. "These early measures"—referring to the original notice to law enforcement officials provision of 1950 and to legislation sponsored by Long in 1967—"were not enforced by HEW and, with a few exceptions, were not implemented by the states," Abe Lavine wrote in a review of AFDC administration.[51] A comparable

51. Abe Lavine, *Administration of Public Welfare in the Case of Aid to Families With Dependent Children* (Durham, N.C.: Welfare Policy Project of the Institute of Policy Sciences and Public Affairs of Duke University and The Ford Foundation, 1977), p. 41.

conclusion was reached by the comptroller general in his agency's study of child support programs.[52]

Eventually, responsibility and independence pushed out front-end privacy. Both the Internal Revenue Service and the Social Security Administration, respectively single-minded about collecting taxes and administering social insurance, at first found it useful to support privacy. According to Long, "The tax-collecting agencies just didn't want to fool around with playing any part or assisting us in setting up a mechanism to collect from those people what should be paid for the support of their children."[53] In 1974, however, Long led Congress to accept a plan creating a federal parent-locator service and requiring states to utilize information from HEW and from the Internal Revenue Service files in finding an absent father and enforcing a child support order against him. Neither HEW nor Internal Revenue gave up easily. "It took us years to make the Internal Revenue Service tell us where this father was," Long has explained. "They did not want to have anything to do with it. They wanted to protect his privacy. . . . Finally, we managed to muscle it through and put it on the President's desk in a bill the President would sign." Having "muscled through" access to income tax data, Long faced administrative reluctance in HEW to reveal social security numbers. "Then the social security people tell us, and then the White House group, these arch protectors of privacy, that it does not violate the letter of the law to provide the social security number 'but we think it violates the spirit of the law to tell you what the man's social security number is.' "[54]

It took eighteen months after congressional passage to muscle through a change in the Social Security Administration's position. At the Social and Rehabilitation Service, the agency then responsible for developing the federal parent-locator service, administrators understood that Long would not process the nomination of William H. Taft to be general counsel of HEW—a nomination that Secretary David Mathews felt strongly about—until Mathews told the Social Security Administration to release the numbers.[55] Senator Long confirms the strategy: "It got to the point where I was resisting appointments in that

52. Comptroller General of the United States, *Collection of Child Support Under the Program of Aid to Families With Dependent Children*, Department of Health, Education, and Welfare, Social and Rehabilitation Service, no. B-164 031(3) (HEW, 1972).

53. *Family Assistance Act of 1970*, Hearings, pt. 2, p. 468.

54. *Congressional Record*, daily edition (July 29, 1976), p. S12822.

55. *Congressional Quarterly*, Weekly Report (April 17, 1976), p. 910.

department to get them to make a decision. They finally made the decision that, yes, States can have the numbers. So, they can get the numbers now, at long last, to help try to make these absent fathers do their duty."[56]

A few months after the Republican administration gave in, Hale Champion appeared before the Senate Finance Committee as nominee for under secretary of HEW in the new Carter administration. Long took the precaution of going over the problem of child support, income tax records, and social security numbers with him and extracting a favorable response. "Mr. Chairman," said Champion, "I think we ought to perform the same way you are suggesting to us."[57] The threat of muscle works too.

The Federalization of Enforcement

Child support enforcement through federal action is actually a legacy of the so-called welfare reform effort originated by the Nixon administration to the surprise of many of those critical of its social welfare policies. Sustaining the argument for a guaranteed-income program required insisting that AFDC provided, in the well-worn phrase, a prima facie incentive for family dissolution via desertion. An income guarantee to intact families would remove that incentive for a poor but devoted father. Income-guarantee proponents could accept a provision that made other deserting fathers—those whose desertion could not be viewed as an act of love—liable to the federal government for family assistance payments made to their dependent families. When the welfare reform proposal was first made, the HEW view was that the language in the proposal gave the secretary authority to tap any income or assets of a deserting father, not simply federal benefits. Although Congress persistently resisted the income-guarantee component of welfare reform, it did salvage the federalization of child support. At first lost because of the reluctance of federal agencies to get into the business of child support collection, Long's ideas on child support backed into public policy status in 1974. Commenting on the adoption in that year of a new and stronger role for the federal government in child support enforcement, Long passed over the unintended help

---

56. *Congressional Record*, daily edition (July 29, 1976), p. S12822.

57. *Nominations of Hale Champion, Thomas D. Morris, and Arabella Martinez*, Hearings before the Senate Committee on Finance, 95 Cong. 1. sess. (GPO, 1977), p. 4.

provided by the welfare reform effort in undercutting opposition. Controversy and earlier objections had been met, according to Long, "by the discussion and the accommodation that occurs among Senators and with those in the executive branch."[58]

Using federal authority to force fathers to meet support responsibilities, unlike using federal policy to strengthen families, is not a vague objective. Long has perfected and refined the child support enforcement program in an effort to reach a clearly stated goal: "What I hope to do is to make it so difficult for a father to escape his support obligation toward his children that you would not have to sue more than about 1 percent of the fathers, and that the other 99 percent will comply."[59] To approach that objective, at least in regard to AFDC families, requires insisting that AFDC applicants cooperate in identifying and locating a father. Different from previous government responses, this response is neither unquestioning nor punitive. Program development has come to the point where the response is a probing one that frankly intrudes into family relations.

The adoption of the child support enforcement legislation of 1974 presumably unleashed federal authority to locate and compel an absent father to become a partner of, if not a replacement for, federal and state governments in supporting his family. An AFDC applicant-mother faces questions: Who is the father? Why is the father absent? Where is the father? Where is the father's last-known location? What effort has been made to achieve child support? With these data in the computer—and with support payments assigned to the state—the parent-locator service is expected to swing into action as necessary, using the father's social security identification number to locate him and any source of income; the Internal Revenue Service is expected to extract child support payments; and the court system is expected to enforce delinquent support orders. Added to the trickle of support payments voluntarily forthcoming without this enforcement superstructure, the new income to state treasuries is presumed to be enough to allow an increase in welfare benefits. Early in 1978 John Dempsey, Michigan's social services director, looked back over his state's support enforcement program and estimated benefits in Michigan to be 7 percent higher than they would have been without the program. "This is a program with no negatives," Dempsey says, adding that it is important whatever

58. *Congressional Record* (December 17, 1974), p. 40323.
59. *Child Support and the Work Bonus*, Hearing, p. 148.

one's political philosophy. Liberals must recognize that the program benefits children, he says, while it is "obviously appealing to conservatives."[60]

The assumption that the child support enforcement issue produces a classic liberal-conservative break— with liberals presumably favoring a soft stance and conservatives a hard-line one—is mistaken. There are conservatives and liberals on both sides. As a senator, Walter Mondale joined Russell Long's child support team, calling support delinquency a "phenomenon [that] is intolerable."[61] As HEW secretary, Joseph Califano embraced the program, describing child support enforcement to a group of specialists as "a sound, worthwhile and extraordinary program."[62] Other liberals have been less enchanted. And though there is plenty of praise from the conservative side, important objections to aspects of the federal enforcement program have come from Caspar Weinberger, among the most conservative secretaries of HEW in the department's history, from Senator Barry Goldwater, and, on two occasions, from President Gerald Ford. The latter, in 1975, termed the enforcement procedure "an undesirable and an unnecessary intrusion of the Federal Government into domestic relations."[63]

Ford's comments, made on signing a broader welfare bill to which Long had attached his child support proposal, were followed up the next year with proposed corrective legislation. Although the House of Representatives readily adopted the Ford-endorsed amendments— amendments that in effect restored the status quo ante by eliminating federal court authority to enforce delinquent support orders, eliminating the federal parent-locator service, and repealing the use of the Internal Revenue Service to collect child support payments—Long had not muscled through a bill only to have it "corrected" before implementation. Instead, the bill that Long eventually maneuvered to passage made some changes in the program, but none of them Ford's "corrections." On signing the new bill, Ford repeated his objections, but it was clear by then that whatever resistance might be forthcoming to the federal activity would have to take the form of administrative foot-dragging. It did. It was then that Long dragged his own feet on

60. Informal remarks at HEW Secretary's Symposium on Child Support Enforcement, March 1, 1978, Washington, D.C.

61. *Congressional Record* (December 17, 1974), p. 40323.

62. Informal remarks at HEW Secretary's Symposium, March 1, 1978.

63. *Public Papers of the Presidents: Gerald R. Ford, 1975* (GPO, 1977), vol. 1, p. 14.

the confirmation of HEW officials important to the administration. Long won, and his victory was confirmed by the Carter people.

Limits on Enforcement

How far should public policy go in insisting that support responsibility may not be abrogated unilaterally? Politicians will accept for the record statements by an organization like the National Assembly for Social Policy and Development that "measures which strengthen the underpinnings of society as a whole" are fundamental to dealing with desertion,[64] but that impeccable judgment diminishes none of the costs of AFDC and none of the outrage of the taxpayer who must support the deserter's children and who doubts that the connection between strengthened underpinnings and a reduction in welfare costs will be made during his lifetime. If desertion followed by nonsupport is "intolerable," to use Walter Mondale's word, is there any circumstance under which the deserter should not be pursued?

The basic child support enforcement legislation of 1974, it will be recalled, required an AFDC applicant to cooperate in establishing paternity and in locating an absent father for purposes of child support collection. HEW's initial regulations authorized "good cause" exceptions in cases of incest and forcible rape on the theory that in such cases formally establishing paternity involves intolerable costs to the mother and child. The 1975 amendments to the statute acknowledged the possibility of other good causes for refusing to cooperate and the possibility of legislative-executive differences on the subject by adding an "in the best interests of the child" exception. The latter required HEW to prescribe standards governing use of the exception and, to President Ford's annoyance, provided authority for a legislative veto of HEW's standards. Whether the best-interests-of-the-child loophole is a "wide-open loophole for professional welfarists to claim blanket amnesty when people refuse to cooperate in finding the father," as an opponent claims, or simply a "loophole only about the size of the eye of a needle," as a defender suggests, depends on HEW regulations. Apropos the latter loophole, one cynical congressman commented, "I can just see whole herds of camels galloping through this one."

When the House Ways and Means Committee was considering the

---

64. *Child Support and the Work Bonus*, Hearing, p. 257.

best-interests exception offered by Abner Mikva, Democrat of Illinois, members agreed with him that the threat of physical harm constituted good cause, but not that psychological or emotional harm did. HEW's first crack at a rule applied the best-interests exception to cooperation in establishing paternity and security support "likely to result in substantial danger, physical harm, or undue harassment to the child or the caretaker relative." Proposed only three months before the 1976 election and received coldly by congressional overseers and public participants alike, it was never adopted. What may have seemed to be a straightforward problem in August 1967, when Russell Long asked HEW Secretary John Gardner, "How about these fathers of these children?" had become a political mess by August 1976.

The publication of the proposed rule brought 1,700 responses from noncongressional sources: private citizens, welfare and child support agencies, law enforcement officials, legal services organizations, advocate groups.[65] Of the 1,500 comments from private citizens, over 90 percent objected to the proposed change, most complaining that it would undermine the enforcement program, encourage irresponsibility on the part of both parents, and add to the taxpayer's burden. Most comments in support of the proposal seemed to come from AFDC mothers reluctant to participate in support enforcement. Some social workers wrote to express a belief that mothers should never be forced to cooperate in establishing paternity and obtaining child support. Legal services groups and child advocacy groups claimed the proposal provided insufficient insurance to the child or caretaker against harm that could result from the enforcement process.

Other critics recommended that the danger of emotional, psychological, or mental harm be included among the good-cause exceptions. A little uneasy about what they might be getting into, department officials convened an intramural panel of experts on child and adult mental health and child welfare to consider a standard of emotional harm. Alas, after much discussion, the general conclusion was that the subjective nature of emotional harm meant that no standard could be definitive. Instead, the panel cited relevant factors—like intensity and probable duration of the emotional upset—that should be taken into consideration in determining emotional harm. State spokesmen responded that inadequately trained welfare personnel could hardly be expected to judge intensity or predict duration.

65. *Federal Register*, vol. 43 (January 16, 1978), p. 2171.

Although the impossibility of the job was confirmed by its own experts, the department nevertheless proceeded to include a standard of emotional harm in what it called "final regulations . . . with a view to possible revision," issued in January 1978—seventeen months, and a change in national administration, after the initial try at a good-cause rule. A more apt characterization of the regulations would have been "possible regulations with a view to revision." As a practical matter, if HEW personnel had cleared proposed regulations with Long before issuing them, a great deal of trouble might have been avoided. Early in February—three weeks after the appearance of the "final regulations"—Long told Secretary Califano of his disappointment in them. The tone was relatively mild.

I think that those regulations suggest that if the mother, in seeking to be added to the welfare rolls, merely states that it might create some distress for her, that she might be afraid of the father or something of that sort, that this would be an adequate excuse for failing to identify the father. . . .

It was my purpose in pressing for child support legislation, to require the mother to cooperate in seeking support from the father if she is going to receive welfare payments.[66]

Though Califano volunteered to "recheck" the emotional-harm aspect of the regulations, no easy accommodation was forthcoming. In mid-March, with the effective date of the regulations at hand, Long again showed "muscle." After the introduction of a resolution to disapprove, he delivered a message to HEW, complete with a challenge to the secretary to take control of his department. "I am very disappointed," said Long, "to see the Secretary of Health, Education, and Welfare going the route of his predecessors, being a Gulliver tied down by a bunch of Lilliputians. He is one of the few men over there, so far as I know, who is in favor of child support. Now the Lilliputians have tied Gulliver down. . . . They have done everything they could to prevent this Nation from calling upon parents to support their children. Now they will kill it by regulation. It is an outrage. . . . They declared war on us when they did this."[67]

It was to no one's advantage to push the resolution of disapproval. None of the principals really wanted war. For his part, Long, after ten years of effort to get a child support enforcement program in place, could not favor the delay that would have resulted from disapproval and a challenge to the constitutional validity of such congressional

66. *Welfare Reform Proposals*, Hearings, pt. 1, pp. 64–65.
67. *Congressional Record*, daily edition (March 15, 1978), pp. S3791–92.

action. Yet such a challenge would have been inevitable. Gerald Ford had been explicit when he signed the child support legislation that carried the provision for a legislative veto of regulations by either house within sixty days of submission. Terming such a provision "an unconstitutional exercise of Congressional power," Ford had instructed HEW to regard the provision as simply a request for information about the proposed regulations in advance of their promulgation.[68] Accordingly, he asked HEW to report to Congress at least sixty days before the child support regulations were to be issued. Even though there was a new president, HEW could not easily back away from Ford's position that a legislative veto of administrative regulations is unconstitutional. This was the particular case on which the line had been drawn, not just a superficially comparable case that could be distinguished or explained away. At the same time, the department did not welcome the idea of taking on the chairman of the Senate Finance Committee by challenging a disapproval resolution. Not only would there now be an intraparty dispute over separation of powers, but there would be a dispute with the committee having jurisdiction over critical aspects of the HEW program. Moreover, Long had correctly characterized Secretary Califano as favoring a child support enforcement program. Even as Long was increasing the pressure to tighten the emotional-harm loophole, Califano was telling a meeting of state and local child support enforcement officials that the program was "sound, worthwhile, and extraordinary," in part responsible for the decline in the AFDC rolls, and a top priority of the department and of the Carter administration. The president was very conscious of it, Califano said.[69] The appeal of child support was not only in its dollar return—HEW claims to have collected $500 million from AFDC cases over the twelve months ending with April 1979—but also in its expression of what Califano described as a "fundamental principle that should drive any society: that individuals must be responsible for their own actions." The child support program, he said, rebuilds not only financial ties, "but family ties as well."[70] More than a year into an administration in which Califano was to be principal adviser on how federal programs could aid and strengthen families, child support provided an opportunity to keep the family policy issue alive.

68. *Public Papers of the Presidents: Gerald R. Ford, 1975*, vol. 2, p. 1149.
69. Informal remarks at Secretary's Symposium, March 1, 1978.
70. Ibid.

Since the continuation of the program served the interests of both Long and Califano, the outcome was certain. By informal agreement, the resolution of disapproval would be allowed to languish and HEW would reopen consideration of the so-called good-cause exception that allowed an AFDC mother to decline to cooperate in pursuing a father because of fear of emotional harm. The reconsideration process included a public hearing distinguished less by novel arguments than by the presence of a well-known Senate Finance Committee staff member as a front-row observer—an obvious reminder of Long's interest.

New regulations appeared at last, ten days before congressional adjournment in 1978. HEW undertook to clarify its view of emotional harm: it must be serious, demonstrable, and have the observable consequence of substantially impairing the ability of the person to function. But the department did not require, for purposes of the good-cause exception, that the emotional harm be "lasting." With the tempest resolved, it is clear that the intensity of the battle over the emotional-harm loophole far exceeded the practical significance of the issue. Good cause is a relatively small cause. Child support collections from AFDC cases are unaffected by the rarely invoked exception. Lawyers, psychiatrists, and bureaucrats can argue endlessly over what is a valid test of anxiety and over how many forms emotional harm can take and over who is qualified to make an emotional-harm finding, but only a handful of AFDC applicants have any interest in these esoteric questions. The HEW position that outraged the chairman of Senate Finance and led to seemingly endless negotiation involving Senator Long, Secretary Califano, and high level staff people on both sides should be thought of as a defense of principle rather than of masses of people. Note, for example, Mecklenburg County, North Carolina, where, a legal aid attorney told HEW's hearing board, 10 to 15 of 1,000 families receiving AFDC seek the good-cause exception. Projected nationally, the figure suggests that of 3.5 million AFDC families, perhaps 3,500 to 5,000 are involved. Allowing for cases of threats of physical harm where the father has a history of assault further reduces the probable number of cases in dispute.

Influential politicians consider it irrelevant that only a trifling number of emotional-harm cases may present themselves. Senator Long and many of his colleagues have come to see the problem as a moral imperative. "If there is someone available who is working who has a duty to support that child, he should be made to do so," Long says. "If this program weren't making a penny, we should still be supporting it as a matter of equal justice."[71] That public dependency should never be tolerated unless responsible fathers are pursued is a proposition that strikes politicians, dependents, and ordinary taxpayers as reasonable. But a broken family supported in part by a reluctant father is no stronger than a broken family supported by public assistance. The former simply conforms more closely to the traditional model of family responsibility. Child support enforcement thus offers the common ground for a coalition of politicians who deplore the erosion of the traditional model and those who deplore the high cost of public assistance.

Early experience showed the stakes in non-AFDC cases to be at least as great as those in AFDC cases, yet there is not a comparable single-minded determination to use federal power and money to compel child support payments from recalcitrant or delinquent fathers whose families are not public dependents. For example, after a period of federal willingness to share state administrative costs (75:25) in non-AFDC cases too, Congress allowed that authority to lapse in 1978. A year later Senator Long was still looking for a bill on which to piggyback both retroactive reimbursement to the states for the missed year and a renewal of reimbursement in non-AFDC child support cases. Moreover, before Long finally found a vehicle, he allowed the administration's trade negotiator to dissuade him at least once from using a trade bill for the purpose.

However extensive the number of its potential beneficiaries, child support in non-AFDC cases just lacks the urgency accorded child support in AFDC. To put it differently, federal intervention bent on enforcing child support responsibility generates less interest when the victims of irresponsible behavior can sustain themselves without public assistance. "Equal justice," the "fundamental principle . . . that individuals must be responsible for their own actions," the federal government's "nationwide responsibility," and the role of child support enforcement in sparing children the effects of family breakup are all precepts with general applicability, but they are easiest to apply to broken families reduced to relief status.

71. Ibid.

CHAPTER FIVE

Neglect and Abuse

"To be helpless and unloved," the psychiatrist and ethicist Willard Gaylin has written, "is the matrix of disaster."[1] Family is a preventive for just such disaster. The family unit, under routine conditions, provides a measure of mutual support that protects each of its members from being left helpless; under optimum conditions, that mutual support is provided with love.

Proponents of family policy expect it to ease the controllable pressures that might otherwise diminish or destroy a family's capacity to give its members the help and love they need. Economic support and social services are the elements of policy most often urged to forestall family dysfunction, although it is far from certain that either has the desired effect. In any event, it is too late for preventive services when family dysfunction has advanced to the point where "helpless and unloved" describes the actual circumstances of part or all of a family— when disaster is already at hand. The neglected child separated from his parents and consigned to foster care in the homes of nonrelatives for indefinite periods and the dependent spouse who is the victim of physical abuse are often at such a point.

The consequences of these two kinds of problems, like other real problems of family dysfunction, can be identified and treated. Advocates of social policy, who make prevention and solution the goals, tend to give less attention than is warranted to identification and treatment. But preventing or "solving" dysfunction associated with parental neglect or rejection, or with violent behavior of a spouse, rather than mitigating their consequences, is still beyond the capacity of public policy.

---

1. "In the Beginning: Helpless and Dependent," in David Rothman and others, *Doing Good: The Limits of Benevolence* (Pantheon Books, 1978), p. 19.

Foster Care

Well-intentioned state and federal responses to the money problems of families with children, like mother's aid laws and then aid to dependent children, assume that children are being cared for at home by at least one parent. But parental care is sometimes impossible even if money is provided. Arranging for temporary or long-term foster care for children without parents or for children whose parents cannot provide home care—whether "for considerations of inefficiency or immorality" or less judgmental reasons like prolonged illness—is a principal component of the public function ambiguously called child welfare. At the behest of the Children's Bureau, the draft Social Security Act of 1935 included a small authorization for federal assistance to state and local child welfare services. This provision, which was approved by the act's planners without much consideration, first became an instrument for financing the training of a generation of social work leaders and later served as the wedge for expanding family-based care over institutional care.

Public officials concerned with welfare, children, and families are under little or no pressure to devote themselves to problems of foster care and adoption, since most of the 2 million children separated from both biological parents for temporary or extended periods are likely to be cared for informally by relatives or friends, without public involvement. That private-support network—described by Robert Hill as a particular strength of black families[2]—makes no demands on the federal-state child welfare system. Inevitably, however, there are children whose need for care cannot be met by the private network. Rarely the subject of sustained attention from policymakers, those children are socially and politically handicapped. They are socially handicapped because many of them are unwanted children whose parents are indifferent to them and because many are the offspring of social outcasts—unwed adolescents, the mentally ill, incarcerated criminals. They are also politically handicapped because those who provide them with services are neither organized nor choose to make demands even on politicians who worry about unequal opportunity and its consequences for social stability.

Given the universal belief in a stable family environment for chil-

2. *The Strengths of Black Families* (Emerson Hall, 1972).

dren, issues of foster care, reunification, and adoption should be of primary concern to family policy proponents. But the conflict between a child's need for permanency and a presumption in favor of eventual reunification with a biological parent is hard to resolve. So is the problem of children for whom permanent placement seemingly cannot be arranged but for whom reunification is also unlikely. Though family policy cannot settle these and related questions, it can illuminate them and make least-undesirable choices. Before and after family policy became a presidential cause, however, administrators responsible for the program at the federal level, not knowing what to do, did nothing with foster care. In Congress, where foster care is small stuff enveloped within more compelling matters, specialists on foster care struggle for attention.

Questions about child welfare tend to be eclipsed because of an accident of history that first worked to their advantage but now affects them adversely in the competition for congressional attention. Since the federal Children's Bureau antedated the New Deal by two decades, Children's Bureau personnel were on the scene in the mid-1930s and able to arrange for the incorporation of child health, crippled children's services, and child welfare items in the Social Security Act. Writing these small, otherwise unwanted efforts into the Social Security Act gave them a good home initially but had delayed costs for child welfare policymaking. None of the programs or even all three together touch a large enough fraction of the general population to command public interest comparable to that given the various social insurance or public assistance titles of the Social Security Act. As a result, the House Ways and Means Committee and the Senate Finance Committee, each over-loaded with responsibility for internal revenue taxation and foreign trade along with social insurance, with public assistance, and subse-quently with medicare and medicaid, have found it convenient either to let child welfare policy just slide along from year to year or to give it short shrift.

The absence of reliable numbers both encourages policy drift and is a result of that drift. To respond to the needs of children not cared for by at least one biological parent, it is useful to know the size and characteristics of the child population involved. That no one can be confident about its size is a sign that national public officials are indifferent to this population. Since HEW did not feel it could get states to report on those aspects of substitute care that are not federally funded, it gave up trying for national totals after 1971. The number of children actually in foster care may be 350,000, as Secretary Califano stated in July 1977,[3] or it may be 502,000, as reported by Ann Shyne and Anita Schroeder of Westat, Incorporated, in an HEW-sponsored study under way at that same time,[4] or it may be larger or smaller than either of these figures.

The 502,000 figure—an extrapolation, not a head count—was developed after an exasperating exchange with HEW officials a few years ago left Representative George Miller, Democrat of California, unable to learn either how many children were in foster care or how much money was spent on it. Miller thought it important to know those numbers whether or not the dollars were federal dollars. Expressing concern about children who "are not wards of the federal government," he asked, "Of those children out there who are not federally funded, are they taken care of adequately or are they not?"[5] Because it came from a new member of the House, Miller's request for data did not provoke instant compliance from the Children's Bureau. But when more senior members of Congress like Senators Walter Mondale and Alan Cranston also spoke up, the bureau stirred. Around the time Mondale became Jimmy Carter's running mate, HEW began planning a national survey of social services to children and their families, the first such survey since 1961. Carried out in mid-1977, this survey was based on a national sample of 263 counties and independent cities in 41 states and the District of Columbia, and yielded the data from which its compilers extrapolated the figure of 502,000 children in foster care. Subsequently, Carter's first chief of the Children's Bureau, Blandina Cardenas, accepted the total, since she came to express concern over "the half a million American children who've been separated from the security of a permanent family."[6]

3. *Public Assistance Amendments of 1977*, Hearings before the Subcommittee on Public Assistance of the Senate Finance Committee, 95 Cong. 1 sess. (Government Printing Office, 1977), p. 58.

4. *National Study of Social Services to Children and Their Families*, prepared for the National Center for Child Advocacy, Administration for Children, Youth, and Families, DHEW (OHDS)78-30150 (HEW, 1978), p. 109.

5. *Foster Care: Problems and Issues*, Joint Hearing before the Subcommittee on Children and Youth of the Senate Labor and Public Welfare Committee and the Subcommittee on Select Education of the House Committee on Education and Labor, 94 Cong. 1 sess. (GPO, 1976), pt. 1, p. 30.

6. "Homes for All Children: Our National Concern," speech prepared by Blandina Cardenas, commissioner of the Administration for Children, Youth, and Families, June 1979.

If 500,000 is accepted as an accurate estimate of the number of children in foster care, it should have had a sharp impact on the Children's Bureau and its friends. It would not only constitute the largest absolute number of foster children ever recorded in the United States, a circumstance that could be attributed to general population growth, but would also constitute a larger ratio of foster children to the general population than HEW or its predecessors reported for 1933, 1963, or 1969. In 1969, among all children under eighteen, 45 in 10,000 were in foster care, down from the 59 in 10,000 in 1933, but up from the 1963 low of 37 in 10,000.[7] With a national population under eighteen of approximately 65 million in 1977, 500,000 children in foster care would represent 77 in 10,000—a rate 71 percent above that of 1969, and more than double the rate of 1963. Perhaps this means that many more children who needed foster care were getting it in 1977 than before, or perhaps it means that too little attention was being paid to exits from foster care, or perhaps it means that even more attention should be devoted to getting a firm count of children in such care.

Comings and going are also uncertain, but there seems to be more in the way of coming-into foster care than going-out. HEW's consultants reported two and one-half years to be the median length of time for children in foster care nationally.[8] In 1977 an audit of foster care by the comptroller of New York City reported that 17,000 children there remained in foster homes for an average of six years. Of 35,657 children in all types of foster care (foster family homes, small-group homes, and child care institutions) in New York during 1976, only 5,431 were discharged to permanent homes, that is, reunited with parents, discharged to relatives, or placed for adoption.[9] In Mississippi nearly two-thirds of the more than 2,000 children in foster care in 1977 had been in welfare department custody for over two years. "Generally the children we get in foster care grow up in foster care," explains an officer of Mississippi's welfare system. "They come at age 5 or earlier, and we can expect them to be with us for 8 to 10 years."[10] Such an expectation, of course, can become self-fulfilling. If the norm is understood to be

7. White House Conference on Children, 1970, *Profiles of Children* (GPO, 1970), p. 147.

8. *National Study of Social Services to Children and Their Families*, p. 119.

9. City of New York Office of the Comptroller, Bureau of Municipal Investigations and Statistics, "Report on Foster Care Agencies Achievement of Permanent Homes for Children in Their Care," E77-403 (May 26, 1977), p. III.

10. *The Sun-Herald* (Biloxi, Miss.), February 26, 1978.

eight to ten years in foster care, case workers and administrators feel no pressure to plan for permanent family settings.

Still, there has been no insistent demand for federal help from the state level. An opportunity was first provided in the early 1960s for the states to share with the federal government the costs of maintaining welfare-eligible children in foster care. This relief served to keep child welfare off the states' list of critical problems. Foster care cases did not increase dramatically like public assistance, where an explosion of clients and costs made state and local governments active lobbyists for change.

In 1977 national leaders interested in family-strengthening public policy might have given special attention to foster care. Yet the new administration first turned away from a reform proposal, embracing it only after a journalist asked for an explanation of the inconsistency between the concern for families expressed during the Carter-Mondale campaign and the negative response by the Carter-Mondale administration to a legislative initiative for foster care reform. After the fact, stalwarts have claimed that the administration would have produced its own foster care bill without media or other intervention if concerned congressmen had been willing to wait. According to this analysis, family policy was a thing to work out sometime, and the administration's first few months—when the concern was with income maintenance and health insurance—was not the right time. No one of importance could be diverted then to take charge of policies for families. But with no one in charge, what might have been a well-coordinated legislative drive became a source of frustration for proponents of change in foster care and a demonstration of the administration's ambivalence about family policy.

Recently attention has been directed to child welfare policy for two reasons. One, there has been a shift from quantitative questions like "Is the case load increasing?" and "Are the costs within tolerable limits?" to qualitative ones like "Is the affected population well served?" and "Is program activity consistent with an interest in providing children a stable family environment?" Two, a new policy-formation axis has evolved—one that compensates for a weak executive agency, indifferent congressional subcommittees, and an unorganized interest group by using foundation resources to develop policy proposals, academics to wrap them in theory, and individual, highly motivated legislators to force congressional subcommittees to examine the proposals.

Federal Neglect of Foster Care

When first proposed in the mid-1930s, the idea of federal financial contributions to child welfare services offended sectarian sensibilities. Catholic spokesmen feared that their existing arrangements, whereby the cost of caring for children committed to Catholic institutions was paid by several large urban governments, including New York, Chicago, Philadelphia, and Pittsburgh, would be jeopardized by federal and state involvement. The architects and draftsmen of the Social Security Act had been unaware that the legislative proposal might interfere with arrangements between local governments and the Church. When so informed, they "offered to accept any revision of the provisions of this particular part of the bill which would be acceptable to the Church representatives."[11] What was acceptable was to drop the requirement that federal money be matched and to add the limitation that federal money be used only in rural areas where there was no adequate provision for child welfare services—and, of course, little likelihood of a sectarian institution for children. In an exquisite example of logrolling, the suggestions of the representatives of the Catholic Church were accepted "with the understanding that they would not object to any other part of the bill and would actively support the measure," an agreement that was faithfully carried out by both sides.[12]

So the Children's Bureau came out of the process with a puny authorization—less than one-fifth of that provided the Public Health Service for its state and local grants—to be allotted among the states according to a rural-oriented formula and to be spent for local child welfare services in predominantly rural areas. (Each state was guaranteed a token sum, the balance to be distributed in proportion to each state's share of the country's rural population.) If the Social Security Act allowed the Catholic Church to continue its organized activity in the child welfare field, this, according to Edwin Witte, the act's principal

11. Edwin E. Witte, *The Development of the Social Security Act* (University of Wisconsin Press, 1963), p. 169.
12. Ibid.

author, was a bargain price to be paid for lobbying help from the secretary of the National Conference of Catholic Charities:

Father O'Grady was in close touch with many members of Congress and proved one of the most valuable supporters of the bill. It is my belief that he influenced a great many members of Congress to support the bill who otherwise would have opposed it.[13]

Further, the small amount of money involved effectively precluded actually financing services to more than a few children, rural or no. Rather than go into rural-area foster care in a small way, the Children's Bureau took advantage of the vagueness of the term "child welfare services" to follow an entirely different path, one that prohibited by regulation the use of federal funds to pay for any foster care of children except in emergency situations. The regulation was not relaxed until 1947, and not removed until 1951. For a decade and a half, the bureau specified that federal money be used for the employment and training of staff and for services to children rather than for the maintenance of children in care. Under the restrictive language of the act, moreover, the majority of workers so employed and trained were local workers in areas predominantly rural—at least until the rural limitation was lifted by the 1958 amendments to the Social Security Act, which undertook to make child welfare services available in urban areas too.

In sum, federal money to pay for foster care simply was not available before 1947 and was not available for use in urban areas until after 1958. Instead, soon after passage of the Social Security Act, states began to use the federal grant money to pay for the graduate training in social work of child welfare personnel. Taking educational leave became common practice among employees of public welfare agencies, and with few exceptions federal funds were used to pay all the costs of such leave for a broad spectrum of child welfare personnel. The educational-leave policies of the Children's Bureau were liberal enough to include use of child welfare money for the training of county welfare administrators and general field representatives of state welfare departments as long as part of their responsibilities extended to the child welfare program. The stipend might cover part or all of tuition, maintenance, and travel costs. Some states paid full salary while a staff member was on educational leave, and some paid a dependents' allowance as well. Uses of the federal appropriation also encompassed special workshops,

13. Ibid., p. 170.

conferences, and book, magazine, and film acquisitions for staff development.

The implicit division of responsibility that made actual foster care service a state financial concern and staff development a federal financial concern could be regarded as sensible enough while the rural restriction kept the federal agency out of the mainstream of foster care and the money was available only in insignificant amounts. One unforeseen result of interpreting child welfare services to mean professional education of child welfare personnel, however, was to put day-to-day decisions about foster care cases in the hands of the least-trained and most transient workers. Those case workers who availed themselves of the educational benefits either would return to the public agency in new supervisory and administrative roles—as befitted holders of graduate degrees—or would shift over to a private agency where psychosocial services were offered to a middle-class clientele. Those case workers in public agencies who did not use educational benefits as an escape route were thought to be of doubtful competence. Public foster care work sank to the very bottom of the social welfare hierarchy.

A Theory to Guide Public Policy

For more than twenty of the forty years between the first federal legislative action in child welfare and the renewal of congressional awareness of the foster care problem in 1977, only a small group of insiders realized that the children involved were not well served by a small program that for a long time concentrated on staff development and that stayed out of the cities. Child welfare's major failure was the continued absence of a theory on which to base public policy for children in foster homes. Is reunification always the goal? Why or why not? Under what conditions may the goal change? Why? When should parental rights be sustained and when terminated? Why?

An important step in the development of modern foster care theory was achieved in 1959 with the publication of the first comprehensive and systematic evidence concerning the return of children in foster care to their biological families. The evidence assembled by Henry Maas in *Children in Need of Parents*—still considered to be a landmark document—demonstrated that children were allowed to drift in so-called temporary foster care for indefinite periods and that they were locked into foster care more and more firmly as time went on.[14] Maas's analysis showed that a child in foster care for as long as two years reaches a "tipping" point after which the odds run against a return to the home from which the child came. Seventeen years later—in 1976— a synthesis of data from recent foster care studies undertaken by five states confirmed Maas's finding: "The studies indicate that a child's probability of returning home decreased rapidly after two years in placement."[15]

On the other hand, a study of status changes involving 624 children who entered foster care in New York City in 1966 and were tracked for the next five years is less pessimistic. At the end of the five-year period, David Fanshel found that 29 of the children had been adopted, 18 had been transferred to state institutions, 227 were still in foster care, and 350 had been discharged.[16] Of the discharges, 135, or 23 percent, occurred during the third, fourth, or fifth year in care. Viewed differently, Fanshel's work can be read as even more encouraging: of the 362 children in care after two years, 37 percent were discharged in the next three years.

One logical inference for policy from the several studies would be a presumption that favored the termination of parental rights after two years and a requirement that an alternate plan for the child's future be developed at that time. Since it is known that after some period a child is not likely to be reunited with a biological parent, a two-year termination presumption would encourage the recognition of reality. The presumption of termination does not mandate termination, which must always depend on individual circumstances, but it does put public policy on the side of permanency over uncertainty. The principle is not different from that used in divorce policy, where an interlocutory decree will commonly be entered at some fixed period before the decree is final. At some moment, lives must be reprogrammed and the persons involved should know when that moment—whether eagerly awaited or sadly accepted—is at hand. In foster care, as in a broken marriage, the outcomes are limited to reconciliation, legal termination, or indef-

14. Henry S. Maas and Richard E. Engler, *Children in Need of Parents* (Columbia University Press, 1959).
15. Shirley M. Vasaly, *Foster Care in Five States*, U.S. Department of Health, Education, and Welfare, Office of Human Development, Children's Bureau, DHEW(OHD)76-30097 (HEW, 1976), p. 54.
16. David Fanshel, "Status Changes of Children in Foster Care: Final Results of the Columbia University Longitudinal Study," *Child Welfare*, vol. 55 (March 1976), p. 145.

inite uncertainty. Knowing when the prospect for reconciliation becomes remote reduces the need to perpetuate uncertainty and invites legal termination with its opportunity for a fresh start.

Still, to say that even a finding of such obvious value as the two-year tipping point clearly shows the way to appropriate public policy underrates the complexity of the issue. Unlike dissolution of the marital relationship, where mutual consent is common, termination of parental rights is often regarded by one of the parties involved, the child, as outright rejection. Throughout the early period of foster care placement, one goal is to provide assurance to a child that he or she has not been rejected by biological parents. Such assurance both facilitates the adjustment to the foster care placement and prepares the way for reunification of the family. As time passes, the child will have growing doubts, but there is no doomsday setting to confront, no agonizing over whether a parent will or will not seek the child's return before time runs out. It is possible to count the number of cases in which a child is reunited with a biological parent within any given period of time, but there is no mechanism that can produce an equally precise count of the number of cases in which a child is damaged more by formal termination than by prolonged uncertainty or vice versa.

Three careful students of the psychological and legal issues presented by the termination of rights have addressed themselves to a general theory that focuses on children's needs rather than on parental rights. Set forth in 1973 in *Beyond the Best Interests of the Child*, the work of Joseph Goldstein, Anna Freud, and Albert Solnit is as creative as any ever done in the field. Its central argument introduces the concept of the psychological parent[s] (who may or may not be the biological parent[s]) as the preferred parent[s] for any child. At birth, a child is placed with biological parents who, unless other adults assume or are assigned the role, are presumed to become the child's psychological parents.

A psychological parent is one who, on a continuing, day-to-day basis, through interaction, companionship, interplay, and mutuality, fulfills the child's psychological needs for a parent, as well as the child's physical needs. The psychological parent may be a biological, adoptive, foster, or common-law parent, or any other person. There is no presumption in favor of any of these after the initial assignment at birth.[17]

17. Joseph Goldstein, Anna Freud, Albert J. Solnit, *Beyond the Best Interests of the Child* (Free Press, 1973), p. 98.

In order to reach a correct child placement decision, it is necessary to combine (1) the right of an intervenor—who may be the state, biological parents, or other persons—to try to disrupt the relationship between psychological parent and child or to establish such a relationship, with (2) an appreciation of a child's sense of time, which "is based on the urgency of his or her instinctual and emotional needs and thus differs from an adult's sense of time." The placement decision then made will be the least detrimental available alternative: "that child placement which maximizes, in accord with the child's sense of time, the child's opportunity for being wanted and for maintaining on a continuous, unconditional, and permanent basis a relationship with at least one adult who is or will become the child's psychological parent."[18]

This formulation obviously rejects two years in foster care, just as it might reject a period as short as six months, as an across-the-board test of whether a biological parent's rights should be terminated in any particular child placement case. The individual child's conception of time and the state of the child's attachment to a psychological parent provide the data needed to permit the choice of the least detrimental alternative. If these data were gathered and the least detrimental alternative test were to be applied to all outstanding foster care cases, a placement decision would be forced in every instance. And if the data and test were applied at regular intervals in all new foster care placements, few of them would be indefinitely prolonged.

Despite the elegance of the Goldstein-Freud-Solnit formulation, it has failed to attract a substantial following in either political or child welfare circles. Many concerned politicians, administrators, and social workers share anxiety over the problem of "drift" in foster care and share a belief that more extensive and more skillful work with biological parents can result in reunification rather than prolonged foster care. "There has to be a tremendous emphasis on delivering services to parents of children in foster care," David Fanshel told a congressional committee a few years ago. "These are our most oppressed group of people. I think people too easily talk about termination of parents' rights. In a democracy I think we should be very cautious of parents taking that extreme step." Urging Congress to make social services to parents an important part of federal foster care legislation, Fanshel complained of "a much too cavalier readiness to early terminate the rights of natural parents."[19]

18. Ibid., p. 99.
19. *Foster Care*, Joint Hearing, p. 76.

This same emphasis on serving biological parents is apparent in a fourteen-page paper on foster care prepared at HEW a couple of years after the publication of the Freud-Goldstein-Solnit argument. Although most of the paper involves the tiresome detailing of the various statutory authorities for foster care–related expenditures, it turns ultimately to the improvement of foster care:

> Foster care programs in this country would be greatly improved by (1) strengthening services to children in their own homes; (2) making these services available everywhere—from the smallest village to the large metropolitan area; (3) providing services to families on other than a crisis basis; and (4) having trained workers who, with adequate supervision and low enough caseloads, can give the special kinds of attention that parents and children need. Children also need more and better foster family homes, as well as more and better specialized group homes and institutions.[20]

Those old ideas could have come from the staff report on child welfare services published by the Committee on Economic Security forty years earlier. The professionals saw fit neither to refute nor to embrace the concept developed in *Beyond the Best Interests of the Child*, but to let it—like the children it addresses—simply grow old without benefit of a plan for its—or their—disposition.

Impediments to Change

Some of the 502,000 children—to accept the Shyne-Schroeder number as the best available count—living in foster family homes, group homes, or residential institutions are there because of short-term family crises at the end of which the affected children will be reunited with their families or freed for adoption. If the proportion approached 100 percent, and short term never exceeded two years, it would be fair to conclude that the child welfare system worked well. The conclusion would be reinforced if it were also demonstrable that the family crises resulting in substitute care did not lend themselves to any such alternative as, for example, homemaker services to help a family in which a parent or parents may be hospitalized, or day-care services to relieve a family of constant care of a mentally handicapped child. But there is no evidential support that the system works well. On the contrary, most reports, studies, and analyses conclude that it works badly.

Thoughtful social workers have known for a long time that the foster

20. "Statement of John C. Young, Commissioner, Community Services Administration," in ibid., p. 48.

care system is a problem. Studies of discrete aspects of the three-sided relationship—overseen by a social service agency—involving biological parents, children, and foster parents provide plenty of evidence that the best is rarely made of a bad situation. Because case workers understandably focus on the fit between child and foster home, biological parents tend to be cast as outsiders. That role makes it easy for biological parents disposed to slough off responsibility to do so, and makes it hard for parents anxious to maintain contact to do so. Neither pattern facilitates reunification.

Almost always, however, deemphasizing the biological parent is the safest approach for the child welfare worker, who carries in his or her head two injunctions: do the child no harm and do not embarrass the agency. If harm is construed as the abuse, neglect, or abandonment of a child, it is more certain to be avoided in continued foster care than in reunification. To ensure that the agency not find itself the center of unwanted publicity for arranging the return of a child who is subsequently maltreated, a worker need only not arrange for the return of a child wherever any shadow of a doubt exists.

But the underlying assumption in foster care is its temporary nature, to which lip service is consistently given. From time to time, then, the child welfare professionals confront the dilemma and urge one another to attend to it by a more careful examination of individual cases. The literature records success stories of individual agencies "cleaning house" by intensifying contacts with parents to achieve reunification or termination of parental rights, by reexamining anachronistic adoption standards, and by putting staff on special assignment to monitor and support biological parents who might otherwise be doubtful about reunification. Recently, even coercion of foster parents has been proposed. "I told a worker," a New York agency director committed to the idea of permanent placement explained to an interviewer, "that foster-parents who have had a child for 10 years should be coerced into adopting her. The child could be placed for adoption with another family, but she could not be expected to adjust well to that implicit rejection by long-time foster parents." Still, the idea of forcing a child on reluctant parents is not universally accepted.

Reports on demonstration projects designed to test ways to resolve cases of prolonged foster care have been at hand for decades, but the beneficiaries have always been too distant from politics to pressure government for program changes, or have lacked the strength to do so effectively. A National Foster Parents Association (NFPA), organized in 1972, could argue in a national conference over the merits of salaries for foster parents as against higher reimbursement payments. But decisions about either one are made separately by fifty states and the District of Columbia, which would have to be separately lobbied on behalf of either objective. That task is beyond the association. Instead, it has emphasized the desirability of competency training, an objective that apparently excites its leaders more than it interests rank-and-file foster parents, only a few of whom have entered preservice training programs.

It is not likely that a foster parents association could ever become a consequential force, because the motives of foster parents are too diverse to lend themselves to a specific program. Some have only altruistic interests—to help children in trouble. Others view foster care as a service for sale and have no qualms about emphasizing the importance of price. Still others are drawn to foster care out of dedication to a black, Hispanic, or Indian ethnic heritage. When the NFPA has a chance to express goals, it is more likely to describe the dimensions of foster care—growth in total numbers of children in care, of abused and neglected children in care, and of children too long in care—than to propose remedies for the system's failings. Exactly because they are among the most docile purveyors of a public service, foster parents initiate no proposals for important change in foster care policy.

None of the four groups involved in the system—children, for whom someone else must speak; biological parents, sometimes too uninterested to speak, sometimes too suspect to be heard; foster parents, not motivated to speak; and child welfare professionals, too insecure about their own role to speak—is an actual or potential policy activist group. Without a disaffected clientele that can make itself heard, and with costs divided between governmental entities so that none is burdened intolerably, the tendency is for arrangements to become automated. Parents voluntarily give up care of their children or judges order removal, foster homes are found, workers in public and private agencies arrange placements, federal and state money is appropriated. As long as no untoward event occurs—for example, outright fraud or other criminal behavior on the part of any of the participants, for which there is low probability—the process goes on unquestioned. Periodically, the practices of one or another child care institution may command attention, but the issue is likely to be confined to alternate views of child rearing rather than to expand into questions about the operation of the foster care system.

Questions about the operation of the system, occasionally raised by only a few troubled insiders, are more likely to be ignored than answered. To know that foster care policy was vulnerable, HEW officials need only have reviewed the agency's own history of slight involvement in foster care, the periodic shift of child welfare issues in and out of the jurisdiction of the Children's Bureau to the point where federal specialists were no longer to be found, and the research on foster care outcomes that HEW itself had financed. That kind of review does not happen without provocation: scandal, sustained pressure from organized groups, or high-level interest—from the White House, the HEW secretary, or the Congress. Any of these may be enough to make one cause *the* cause of the moment. Without scandal, pressure, or political interest, however, there is little probability that an old program will be rescued from the depressing monotony of routine renewal at HEW and reexamined in the light of new knowledge and new needs.

Foster care has been no First Lady's "principal interest," nor has a secretary of HEW taken it on as a personal crusade. Consequently, it did not receive the high-level attention in the late 1970s that was briefly accorded mental health policy and the dangers of cigarette smoking. Because foster care neither makes a substantial difference in the federal budget nor involves millions of people, it does not automatically command attention. Scandal does provide occasional visibility, but it is scandal usually limited to child-rearing practices in a particular setting rather than intolerable scandal entailing fraud in benefit claims or other continuing misuse of public money.

Foster Care Reform as Family Policy

If there were a way in which a family policy concept could guide improved public responses to the continuing problem of children in need of parental care, it should have been apparent between 1977 and 1980 during consideration by the Carter administration and Congress of the most important proposal for child welfare reform in a quarter-century. Injecting the goal of family policy into the debate provided no guidance, nor did it simplify complex problems. Different views of how to discourage needless or prolonged foster care—indeed of what constitutes needless or prolonged foster care—could not be accommodated.

Developing congressional interest in foster care and the related issue of adoption subsidies might have been only a lingering dream of some academics working in a University of California Childhood and Government project and of officials of the Edna McConnell Clark Foundation—where demonstration programs on foster care and adoption reform have been emphasized since 1973—had it not been for the steady determination of Representative Miller to call attention to what he has termed a "continuing crisis in foster-care." (There is no doubt about the "crisis" in California, a state with the highest total expenditures for non-AFDC foster care and second to New York in expenditures for AFDC foster care. State and local costs in California for foster care were about $1.25 billion in 1979.) In 1977 Miller, the only member of the House of Representatives who calls children and families his major legislative interest, offered his colleagues an assessment of foster care policy. "A system," he said, "designed to provide short-term care for a child, while family difficulties—in over 90 percent of the cases, parental problems—are addressed with appropriate services, has become, instead, a system of indeterminate, long-term placements in which little if any effort is made to restore the original family or, failing that, to place the child in a suitable adoptive home."[21]

In his second term, Miller, helped by fellow California Democrats who served as chairman of the Subcommittee on Public Assistance of the House Ways and Means Committee and chairman of the Senate Subcommittee on Children and Youth, pushed his foster care reform proposals far enough and fast enough for them to be later coopted by the Carter administration as its first substantive family policy proposal. While HEW and Domestic Council officials stood silent about what family policy might include, Miller forced the issue in 1977 by proposing comprehensive legislation dealing with (1) preventive services that might preclude the need for some foster care; (2) post-placement services directed to reunification; (3) improved procedural and due process protections for children and families in the foster care system; (4) improved information systems about children in foster care in order to track their status; (5) subsidies to adopting parents to encourage permanent placement of children. The proposal did not purport to be

21. *Congressional Record*, daily edition (June 14, 1977), p. H5822.

a solution to the dilemmas of child placement. It did confront them, however, and suggested techniques for easing the consequences for children, biological parents, foster care providers, and adoptive parents.

Within six weeks Miller's bill had been incorporated into high-priority public assistance amendments and approved by the House subcommittee. A month later, under suspension of the rules, the House passed the public assistance bill, which, in its child welfare services title, changed the preexisting authorization for federal grants to the states into an entitlement. The result would have been to ensure the annual distribution of $266 million in federal grants for child welfare services rather than to maintain the authorization-appropriation distinction that regularly yielded only $56 million of the $266 million. Other relevant titles would have extended federal matching for AFDC children in foster care beyond court-ordered placements to include voluntary placements, and also extended federal matching for foster care beyond private small-group homes to include public group homes.

Ironically, this was too swift a pace for the new administration. A few days before House action, at a meeting he called to obtain suggestions for HEW action, Secretary Califano told representatives of children's and youth advocacy groups that the president opposed the additional funds that would be made available under the pending legislation to reform foster care. Califano thus affirmed a position previously taken by HEW. During the next month, however, several things happened to change the administration's position: the potential embarrassment to Vice-President Mondale—once the Senate spokesman for children and families—was called to his attention from the outside; the strong possibility that Congress, early in the life of the administration, would ignore the president's reported wishes was called to Califano's attention from the inside; and the desirability of quickly showing a liberal stance on a family issue to blur the administration's hard line on medicaid abortions became so evident that neither outsider nor insider was needed to call attention to it. The administration reversed itself and gave support to increased spending on child welfare services.

Califano joked—not for the hearing record—that the initial opposition dated to a time so soon after Carter's inauguration that Office of Management and Budget personnel thought they were still working for the Ford administration.[22] For the record, the secretary offered renewed assurance that the Carter administration would give "special emphasis to policies and programs that strengthen and support the family." Acknowledging a debt to the legislation developed by the House Ways and Means Committee, Califano thereupon took title to the foster care legislation in the name of his leader:

> The President is concerned that his administration should not only propose programs to aid the family but also reexamine and reform existing policies that harm rather than help maintain stable, supportive family units. The proposal the administration presents today is another demonstration that the President will keep his campaign pledge.[23]

Prospects seemed good for new federal foster care money targeted to services rather than client maintenance. The House-passed foster care and child welfare services bill, which incorporated provisions espoused by advocates of prevention, reunification, and adoption, was characterized by the secretary of HEW as "the keystone to the administration's policy on families." But Senator Daniel P. Moynihan—a proponent of family policy long before he chaired the Senate Public Assistance Subcommittee—exposed the shallowness of the administration's work toward developing a family policy. Moynihan reached into the political literature of social services to resurrect a question that program administrators years before had anticipated would be raised by budget examiners: what do you know about services now that you did not know last year?[24]

The question opened the way for subcommittee moderates like Robert Packwood to challenge the restriction on state use of new money as out of keeping with the change of philosophy in Congress:

> I listened over and over. Joe [Califano], you said it. They live in Warrensburg, Mo. and we live in Washington, D.C. You used "they" and "we." Those people disagree.
>
> Pat [Moynihan] has put his finger on it. You are going to have to come to a decision. You are either going to give "they" the money and "they" may not spend it right, "they" might spend too much for day care and not enough for foster care; "they" might not spend it the way "we" think they ought to spend it. But you cannot have it both ways.[25]

22. *Washington Post*, July 13, 1977.
23. *Public Assistance Amendments of 1977*, Hearings, p. 58.
24. Ibid., p. 76.
25. Ibid., p. 78.

In the end—an end that was long in coming—this child welfare bill died, a victim as much as anything of the special scrutiny accorded it as the "keystone" of the administration's policy on families. Moynihan decided Califano did not know "one damn thing" about foster care and adoption that was not known before he sponsored the bill, that the department provided no evidence whatever about the proposal "except that it sounds like a good idea." Other members of the Senate Finance Committee were unwilling to restrict new money to services; some others were unwilling to provide financing for AFDC children placed in foster care voluntarily unless it was accompanied by a ceiling on federal AFDC–foster care expenditures; and still others would have limited federal matching for foster care in large private institutions. In sum, once the small federal financial and regulatory involvement in foster care gave promise of giving way to a family policy showpiece, HEW moved to put its mark on the plan, and both public and private child care agencies and intermediaries moved to protect their separate interests.

At one point, the Finance Committee tentatively approved a staff proposal to place the child welfare services title of the Social Security Act under the act's Social Services Title XX, which maximizes state discretion in the distribution of social services among competing causes. Since under traditional arrangements about $56 million was assured for child welfare services, and under the House-passed bill $266 million would be, the child welfare lobby rushed to defend the "collaborative federal-state child welfare program," that is, the earmarking of federal money for child welfare services. "Child welfare services and, hence, the welfare of the children they are designed to protect stand in mortal danger," said Joseph H. Reid, director of the Child Welfare League of America,[26] which, under the circumstances, also stood in mortal danger. Working through Senator Herman E. Talmadge, Democrat of Georgia, friends and dependents of the child welfare services title protected it, but too many issues had now been opened, with too little data available to resolve them, for the bill to move along easily.

As it did with the question of continuing a separate child welfare services title, the Finance Committee backed and filled on the proposal

26. "Statement of Joseph H. Reid on the Need for Child Welfare Services," *Child Welfare Planning Notes,* Child Welfare League of America, Hecht Institute for State Child Welfare Planning, Bulletin 7 (July 28, 1977), p. 2.

to reduce the federal matching funds paid for foster care in institutions housing more than twenty-five children. When Moynihan asked for a reconsideration of the initial decision to reduce those funds, he argued that there was no evidence that large institutions are ipso facto bad for children, but that the arbitrary penalties based on arbitrary norms, which required change in established practice, would ipso facto be disruptive to hundreds of such institutions. The view had been pressed on Moynihan and others by leaders of child care agencies—and by state officials who had had just enough experience with deinstitution-alization not to like the idea of having to undertake it. But with invidious comparisons being made between the annual cost of foster care in New York institutions ($14,000) and the annual cost of foster family care in Wisconsin ($1,560), members understood that they were likely to hear more on the subject.

The Senate Finance Committee did report a bill. For some of the child advocates from the Child Welfare League and the Children's Defense Fund, any measure would have been satisfactory if it provided for increasing the money for child welfare services and paying it on an entitlement basis; extending AFDC foster care payments to children voluntarily placed; mandating placement of children in "the least restrictive setting"; requiring periodic case review; and offering federal subsidies to encourage adoption of hard-to-place children. The com-mittee met about half of those objectives and added a provision of its own that would have gradually transformed so-called uncontrollable federal spending in AFDC foster care into a closed-end authority ultimately limited to 175 percent—or about $350 million annually—of 1977 expenditures. Though the committee extended AFDC foster care to include children in public as well as private facilities, it limited the extension to new placements in public institutions housing no more than twenty-five children, specifically prohibiting payments for chil-dren already in such institutions. If permanent, family-type placement is the goal, the Finance Committee majority said in effect, the govern-ment should gradually restrict spending, not authorize spending on a whole new group of voluntarily placed children, approach increased spending for services warily by using services money for tracking and case review, and emphasize subsidized adoption.

Under the chairmanship of Russell Long, the Senate Finance Com-mittee normally brought to the floor in each Congress only one bill amending the Social Security Act. Accordingly, child welfare was entangled with a variety of more or less related welfare and social security provisions. The tangle worked to delay calling up the bill: HEW, the Finance Committee, the White House, and welfare groups negotiated, traded, and otherwise bargained according to a well-known if imperfectly understood pattern whereby either an important trade or tax bill or some such esoteric measure as one to change the duty on synthetic rutiles can become the vehicle, as necessary, either for speeding the passage of particular welfare-related items, or making them veto proof. Those items most earnestly sought by the administration are least likely to be given an early ride on a convenient synthetic rutile or comparable bill and are most likely to be held for their hostage value. The inevitable result is a last-days-of-session pressure to come to an agreement on important welfare policy items. Under ideal conditions, before time runs out such an agreement will be reached among committee staff personnel, subcommittee leaders, administration lobbyists, and interest group spokesmen with the skill and stamina still to be arguing a position. Any one of the four forces is often able to impose a veto on a bill because the competition for a place on the end-of-session must-list is intense enough to discourage congressional leaders from calling up bills that can lead to serious political trouble.

Fifteens months after House passage, George Miller fretted about Senate inactivity. "The legislation, unfortunately and unnecessarily, has been stalled in the Senate Finance Committee where it has not only been weakened, but also burdened down with wholly irrelevant welfare amendments," Miller complained, adding that the measure could and should have been enacted a year earlier.[27] Moralizing by a junior House member about the behavior of one of the Senate's most powerful committees is neither welcome nor likely to have much effect. By then, however, Miller knew that a standoff between House and Senate over differences in the child welfare provisions was highly probable. On top of that frustration, he did not know how much of a complication might be created by other welfare amendments included by the Finance Committee.

Nor did the administration feel any less frustrated. Though it re-

27. *Congressional Record*, daily edition (September 6, 1978), p. E4803. Mil' :r again complained about Senate behavior in May 1979: "There are half a million foster children who need this legislation, and those who are truly concerned about their well-being are tired of the delays and the political machinations of a few who simply do not seem very concerned about improving the system and the lives of these children." Ibid., May 14, 1979, p. E2250.

jected the omnibus welfare bill reported by the Finance Committee, it would have liked to salvage the child welfare provisions. Indeed, one Sunday morning a deputy director of the Domestic Council tried practicing shuttle diplomacy as he went from the Finance Committee staff in one room, to Miller's administrative assistant in another, to HEW staff in yet another. No treaty resulted. How much to pay for child welfare reform, as they defined reform, split proponents of the House-passed bill, who did not even learn the asking price until a few days before the deadline for doing business.

The asking price turned out to be acceptance of the Senate Finance Committee's version of adoption subsidies, foster care reform, child welfare services, and an AFDC foster care spending ceiling in a package that also restricted earnings of working AFDC recipients. Agreed to by Moynihan, Long, and Alan Cranston, nominally administration spokesman in the Senate on family and children's issues, the package was grafted on to the 1978 tax reduction bill. However the excess of benefits over costs may have been calculated by Cranston, who rejected a warning from the head of his own state's Association of Children's Residential Centers that "a ceiling would be disastrous," the resident lobbyist of the Child Welfare League made a different calculation. He judged the proposed ceiling on federal payments for AFDC foster care to be intolerable. The league organized an opposition network that operated a special "foster care clearinghouse" for duplicating and distributing mailgrams and telegrams solicited and received from league members and affiliates. Besides associations of residential centers and homes for children, the league network included both the American Parents Committee and the formidable National Conference of Catholic Charities. The network's strategy was to concentrate on delivering to the House Public Assistance Subcommittee chairman, James Corman, Democrat of California, "a very simple and direct message": to oppose the entire package in conference committee. This strategy succeeded.

Foster care reform legislation was fought over in the last days of the Ninety-fifth Congress by professionals in and out of Congress with different perceptions of what was involved. Child Welfare League spokesmen perceived the fight as a holy war against closed-end spending, an evil philosophy that could limit public funds for league members and the children they serve, and as a chance to outmaneuver both Senator Long, an old antagonist, and the Children's Defense Fund, an effective competitor for leadership in child advocacy. George Miller and his House colleagues perceived their just cause as having been fouled in the Senate and struggled to restore purity. The Senate Finance Committee perceived its work as having been a realistic and hard-headed improvement on the "soft services" approach of the House bill with which the administration—ignorant about the issue—had gone along. The administration perceived a complex parliamentary tangle that could unravel in unpredictable and possibly unwelcome fashion.

Aware of cross pressures from child advocates, and reluctant to jeopardize its relations with either the Senate Finance or the House Ways and Means Committee over an issue that it had been shamed into embracing and that it had thought to be noncontroversial, the administration temporarily abandoned its family policy "keystone." Skirting the dilemma of parental rights versus permanency for children, HEW sent a letter to Capitol Hill indicating a willingness to forget the whole thing. The foster care reform effort that had appeared to be a romp when it was initiated nineteen months earlier instead was stalled for two more years.

Quid without Quo

One procedural problem and one substantive problem acted to maintain the status quo in foster care and adoption policy in the Ninety-fifth Congress. The procedural problem was timing—the end-of-session pressure and the advantage it gives to the status quo when it is a workable alternative to proposed change. The substantive problem was the proposed ceiling on AFDC foster care payments. On the latter question, most child advocacy groups were content to accept a ceiling in return for a guarantee of increased money for preventive and protective services. But that quid pro quo did not satisfy the Child Welfare League, whose determined and indefatigable lobbyist succeeded in killing the bill. The underlying issues—Does unlimited money perpetuate bad practice? Will a constraint on money change practice for the better or only cut off otherwise eligible beneficiaries? Is there a trade-off between preventive services costs and foster care costs?—remain in dispute.

Neither George Miller nor the Child Welfare League's not-so-friendly competitor, the Children's Defense Fund, believes the foster care ceiling to be more than a symbolic issue. Though they give pro forma opposition to the ceiling, neither would trade other foster care reforms for the retention of an open-end spending authorization. Both accept implicitly if not explicitly the validity of the position taken by the Senate Finance Committee, namely, that tracking, adoption subsidies, and other reforms will reduce the need for AFDC foster care, making the limit on spending a matter of theoretical interest. "I can live with it; it would have no practical effect" is the view expressed in these quarters.

William Pierce, former legislative policy strategist for the Child Welfare League, sees the issue somewhat differently and regards himself as a more experienced judge than those advocates who disagree with him. "Suppose," he asked an interviewer, "there had been a cap imposed on AFDC spending in the sixties when the 'rehabilitation instead of relief, services instead of support' public assistance amendments were enacted? Everyone—with liberal reformers in the vanguard—believed it was to be a new era of reduced need for AFDC. Yet in 1961 there were 3.5 million AFDC recipients and in 1977 there were 11 million. Could 11 million have been served if it had been necessary to fight annually over an increase in the cap?" And Senator John Heinz, Republican of Pennsylvania, recalling the parlous consequences of a ceiling imposed on food stamp spending, has said, "If you like the cap on food stamps, you'll love the foster care ceiling."

The implication deserves more serious attention than those stung by disappointment over the initial loss of reform legislation or ecstatic over subsequent passage have been willing to give to it. To agree to a ceiling on any kind of substitute care is to agree that its growth cannot be defended beyond an arbitrarily fixed point. But if the service is a bad one, it should be reduced, not just subjected to a limit on growth. If the true extent of need for it is thought to be calculable, the debate should turn on that calculation. If a ceiling is fixed on the basis of hunch or uninformed speculation about true need, it is unconscionable.

A ceiling on AFDC foster care assumes that preventive and reunification services will reduce separations of AFDC children from their homes and that where there is separation a new emphasis on adoption—with adoption subsidy payments—will cut away at prolonged AFDC foster care. Let even the true believer beware. What kinds of additional services, Arabella Martinez, then assistant secretary for human development services, was asked, would be available under proposed foster care and child welfare reforms to move the program away from a foster care emphasis. "One is in terms of really counselling families," she answered, "and working much more closely with the family and child."[28] But "really counselling" is an old answer and a vague one. Skeptics have cause to infer from it that HEW has no new plans but felt the need to get a child welfare bill passed.

That conclusion gained credibility prior to the eventual enactment of a child welfare bill in 1980. The department continued to support a ceiling on AFDC foster care funds even after the deletion of an entitlement provision assuring new money for preventive services. Without that provision, the ceiling on AFDC foster care money—once a quid pro quo for a fivefold increase in preventive services money—became a quid without a quo, yet HEW did not back away from this new arrangement that threatened costs without benefits. Having belatedly supported child welfare legislation in 1977, when Califano called it "the keystone to the administration's policy on families,"[29] HEW thereafter showed less sensitivity to substance than to the passage of any bill that it could score as child welfare reform. The bill that finally passed includes a complicated provision that phases in a ceiling on AFDC foster care spending as appropriations for child welfare services increase. But whether those appropriations will increase is problematic. Some child advocacy groups, badly in need of a legislative success story to report, appeared willing to accept a bill that might help locate children in foster care without giving assurance of doing much else.

So despite the reform legislation, the hardest questions remain unanswered—some perhaps unanswerable. What is it about the parental bond that allows some parents to be indifferent and some actually hostile to their children while others, similarly situated, struggle fiercely to care for their children? Can parental neglect be predicted and forestalled? Under what conditions should parental rights be terminated? Is family always to be preferred over institution? Which reluctant parents should be pressed—through counseling or in any other way—toward reunification with a child in foster care? When is foster care a desirable reaction to a family problem?

These questions invite "It all depends" as answer. But before adopt-

28. *Department of Labor and Health, Education, and Welfare Appropriations for 1979*, Hearings before a Subcommittee of the House Committee on Appropriations, 95 Cong. 2 sess. (GPO, 1978), pt. 6, p. 570.

29. *Public Assistance Amendments of 1977*, Hearings, p. 61.

ing a legislative keystone, sponsors can reasonably be asked to show that they have thought about the questions and about the limits of making families strong by government action.

Domestic Violence

Adults form the basic family relationship voluntarily. The traditional "I do" marriage ceremony requires the consent of each partner, and though various forms of parental and peer pressure may push an uncertain bride or groom into marriage, few persons could be expected to consent to legal marriage or to cohabitation if they expected severely abusive behavior from the partner. If violence does occur in a family, the victim will respond as he or she may respond to any other gross indignity: by forgiving; by accepting without forgiving; by having recourse to the law; by seeking therapy for spouse, self, or both; by abandoning the marriage; or, with a combination of these.

The chosen response to violence will most likely depend on the abused spouse's perception of the abuser's emotional and physical health, the victim's own emotional and physical health, the presence or absence of children, and practical considerations—Will it happen again? What danger am I in? Where can I go? How can I exist? When violence is met with forgiveness or with resigned acceptance, its appearance is unknown to all but the principals, and there is no deterrent effect. Nor does recourse to the police or to therapy, unless the victim also abandons the abusing spouse, provide protection against recurrent episodes. Abandonment, however, puts an abused spouse at a legal disadvantage against an abuser who feels justified, or fears the loss of children, or is genuinely contrite, and fights against ending the union. Without money or home or job skills or confidence, a victim of family violence may conclude that there is no practical choice other than to be accepting, if not forgiving.

That absence of a practical choice is especially unacceptable to women concerned about women. Stimulated by both compassion and outrage, they have expanded awareness of spouse abuse beyond habitués of family courts—first to executives of philanthropic foundations, then to officials in the National Institute of Mental Health and the Law Enforcement Assistance Administration who give demonstration grants, and finally to a few state and federal legislators. The goal is to offer a friendly haven, a community-based shelter, as an alternative to disaster for those who are helpless and unloved.

Spousal violence falls in the class of "hidden" social problems—indefensible events or circumstances known to exist but unlikely to be measured and responded to because those involved often prefer to or are compelled to remain "underground." Its victims depend for change on social altruism rather than organized self-interest. Women, organizing on behalf of women's self-interest in general, brought more than social altruism but less than actual self-interest to the spousal violence cause. Whatever might be done by public action would not bear directly on the self-interest of the organizers of particular local shelters, but many of the women responsible for developing them describe the activity as an exercise in "sisterhood" rather than as a work of charity by the privileged on behalf of the underprivileged.

Usually a multiethnic community group organized to provide services to women in crisis situations and to advocate women's concerns will extend its activity to the support of a residential shelter. Gender identification means that the interest of women's advocacy groups in a public response to domestic violence is different from the interest, say, of middle-class groups on behalf of improved food stamp benefits for the poor. But the interest is also different from one that might be mounted by organized groups of abused spouses themselves. The instructive comparison may be with the war veterans' organizations that fight for public benefits for the needy minority of the fraternity. American Legion leaders are usually not themselves on the pension rolls and do not expect to be, but they could be if their luck were bad. Shelter organizers generally are not battered spouses, but they feel they might have been if their luck had been bad.

The community-sponsored shelter program is a grassroots invention and a phenomenon of the 1970s. Previously, the only emergency assistance likely to be provided a woman with children fleeing from an abusive spouse would be an overnight stay in a hotel, financed by a local public or private welfare agency's emergency-services unit. The agency might then try to work out a longer-range plan, but extended shelter was not an available option. When, in 1971, a St. Paul, Minnesota, women's group undertook to respond to other women's questions about family law, it became aware of the limited options facing abused women without independent resources. Member volunteers began to offer shelter in their own homes while seeking support for a more formal program. The group incorporated, a state welfare department grant-in-aid provided funds for salaries for shelter workers, and a St. Paul–based private foundation—the Bush Foundation—made a grant for the down payment on a house and its rehabilitation. With operating funds from other foundations and from the local mental health board, in October 1974 St. Paul's Women's Advocates opened the first shelter in the United States for battered women. Sometimes with YWCA help, often with financial help from church groups, community-sponsored shelters thereafter appeared in Pittsburgh, Fort Wayne, Baltimore, and other cities.

Inevitably, regional networks emerged. By 1978 the National Coalition Against Domestic Violence, a clearinghouse and coordinating unit, claimed to represent over 300 grassroots groups providing either shelter or other direct services to victims of abuse. Its national program is set forth with exquisite clarity by Bonnie Tinker of Portland, Oregon, the coalition's chairperson: "If you want to help us, give us as much money as you can, as quickly and as directly as possible." Tinker also makes clear why the community-based shelters believe their claim for direct federal support for services to be better than claims from the research community or from a federal family-service bureaucracy. "We are the essential source of the great national outcry about battered women," says Tinker. "Most of us began with little or no funding, administrative expertise, or established community support. Through the last few years, however, we have sheltered thousands of women and children. . . . Our programs, which rely upon the peer self-help model, provide an effective alternative to tolerating violence."[30]

Led by the American Home Economics Association, four "family-oriented" organizations that collectively constitute a national advocacy group known as the Council of Family Organizations (COFO) decided in the late 1970s that domestic violence legislation would be a good entering wedge for the development of federal family policy. At the time the Carter administration had stated its interest in family policy, but had yet to produce its own program. Congress was thought to be wary of family-intervention legislation that lacked a clear protective purpose. COFO leaders identified assistance to victims of domestic violence as a family policy cause the administration might embrace. Some back-bench members of Congress thereupon proposed a limited

---

30. *Domestic Violence*, Hearings before the Subcommittee on Select Education of the House Committee on Education and Labor, 95 Cong. 2 sess. (GPO, 1978), pp. 310–11.

categorical grant program to help local community units provide emergency services to battered women.

Though less visibly a goal of family policy people than child care or income guarantees, shelters for victims of domestic violence cost much less and seem less controversial. No organized opposition emerged. A Congress suspicious of programs invented by federal bureaucrats might have been expected to be receptive to one with grassroots origins—all the more so in view of the small amount of money proposed. But subsequent legislative developments exposed congressional reluctance to buy up local programs and congressional doubts whether family problems are susceptible to a public policy solution. A bill that authorized federal grants to community shelters to shore up catch-as-catch-can support provided by church groups, individuals, and voluntary social service agencies lost on the House floor in 1978, and lost again in 1980. Its problems illustrate the point that kindly thoughts about families are not politically self-executing.

Victims, Analysts, and Public Officials as Policy Beneficiaries

Not a family policy success story, the legislative activity regarding domestic violence served instead to make the family policy cause suspect. The Carter administration, clearly unprepared on the subject, took an ambiguous stance that created doubts about its interest in family matters, embarrassed several of its legislative allies, and weakened its own Administration for Children, Youth, and Families in the eyes of congressional personnel and of interest groups with which the agency deals. Before hearings were scheduled, Margaret Costanza, then the president's assistant for public liaison, arranged a White House meeting among community shelter sponsors, administrative-agency officials, and congressional staff. At least one congressional sponsor mistakenly perceived that invitation as evidence of a strong White House interest in the problem of family violence. Actually, Costanza's action merely showed that the family violence issue had attracted the White House's most rapidly falling star, who would soon leave office and whose interest did not necessarily imply any interest at the White House other than her own. Other misperceptions of administration interest followed.

Later, sponsors inferred that sending the commissioner of ACYF—rather than one of several assistant secretaries with relevant responsibilities—to testify at House and Senate hearings showed that the Department of Health, Education, and Welfare had no strong views on domestic violence—or perhaps no views at all. If the message the commissioner carried had frankly acknowledged that the administration preferred not to deal with the subject yet, because it had not decided what to do, House and Senate sponsors might have understood they were entirely on their own. Instead, by testifying that the subject was "important" while indicating that her superiors had no particular plan to propose,[31] the commissioner allowed sponsors to assume that they could count on the administration to lobby for whatever they advanced. But that was too optimistic an assumption to make. All the while talking family policy, the administration neither developed its own domestic violence program nor embraced one developed elsewhere.

Barbara Mikulski, a Baltimore social worker turned congresswoman and sponsor of a domestic violence bill, became the first member of Congress to ask why, if HEW has been aware of spousal violence, it took so passive a role on policy. The ACYF commissioner's answer—given when the Carter administration was fourteen months old—is informative. Violence is a family issue, she said, whereas ACYF had focused on children and youth categories like child abuse and runaways.[32] In short, long after the administration's rechristening of the Office of Child Development as the Administration for Children, Youth, and Families, the agency continued to be without a family focus.

Mikulski, who was not a member of either the subcommittee or the full committee with jurisdiction over domestic violence proposals, had no ready platform from which to continue to ask questions. If she had had one, her questions would have sharpened congressional understanding of alternative approaches to violence legislation—one that simply provides federal money to help community groups establish and maintain shelters, another that tends to label domestic violence as a mental health problem, and yet another that puts domestic violence prevention within a family policy focus. The first approach—limited federal support for community-based shelters—is a modest and ra-

31. Ibid., pp. 104–05; *Domestic Violence, 1978,* Hearings before the Subcommittee on Child and Human Development of the Senate Committee on Human Resources, 95 Cong. 2 sess. (GPO, 1978), pp. 241–43.

32. *Domestic Violence,* House Hearings, pp. 78, 105.

tional response to an ugly reality of family life. The approach that ties domestic violence to mental illness—if the connection is to the victims as masochists rather than the perpetrators as aggressors—is an unwarranted connection hard to defend.[33] The amorphous "family focus" approach to domestic violence that ACYF talks about but does not act to put in place only tends to blur the modest character and specific goals of the shelter approach.

Shelter sponsors, driven by a belief in the sisterhood of women, are interested in public policy to get help paying the bills. But the problem of domestic violence also attracts two other groups that have less direct ties to the phenomenon itself or to the operation of the shelters. One group consists of research analysts who probe for incidence rates and details in the hope of finding a cure. The other comprises government officials who have been interested in folding domestic violence into some broader federal approach to family dysfunction on the theory that all problems of families are interrelated.[34] Clear-cut differences among the three groups became increasingly apparent as spousal violence changed from a problem responded to only at the level of the local police blotter to a problem eliciting proposals for big-stakes federal legislation.

One proposal—viewed more favorably by researchers and bureaucrats than by shelter operators and victims—would put the director of the National Institute of Mental Health (NIMH) in effective control of federal spending. He would be able to distribute grants and contracts in three areas, as he saw fit: research into the causes and means for prevention and treatment of domestic violence; training programs for law, mental health, and social service personnel; and demonstration projects of several kinds. Baltimore's Mikulski, whose social welfare orientation is in community organization, dislikes that plan both in itself and because of its tie to HEW. To put the program in NIMH, she complained, is to say that battered women have a mental health problem rather than a social problem. Viewing with alarm the consequences of such a judgment, Mikulski recalled the history of NIMH implementation of a comparable program:

Our Federal legislation established a program at the National Institute of

33. For testimony that quotes a police captain as saying, "Any woman who stays in a home with a violent husband, who has repeatedly beat her, has to be masochistic and enjoys the beatings," see *Domestic Violence, 1978,* Senate Hearings, p. 82.

34. *Domestic Violence,* House Hearings, p. 105.

Mental Health which treated the rape victim as if she were mentally ill. A lot of dollars got spent on research. Another large part got spent on expensive demonstration projects that had a heavy research emphasis, and direct service was given a very low priority. A little money did dribble down to the community, but instead of going to the grassroots citizens who raised the problem, the money went to traditional agencies, many of whom had brutalized the victim previously.

The similarities between the issues of rape and battered women are overwhelming: The guilt felt by the victim and the grassroots way in which the issue has been resolved, and now I fear that if we follow the same style, that we very well might create the same type of program.[35]

To avoid such an outcome, Mikulski offered her own bill, which emphasized service delivery and bypassed HEW in favor of ACTION, the umbrella agency for volunteer programs that incorporated the Peace Corps and Volunteers in Service to America (VISTA), the so-called domestic Peace Corps. "HEW," she said, "in many ways is so overcentralized, so much emphasis is on hiring coordinators of the coordinators, rather than on people at a grassroots level, and it is so oriented to a Washington mentality that it loses its perspective on direct services. . . . The think-tanks, the group, the crowd that I call the grant junkies, are very often so involved in studying the problem that there is no stake in solving the problem."[36]

Neither the NIMH nor the ACTION approach, both offered in June 1977, could show any political strength. As for the former, the HEW leadership, still new and thinking in terms of big programs, was not going to waste energy on a proposal to spend just $20 million annually on an NIMH-managed program. Indeed, there was no disposition to support a new program in NIMH, since HEW Secretary Califano was preparing to relieve Bertram Brown, then NIMH director, of his job. The administrative location of a federal domestic violence program was far too doubtful a mental health issue to interest the National Committee Against Mental Illness, an effective private lobby. Nor could NIMH lobby for itself. Unlike some of the national institutes doing research on physical health, NIMH has no in-house lobbying strength. On the university campuses, among the few academics who had an interest, none were research heavyweights whose support would make a difference. Within the consumer community, battered women were themselves unorganized. The women's groups responsible for the shelter

35. Ibid., p. 37.
36. Ibid., p. 36.

movement argued that an image of mental illness should not be attached to the problem of abused women, and that research should be done not at NIMH but at the local level by the service providers who know the problem.

As for a program centered in ACTION, its time was past. For 100 years, women's groups said, women had volunteered while men had worked. Women should no longer be asked to volunteer their time when other people are paid for comparable service. After beginning shelter programs with their own resources, sponsors were seeking the security and the respectability associated with money from grants. "We do not wish to relegate shelter programs to the realm of voluntarism. We feel that the very base salary for a staff member of a shelter program is $800 per month," the California Coalition [of service providers] Against Domestic Violence told House members before sponsors agreed on an approach. From the other end of the country, John Moakley, a Democratic congressman from Boston, where an emergency shelter in the South End depended on a staff of twenty-eight volunteers and on private financial donations for its round-the-clock services to abused women, also rejected voluntarism as a permanent arrangement: "We cannot rely upon the good will and kindness of volunteers who are continually in a state of uncertainty, never knowing where their funding will come from."[37]

Only Mikulski ("I was there when Sargent Shriver and Dan Thursz conceived of VISTA and what ultimately became ACTION") seemed prepared to take a chance on ACTION. George Miller told Sam Brown, the director of ACTION, the reactions of support groups in California to the idea of using ACTION personnel in shelters: "There is a very quick shudder at the idea that ACTION would train somebody in Wyoming and send them to Berkeley to deal with the problem."[38] With that quick shudder, ACTION's long-shot chance to become the lead agency in a federal spouse-abuse program—if there were to be a program—disappeared.

Finding a logical administrative home for a proposed domestic violence program developed into the most vexing problem for sponsors. Here was a family policy issue of uncertain magnitude but certain

37. Letter to Representative John Brademas from Sue Martin, for the California Coalition Against Domestic Violence, March 15, 1978, in ibid., p. 698; "Prepared Testimony of Hon. John Joseph Moakley," ibid., p. 607.
38. Ibid., p. 103.

existence. No proposals to respond to it could be faulted as wildly extravagant. No entrepreneur stood ready to get rich at public expense. Since grassroots groups responsible for first taking up the cause rejected permanent association with either a mental health or a voluntarist agency, the Administration for Children, Youth, and Families would have seemed to be the logical administrative home, at least by default. When supporters came together to seek agreement on a bill to move to the floor, however, even the case for ACYF collapsed as it became evident that the agency had no operating program concerned with families as organizational units. Moreover, its attempted response to questions about plans for discharging the "families" responsibility of its name dwelt on the reform of child welfare services as a way for the agency to become "more family-supportive"—a tie to domestic violence so forced and disjointed that listeners correctly believed ACYF still to have an exclusive orientation toward children, to be an Office of Child Development by another name.

Eventually, George Miller, the California Democrat who made himself House spokesman for both adult and child victims of family dysfunction, put together a bill that sidestepped the question of where in HEW administrative control would lie and that also minimized any federal administrative discretion. Pushing aside NIMH, ACTION, and ACYF, Miller would have established an Office on Domestic Violence in the Office of the Secretary of HEW, to avoid any sign of preference for one orientation over another. (But since an office in the Office of Secretary would inevitably be reassigned by the secretary to the control of one of his assistant secretaries, the practical effect of the Miller arrangement would have been to delegate the decision to the secretary of HEW.) A Council on Domestic Violence composed, in the majority, of shelter operators and spouse-abuse victims would control grants and approve regulations. Grants, which could not be made until a program had operated for six months, would be limited to $50,000 a year, could not be renewed beyond three years, and could not account for more than 25 percent of the shelter's budget. Noting that government agencies and academicians were already conducting "voluminous research" on domestic violence, Miller downplayed research other than shelter-based research that would help in understanding usage patterns and other operating factors.

Miller's bill was acceptable both to those who favored NIMH as the lead agency and to those who favored ACTION; the chairmen and ranking members of the subcommittee and the full committee supported it; the House majority and minority leaders also supported it; and Democratic Whip John Brademas would handle it on the floor. It seemed a safe bet for the suspension calendar—the parliamentary rapid-advance track for noncontroversial measures. "We had liberals, we had conservatives, we had everybody," said one staff aide who had worked on the bill from its earliest days. What supporters did not have was an expression of administration interest. Nonetheless, one opponent who insisted that "this is a program that is almost doomed to failure in the beginning," at first doubted whether more than a couple dozen negative votes would be recorded.[39] That estimate was just as wrong as the leadership's assumption that there would be a two-thirds favorable majority. Like counting the incidence of spouse abuse itself, counting the House is a tricky business.

The bill failed, victim of a combination of hidden weaknesses. Members were uninformed about what had been swept up under the heading "domestic violence," and were not given positive signals from HEW, the White House, or any organized interest group in a position to be heard. Many members were suspicious of the "crisis" or "epidemic" character of the problem and edgy about authorizing a total of $125 million under suspension. In effect, too many members had doubts of some kind that could not be resolved under the procedural shortcut. As some of the House's leading liberals—among them Abner Mikva of Illinois, chairman of the Democratic Study Group, and David Obey of Wisconsin, who was to succeed Mikva as chairman—recorded themselves as "nays," it became a rout. The bill that needed a two-thirds majority to pass failed finally to get a simple majority, losing 201 to 205. "There's no logic to why these [suspension calendar] votes go the way they do," Representative Morris K. Udall of Arizona, a liberal who voted for the bill, has explained.[40] "We've got to draw the line somewhere on new programs" was Mikva's way of making the point that the logic lies in opposing new spending programs in sensitive fields about which a member is both substantively and politically uninformed.[41]

39. *Congressional Quarterly*, Weekly Report (May 27, 1978), p. 1335; *Congressional Record*, daily edition (May 23, 1978), p. H4430.

40. Elizabeth Drew, "A Reporter at Large: A Tendency to Legislate," *The New Yorker* (June 26, 1978), p. 89.

41. *Washington Post*, May 24, 1978.

The more domestic violence was connected to family policy, the more vividly congressmen recalled local reactions to federal child care legislation, reactions to the abortion controversy, and reactions to issues like aid to parochial schools and school prayer. No one ever made it plain that the purpose of this bill was to meet an unmet need for emergency shelter, not to make the federal government a family referee. Although administration witnesses made committee presentations too inconsistent and too imprecise to qualify as support for the bill, its managers, without first counting votes, let it come to the House floor via a procedure normally reserved for widely supported noncontroversial measures. They learned that no bill involving the federal government in any aspect of family relations is noncontroversial. "Who needs it?" flashed through enough congressional minds to kill a modest plan that probably would have done better had it not been burdened with the family-focus hocus-pocus.

Four months after ignominious defeat on the House floor, domestic violence legislation almost made a back-door reentry. After having passed easily in the Senate, where it might accurately have been said that "we had liberals, we had conservatives, we had everybody"— only Harry F. Byrd, Jr., the Virginia Independent, insisted on being recorded in opposition—the bill won a favorable response from the House Rules Committee a few weeks before adjournment. Had it not been for the earlier effort, which reflected adversely on the judgment of the leadership, the domestic violence bill would have reached the floor in the normal order of things. But given its history, the still-embarrassed House leadership let the bill lie, and time ran out. Ironically, had it come back to the floor, it might even have managed the two-thirds majority originally sought under suspension. Liberals might have become aware of the bill's limited scope, and conservatives might have overcome their pique at confronting a $125 million authorization on the suspension calendar. Insecure members who follow the crowd on suspension votes might then have found most of the crowd voting aye.

Abuse of Numbers

Junior congressmen may be satisfied with modest successes affecting limited numbers, but cabinet officers and White House staff pass over small gains and look for big payoffs. In domestic violence, an abuse of numbers appears to be a problem common to politicians, analysts, and advocates. Despite a declaration by President Carter that "each year three to six million acts of severe violence occur in American homes,"[42] whether the actual incidence of domestic violence could qualify it as a big-payoff issue is hard to establish. Even more than with other manifestations of family dysfunction, the count of violence is uncertain. No one is obliged to report acts of domestic violence, nor is any agency responsible for reporting statistics. Most congressional proponents of federal legislation on the subject do no more than pick their way around actual numbers while insisting that they are consequential. A principal sponsor, Lindy Boggs of Louisiana, for example, admits a serious lack of reliable information on the nature and incidence of domestic violence yet finds it "drastically underreported."[43] Senator Jacob Javits, the New York Republican who cosponsored a Senate bill, calls domestic violence "widespread" and of "vast dimension,"[44] and other sponsors use comparable terms. None suggests that the data are too shaky to justify national legislation.

But they are shaky, as became evident when ACYF commissioner Cardenas, leaving "greater detail" to others, claimed to have "learned that spousal violence occurs in epidemic proportions," and Gerald Klerman, administrator of the Alcohol, Drug Abuse, and Mental Health Administration, gave a Senate subcommittee the evidence for his judgment that the amount of violence in the family is "extremely high."[45] Klerman based that judgment on the results of a national sample survey of 2,143 people. Undertaken by three sociologists with a grant from Klerman's agency, the survey, according to Klerman, found that one out of six couples—when projected to cover the U.S. population, an estimated 7.5 million couples—had a violent episode during the survey year. The researchers, Klerman said, defined violent episode as "ranging from slapping to severe physical assault." One of the academic investigators involved, Suzanne Steinmetz, reported to the same Senate subcommittee that "marital violence is a wide-spread, all pervading phenomenon."[46] Using responses from three samples— a random sample covering just fifty-seven families in a Delaware

42. "Memorandum for the Secretary of Defense, et al.," creating the interdepartmental Committee on Domestic Violence, April 27, 1979.

43. *Congressional Record*, daily edition (June 21, 1977), p. H6282; *Domestic Violence*, House Hearings, p. 55.

44. *Congressional Record*, daily edition (March 20, 1978), p. S4165.

45. *Domestic Violence, 1978*, Senate Hearings, p. 251; ibid., p. 263.

46. Ibid., p. 304.

county; a random sample in New Castle County, Delaware, and county police statistics; and the NIMH-sponsored survey mentioned above—Steinmetz reaches conclusions about "severely battered women":

> In a given year, you are likely to have 3½ million severely battered women. I am talking about the kind of women that would need shelter or some kind of hospital intervention or police intervention. I am not talking about hitting or slapping. You are also, in that same year, likely to have 250,000 battered husbands.[47]

To reach his 7.5 million figure, Klerman adds to Steinmetz's 3.5 million severely battered cases a presumed 4 million episodes involving three categories not deemed "severe and high-injury risk violence." These acts of lesser violence appear in the survey schedule as "threw something at the other one," "pushed, grabbed, or shoved the other one," and "slapped the other one."

Both Klerman's total of 7.5 million "violent episodes" and Steinmetz's figure of 3.5 million "severely battered women" take on importance because the work done for NIMH turns out to be the only reported effort at a comprehensive count. To depend on it is to invite doubt and confusion. If one begins with Steinmetz's reported estimate of 3.5 million women severely battered "in a given year"—reduced to 3.3 million in her formal paper filed with the subcommittee—and recalls that the national sample survey yielded 2,143 completed interviews from a stated universe of 47 million couples, the estimate of behavior characterized by the researchers as severe battering of women seems to depend on reports from about 7.5 percent of the respondents. In another place, however, Steinmetz's senior research colleague, Professor Murray A. Straus of the University of New Hampshire, indicated that just 6.1 percent of the sample couples were involved in severe violent acts during the survey year, and further indicated that 3.8 percent of the sample were cases of severely battered women.[48] And he gave a subcommittee of the House Science and Technology committee a much lower figure than Steinmetz's 3.5 million:

> The data on the 2,143 couples in our sample show that, for the twelve month period preceding the interview, 3.8% reported one or more physical attacks

---

47. Ibid.
48. Murray A. Straus, "Normative and Behavioral Aspects of Violence Between Spouses: Preliminary Data on a Nationally Representative USA Sample," paper read at the Symposium on Violence in Canadian Society, sponsored by the Department of Criminology, Simon Fraser University, March 12, 1977, esp. tables 1 and 2.

which fall under our operational definition of wife-beating. Applying this incidence rate to the approximately 47 million couples in the USA, means that in any one year, approximately 1.8 million wives are beaten by their husbands.[49]

Straus's presentation characterized wife-beating and child abuse as the aspects of family violence that most urgently need remedial action. Still drawing on the research team's own sample survey findings and definitions, however, Straus indicated that in the survey year more couples reported severe violent attacks of husband-beating than reported comparable attacks of wife-beating—4.6 percent against 3.8 percent. If the spectrum of violent acts is expanded to include Klerman's three lesser categories, violence committed by husbands on wives is reported to have occurred in the survey year at a rate only slightly higher than violence committed by wives on husbands—12.1 percent and 11.6 percent, respectively.[50]

So the incidence data collectively presented to Congress by NIMH grantees and the administrator of the agency would allow a previously uninformed congressman to conclude that in any year there are 7.5 million victims of violent acts by their spouses, or that there are 3.5 million severely battered women, or that there are 1.8 million wives beaten by their husbands in a fashion that carries a high risk of serious physical injury to the victim. The same previously uninformed congressman would have had to pore over the citations and trace them back, however, to learn that the incidence of spousal violence—as revealed, at least, by the national sample survey—is evenly distributed between husbands as perpetrators of violence and husbands as victims of violent acts by wives. He could not learn from the data presented or cited, or from oral testimony, to what extent individual respondents reported violent acts by both partners.

If the evidence of need offered by NIMH and its academic beneficiaries leaves some legislators unpersuaded and confused, no reassurance comes from looking elsewhere. Various other groups professing an interest in the issue have no reliable data, but some have been remarkably creative in the use of numbers. An example is seen in a 1978

49. Murray A. Straus, "National Survey of Domestic Violence: Some Preliminary Findings and Implications for Future Research," paper prepared for hearings on "Research Into Domestic Violence," Subcommittee on Domestic and International Scientific Planning, Analysis, and Cooperation, February 14, 1978, p. 4.

50. Straus, "Normative and Behavioral Aspects of Violence," p. 11.

statement from the American Bar Association's (ABA) Section of Individual Rights and Responsibilities asserting that Federal Bureau of Investigation (FBI) statistics "reveal that the number of domestic beatings are three times as prevalent as the number of rapes, and there is a rape reported every three minutes."[51] They reveal nothing of the sort. If there were "a rape reported every three minutes," that would mean 175,000 rapes annually. What the FBI's Uniform Crime Reports for 1976—the last year on which the ABA statement could have been based—actually show is one forcible rape reported every nine minutes, or a total of about 57,000 forcible rapes known to law enforcement officers.[52] If, as the ABA statement maintained, there were a rape reported every three minutes and domestic beatings were three times as prevalent as rape, domestic beatings would exceed 525,000 annually. Tripling the actual FBI figure of forcible rapes reported yields a more modest 171,000 presumed beatings. But Uniform Crime Reports do not deal with "domestic beatings" as a discrete category. The reports do indicate a total number of arrests (72,000) for "offenses against family and children"—a much broader category than "domestic beatings"—nearly three times greater than the number of arrests (26,000) for forcible rape.[53]

To arrive at its conclusion that the number of persons affected by domestic violence is "staggering," the American Bar Association says that the FBI "estimates that the figures for reported crimes represent less than 10% of the total number of 'wife-beatings' that occur."[54] Now "wife-beating" is subsumed in Uniform Crime Reports within a so-called Part II offense category termed "offenses against family and children" that lumps together "nonsupport, neglect, desertion, or abuse of family and children." Only arrests—as distinguished from all known incidents—are reported for Part II offenses. There are no "figures for reported crimes" in this category. The total number of arrests for offenses against family and children, however, is 72,000. If one assumes the extreme case of zero arrests for nonsupport, neglect, or

51. "Statement of Sara-Ann Determan on Behalf of the American Bar Association," in *Domestic Violence, 1978*, Senate Hearings, p. 282.

52. U.S. Federal Bureau of Investigation, Uniform Crime Report, *Crime in the United States, 1976* (GPO, 1977), p. 16.

53. Ibid., p. 173.

54. *Domestic Violence, 1978*, Senate Hearings, p. 282.

desertion—that is, that *all* arrests for offenses against family and children involve spouse abuse—and allows for, say, ten times more incidents than arrests, the "wife-beating" total could be forced to an outer limit of 720,000.

Suppose, however, that number includes only simple assaults—slappings, shovings, and so-called pushing around—whereas actual batterings come in as "aggravated assault"—unlawful attack by one person upon another for the purpose (whether successful or simply attempted) of inflicting severe bodily injury. Because they are Part I offenses, all known aggravated assault offenses, not just arrests, are reported. Again, if one accepts the absurd—that *all* aggravated assaults are cases of spouse abuse—the outer limit of aggravated assaults on a spouse would be the total known aggravated assaults in the nation.

In sum, assigning zero values to nonsupport, neglect, and desertion, counting *all* arrests for offenses against family and children as involving physical abuse of a spouse, multiplying the arrest number by a factor of ten to account for incidents where there is no arrest, and adding to that product, as spouse abuse, every known aggravated-assault offense in the country produces a deliberately inflated total of just over 1.2 million incidents of spouse abuse. Such an exercise would involve patently invalid assumptions, and the ABA of course did not make them. On the other hand, it did refer to and cite FBI statistics in arguing that domestic violence affects a "staggering" number of people.

Any postmortem on the fate of domestic violence policy should examine the data base from which proponents sought to enact a national program. Not only the ABA's somewhat loose use of FBI data, but the bases for each of the estimates—Klerman's 7.5 million, Steinmetz's 3.5 million, Straus's 1.8 million, and the ABA number whether taken as 526,000 or 1.2 million—invite doubt about whether any incidence figure is to be trusted. It may be argued, of course, that physical assault within the family is an evil against which a national program should be directed whether there are 1 million or 3 million incidents annually, that slapping is no more to be countenanced than is more severe assault, and that shelters represent the only prescription available. Yet to be effective, program design must take into account whether most of the victims require emergency shelter facilities or whether they require outpatient mental health therapy or legal counseling. Data are never adequate, but even inadequate data can be suggestive—if properly gathered and accurately reported.

Failure versus Success

"The sponsors were stunned by the House vote," *Congressional Quarterly* reported after the loss of the domestic violence bill in 1978. Viewing spouse abuse as a major social ill, those sponsors anticipated at least as positive a vote as there had been on child-abuse legislation in 1975. The difference in outcomes is a reminder that strategies and techniques are as important determinants of social policy as theories and principles.

To begin, the drive for federal child-abuse legislation capitalized on factors more directly relevant to it than the endorsement of strong families by high-level public officials. Those factors included the support of prestigious professional classes, a long history of organized private concern and an established record of public intervention, and, with Walter Mondale, an ambitious subcommittee chairman eager to take on an opposition administration that could be tagged unresponsive to human need. So policymakers who adopted the child-abuse cause in the mid-1970s—a hundred years after the organization of the Society for the Prevention of Cruelty to Children—found they could depend for support on the determination of physicians, especially pediatric radiologists, in several parts of the country to document the problem. When violence between couples became a concern, no comparable group of outraged physicians lobbied for legislation. Either American medicine has not thought to study the phenomenon of spouse abuse, or proponents of legislation on the subject have not thought to involve physicians in making their case, depending instead on direct accounts and surveys. Justifiably or not, the absence of medical testimony affects the attitude of some policymakers, who regard both macrodata projected from sample surveys and first-person accounts of discrete incidents as insubstantial grounds for national legislation.

The amount and quality of social research also made a difference in the legislative staging for child abuse and for spouse abuse. Reports and data on child abuse have been amassed over the hundred years since a New York judge issued a special warrant to protect one Mary Ellen Wilson from abusive treatment by her stepmother. The long history of intervention gave additional legitimacy to modern child-abuse legislation. Parallel activity in domestic violence lacks the character and depth of the work on child abuse and, at least by comparison, appears quick and dirty.

Finally, unlike child-abuse legislation, domestic violence legislation could not be pushed as either a party or a congressional response to administration unawareness of or indifference to a social problem. In 1973 Walter Mondale, unhappy with HEW's failure to take action on child abuse, had turned the issue into a congressional and a party cause. When a Nixon administration spokesman, arguing against the child-abuse legislation, told Mondale, "Our first position is not to resort immediately to some new federal mechanism to find the answers,"[55] Mondale rejected the advice and led the fight for a federal program. Later, the domestic violence bill was unable to overcome the indifference of the Carter-Mondale administration, which, in its turn, showed no desire to resort immediately to some new federal mechanism to find the answers. But with Congress and the administration controlled by the same party, a partisan attack was precluded. Moreover, the Carter administration sent confusing messages: on the one hand, assurances that its inactivity did not imply a lack of interest or awareness; on the other hand, the designation of a powerless official to carry the assurances. To the disappointment of supporters who had hoped for help, neither White House nor HEW congressional liaison staff marshaled data, lobbied members, or took vote counts.

Outright opposition is easier to overcome than an ambiguous response from a supposed political ally. Frankly opposed to any federal activity to combat child abuse, the Nixon and Ford administrations appeared fair game for a careful congressional initiative. A mistaken assumption that the Carter administration, avowedly concerned about families, would advocate legislation against domestic violence made supporters overconfident. In committee appearances that neither congressmen nor witnesses enjoyed or benefited from, HEW officials incorporated domestic violence into their professed broader concern for families, without making substantive contributions. ACYF commissioner Cardenas, for example, remarked that spousal violence often occurs separately from other forms of violence, but then again, that child abusers are often spouse abusers, and that there are many forms

55. *Child Abuse Prevention Act, 1973*, Hearings before the Subcommittee on Children and Youth of the Senate Labor and Public Welfare Committee, 93 Cong. 1 sess. (GPO, 1973), p. 94.

of violence within the family.[56] While presumably addressing the question of spouse abuse, HEW officials have been likely to describe other programs: child-abuse treatment centers, a comprehensive-emergency-services demonstration program that does not specifically focus on abused spouses, and research and demonstration projects to prevent criminal violence against the aged. As for strategies and programs directly tied to spouse abuse—for example, emergency welfare assistance—ACYF has neither made proposals nor stayed abreast of those made by private groups. When ACYF categorized domestic violence as a serious problem that needs to be attacked via a family focus, it had neither a domestic violence program nor a family focus.

Rather than chance another encounter with skeptical legislators, the Carter administration joined Senator Alan Cranston in a staged retreat. Cranston, who took a domestic violence bill through the Senate once, chose not to push his luck with a second try until House passage could be assured. Formally withdrawing "at the present time," Cranston emphasized the importance of getting the administration involved as much as possible. The president appointed an Interdepartmental Committee on Domestic Violence with instructions to formulate a work plan to guide future actions. "This Administration," President Carter wrote, "is committed ultimately to the cessation of such violence and immediately to the relief of those who suffer its consequences."[57] Within HEW, the Office on Domestic Violence has been established to gather and disseminate information and coordinate activities.

The Carter administration never accomplished much either "ultimately" or "immediately" in the way of domestic violence policy. The case made for it by the administration was restricted to the president's characterization of domestic violence as a growing crisis—a judgment based on suspect data. Cranston did try again, but even a watered-down bill was finally abandoned in the face of a threatened filibuster in the lame-duck session after the 1980 election.

56. *Domestic Violence*, House Hearings, pp. 81–82.
57. "Memorandum for the Secretary of Defense, et al.," April 27, 1979.

PART THREE

The Limits of Policy

CHAPTER SIX

The European Way?

THE DISCOVERY or acceptance of family as an organizing entity for child development, social services, and public welfare policy does not ipso facto produce new ideas and initiatives, nor does it necessarily make old ideas more marketable. A negative income tax neither gains strength nor changes character if called a family assistance plan. Proposals for preschool child development that have been blocked do not become unblocked if relabeled child and family services proposals. Yet by widening the limits of intervention, an emphasis on families widens the range of acceptable policy models. The search then turns to policy models once ignored or dismissed as beyond the pale. Accordingly, as "family policy" increasingly became the way of describing social services and public welfare programs, the attention given European family policy practices grew. With support from Carnegie Corporation, the Ford Foundation, the German Marshall Fund, and other foundations, the examination of European programs—with a view to transferability—became urgent and popular.

Unlike stealing designs for military hardware, borrowing social programs from another nation is an acceptable practice, perhaps an inevitable one. "The invention and diffusion of social programs does not appear to be a random phenomenon," Hugh Heclo concludes after showing that the international diffusion of income-maintenance programs did not simply occur but followed "a few regularities" in the process. The adoption in one country of protection against one cause of income interruption was followed by its adoption in other countries; the adoption of protection against various causes of income interruption systematically followed one another in the same country; the period for widespread diffusion held between fifty and eighty years for each form of protection.[1]

1. Hugh Heclo, *Modern Social Politics in Britain and Sweden* (Yale University Press, 1974), pp. 10–11.

According to Sheila Kamerman and Alfred J. Kahn—the leading American entrepreneurs of cross-national studies of social policy—mass media, jet planes, and international conferences are now shrinking the time period for international diffusion. If it took fifty years for Bismarck's social insurance program to reach the United States from Germany, it took only a little more than a decade for service programs for the aged to move from the advanced European nations to the United States, say Kahn and Kamerman. "Obviously," they claim, "there is occurring in all our countries an international transmission of social policies, and North America will no longer be left out of the international social policy debate. Central to this debate at present is the question of family policy."[2]

Not so obviously. The conclusion may be valid for the discussion of social policies by international "working parties," but unwarranted when extended from scholarly discussion to the adoption of social policies in the United States, and not sufficiently hedged as far as family policy is concerned. International transmission occurs over a selective network. If the United States were to emulate any European family policy, it would be the policy of one or another of only those few European industrial democracies with which this country identifies most closely.

Yet for all the foundation support, mass media, jet planes, and international conferences, American policymakers, hard put to assemble a family policy based on proposals from American academics, would be equally hard put to build on the family policy practices of Great Britain, France, West Germany, or Sweden. Instead of having a comprehensive package of inoculations and therapies to prevent and repair family breakdown, each of those nations—like the United States—confronts limits. So each emphasizes some goals and passes over others. Much of the family policy literature that describes foreign programs is social history of bygone eras or is children's policy or welfare policy relabeled. Studies of cross-national surveys and interviews with European academics, social welfare practitioners, and politicians interested in children and families only reinforce the conclusion suggested by domestic research: that family policy is a chimera—a fabrication of the mind that sees an elixir of family strength in policies that redistribute income, that encourage or discourage procreation,

2. Sheila B. Kamerman and Alfred J. Kahn, eds., *Family Policy: Government and Families in Fourteen Countries* (Columbia University Press, 1978), p. 15.

that stimulate early childhood education, that encourage mothers to stay at home with young children, or that advance women to equality with men.

Notes on Western European Family Policy[3]

Respondents in Western Europe are puzzled by the sudden American anxiety over family policy, sympathetic to the American ambivalence about abortion as a right, numbed by the size of the American research investment in child development, and indifferent to the American interest in child care as a technique to reduce welfare cost. For them, the key social policy issue for the future is equality for women. And equality means not merely choice for mothers between mothering and working, but a formal recognition that all family functions except carrying a fetus and nursing an infant can be performed by either men or women. From that base, the questions raised have to do with timing, with perceived consequences, and with techniques: whether the women's issue can be delayed or whether it is already the most important of all social policy concerns; whether trade unions and government will continue to resist women's pursuit of greater opportunity outside the home as being a threat to men's jobs and governments' pronatalist policies; whether males will continue to resist assuming household responsibilities; and which of the measures designed to accomplish greater equality will really get the job done.

The awareness of the social importance and implications of the theme "equality is the goal" is universal, but differences in policies are greater than similarities because support for the implementation of equality is uneven. The theme is stated less frequently in Britain and France than in Sweden. Coping with it is especially troublesome in the

3. These notes are an updated version of part of a paper I submitted in August 1977: "Early Childhood and Family Policies: A Position Paper for Staff and Trustees of the German Marshall Fund of the United States." My discussion of European family policy reflects on-the-scene notes from six weeks of open-ended interviewing among academics, social welfare practitioners, and politicians concerned with family policy. The project was facilitated by my earlier participation in the International Working Party on Family Policy at Arden House, Columbia University, Harriman, New York, in April 1977. Neither the German Marshall Fund nor the organizers of the International Working Party necessarily agree with the views expressed here, and neither should be held responsible for them.

Federal Republic of Germany (FRG), where mother-in-the-home remains a value highly prized.

West Germany: "We Have a Special Past"

Competing approaches to policy evident in the FRG make that country of particular interest. Despite the formal acceptance by both major political parties of the principle of egalitarianism in family life, the most extreme position actually discussed is the free-choice position: women who want to work should have the chance to do so; women who want to stay home should have that choice. Moreover, the public policy incentives most often mentioned are those that tilt toward the home; one hears little about policy options that would facilitate increased labor force participation by women.

Kindergartens are a case in point. Since 1970 there has been a 25 percent increase—to about 60 percent—in the portion of the three- to five-year-old child population in kindergarten. The Social Democrats (SDP) take particular pride in that increase because of the SDP position that kindergarten development is the preferred way to help women who are seeking emancipation from household ties. Unhappily, the absence of a school lunch program coupled with the reluctance of teachers to work afternoons greatly reduces the value of kindergarten for the mother who would like to work. Yet there is no sign that the federal government will use its authority to initiate *Modelleinrichtungen* (innovative techniques) to demonstrate the tie between a school lunch program and greater labor force participation among mothers of young children.

Some scholars and some politicians in the FRG believe that proposals explicitly oriented to the early separation of children from the home through any kind of state-sponsored program are doomed because of experience under National Socialism. Consequently, if mothers are to be given equal opportunity in the labor force, the way will not be eased by state-supported early education or child care. The closest approach to any such state-supported activity in the seventies was the extensive—for Germany—*Tagesmütter* (day mothers) experiment, a neighborhood day care demonstration planned and managed through the research enterprise in Munich (Deutsche Jugendinstitut) of the federal government's family ministry. Although a very small number of children were involved—perhaps 200—sociologists at the Jugendinstitut hoped at least to shift day care from its present largely private auspices to the public sector, to end the unregulated market in the selection of day mothers, and to improve the status of the day mother generally.[4] Over the long haul, they also look to an expanded system that could first assist mothers who work out of economic necessity, then provide all mothers an honest mothering-working choice rather than a paper one. Among the most avant-garde, who talk of the American investment in child development research, there is even a vision of day-care centers emphasizing cognitive development. In real life in the FRG, however, the principal investigator in the Jugendinstitut's project was under no illusions and solicited job offers long before his project was completed. The judgment of the University of Cologne's leading sociologist in this field is that "the public resonance being channeled by the churches and some family organizations has been critical to such a degree that it appears to be highly improbable that 'Tagesmütter' ever will become institutionalized on a broader scale in the FRG."[5]

The family policy problem that many West German leaders really believe most compelling is the decline in the birthrate. As with state intervention in child rearing, any state effort to increase the birthrate gives rise to anxiety. "We have a special past on the population subject," explained a member of the federal Bundeshaus who is chairman of his party's legislative group on family issues. "I prefer to worry over the quality of life than to worry over stressing the need for 60 million people." Not all politicians can afford that preference. A falloff in the birthrate from 17.7 births per 1,000 population in 1965 to 13.4 in 1970 and to 9.8 in 1976 presents a practical problem that threatens the quality of life for an important segment of the population. Like that of the United States, the FRG social security system depends for its future stability on a working-age population large enough to sustain the retired population. In the 1960s, when the availability of women for employment was an important element in West German economic growth, government looked favorably on female participation in the labor force. Thereafter, the federal government made no effort to encourage institutionalized child care. Working wives continued to work rather than have children; new wives did the same. Young

---

4. Arbeitsgruppe Tagesmütter, *Das Modelprojekt Tagesmütter* (Munich: Juventa, 1977).
5. Friedhelm Neidhardt, "The Federal Republic of Germany," in Kamerman and Kahn, eds., *Family Policy*, p. 235.

couples, in sum, have apparently chosen to go childless or to limit the size of their families.

The convergence of economic slowdown, unemployment, the fall in the birthrate, and the relative weakness of women in FRG political leadership appears to brighten the prospects for a government payment known as *Erziehungsgeld* (education money), long favored by the now out-of-power Christian Democrats (CDU). Building on its traditional approach to questions of family life, the CDU talks of education-money payments for mothers who will devote themselves exclusively to the "early education" of their children during the first three years of life. The attraction is plain enough for unemployed mothers and for tradition-minded mothers, as well as for mothers in low-status work. As a political matter, *Erziehungsgeld* is expected to appeal to that part of the male labor force concerned about job competition from women. And, all at once, a government adopting the allowance will have a response to middle-class intellectuals who claim that government demeans the social role of the mother by failing to give it formal recognition.

Although the SDP is avoiding the issue for the time being, it seems unlikely that it can continue indefinitely to express faith that technological progress will make it possible for smaller numbers of young people to care for the needs of larger numbers of old people. Paying mothers to "educate" their own infants—or paying fathers to do the same—is the most probable FRG family policy development on the horizon. If it should come to pass, however, it will be declined by successful professional women not willing to interrupt their careers for so long a period. A distinctly pronatalist public policy that takes the form of money payments to induce exclusive dedication to parenting does not suit the needs or the ideals of these professional women. It may indeed be impossible for West Germany to resolve the sometimes contradictory pressures stemming from an economic slowdown, a resistance to government-imposed family policy, a rising demand for equality of opportunity for women, and a sharply falling birthrate.

Great Britain: Agonizing over Privacy

Early childhood–family policy concerns in Britain are more comparable to those in the United States than to those on the continent. The British tendency is to back away from family policy per se—no legislation, no government bureau carries the "family" label—by using categorical programs. The historic tendency of the social security system—still not entirely overcome—to preserve male work incentives and the flourishing children's research business are similarly reminiscent of American practices. So is British anxiety about exposés of low-quality private day care. Research and evaluation efforts and a disposition to focus on children of deprivation are both evident in Great Britain and the United States, but not in France, West Germany, or Scandinavia. And though pronatalism has not been absent from British policy, its limited impact again puts Britain closer to America than to the continent.

Equally persuasive cases can be made for saying that early childhood and family matters should be and are a major concern of British social policy and for saying that British social policy quite properly has avoided intervention in early childhood and family matters, regarding them as private relationships. In a thoughtful paper that helps to explain how explicit policy is made to seem only implicit and how implicit policy is made to seem entirely explicit, Roy Parker and Hilary Land remind the reader of H. G. Wells's observation that many are fearful that in seeking to save the family they should seem to threaten its existence.[6] That worry is very much in evidence in Great Britain, where it is possible to hear expressions of impatience with foundation-financed cross-national social policy studies that have "only one way of viewing a solution—more public participation."

Britain's Conservative government, elected in 1979, inherited from its Labor predecessor no family policy issue that will demand official attention in the close future. Granted that Britain has come to be a relatively poor country, and that reactions are affected by that worrisome truth, it is only a partial explanation of what has been almost a studied unwillingness to reach a consensus on any kind of government intervention in the family. What has resulted, therefore, is a wide diversity of views and concerns. Some who think that children's cognitive development is important do not also link it to day care for children and equal employment opportunity for women. Some who take firm traditionalist positions deploring the unwillingness of mid-

6. Hilary Land and Roy Parker, "United Kingdom," in ibid., p. 360. Land has come to fear just this phenomenon in connection with family policies emphasized by British and French politicians that regard "families in which men are breadwinners and women are first and foremost wives and mothers . . . as 'normal' or 'natural.' " Hilary Land, "The Changing Place of Women in Europe," *Daedalus*, vol. 108 (Spring 1979), p. 90.

dle-class women to accept the housewife role also urge public investment in early cognitive development. Some others view family and early childhood matters solely as a categorical question—"services must be provided children in deprived areas," "make sure children have access to play," and so on—or as an income-maintenance problem that presupposes the single-parent family to be the family policy issue. After a relatively promising start a few years ago, implementation of the 1967 Plowden Report recommending nursery education for many three-year-olds and most four-year-olds has stopped.

As for the role of specialists and interest groups, the National Children's Bureau, the voluntary organization concerned with children's needs, and thus the British equivalent of the Child Welfare League of America, devotes much attention, as does its American counterpart, to categorical problems.[7] Its publications list is dominated by titles dealing with abuse, adoption, foster care, chronic medical problems, handicapped children, residential care, and the like. Recent projects developed and carried out at its Children's Centre have dealt with children at risk (that is, those who are educationally, economically, or socially disadvantaged), with disruptive junior-school children, and with the problems of young people growing up in foster care, all reasonable reflections of the present British definition of early childhood and family policy questions. Neither working mothers nor redistribution of family roles is on the Children's Bureau's agenda. To make this point is not to denigrate the bureau's very useful work, but to emphasize that its work coincides with the concerns of governmental policy.

That coincidence is less evident in reviewing the work being done at the University of London's Coram Research Unit, where parent-child relations are an important subject of research. Scholars there have tried to push the government forward, especially on the issue of child care. Without directly confronting the question of deliberate policy to ensure women equal opportunity, Coram's researchers have expanded stud-

7. The bureau's most original work is the National Child Development Study (1958 cohort), a long-term multidisciplinary follow-up investigation of virtually all the children born in England, Scotland, and Wales during the week of March 3, 1958. The cohort numbers 17,000. Follow-ups have been undertaken when the children were seven, eleven, and sixteen years old, and the plan is to continue studying their growth and development at least until they have themselves become parents. See Mia Kellmer Pringle, *The Needs of Children* (Schocken Books, 1975), pp. 10–11. A summary of the findings from the third follow-up is in Ken Fogelman, ed., *Britain's Sixteen-Year-Olds* (London: National Children's Bureau, 1976).

ies of the value of nursery services for children to cover the value of such services for young mothers. Using survey data, some of it self-generated, Coram personnel showed that there is a widespread, unsatisfied desire in Britain for preschool services: about one-quarter of the parents surveyed want all-day care for children over one, an additional 30 percent want all-day care for children from the age of two, and 60 percent want this care for children aged three and four. These findings, together with survey findings that among working-class mothers of young children, two in every five suffer from depression, anxiety, and low self-esteem, were interpreted by Jack Tizard of Coram: "The constant strain of child care is in part, and perhaps in large part, responsible. The seriousness of the position of families with young children, especially mothers, has been largely ignored."[8] Rather than improved child allowances, or equal employment opportunity for women, the researchers concluded, the universal expansion of nursery school services so that they are available on demand is the most important issue of social policy.

The disposition at Coram—as at comparable American research centers—is to put the early childhood issue in developmental terms that go beyond "women and work" and emphasize the importance of comprehensive programs for the child's development as well as for the mother's convenience. This attitude produces a feeling of déjà vu for any student of the American child development policy debate of the 1970s. So does the absence of a government policy response and the apparent low level of public interest in child development problems as opposed to bread-and-butter ones.

France: Deliberate Contradictions

Family policy in France is essentially an income-maintenance policy that evolved out of a pronatalist policy now widely understood to be unsuccessful.[9] The outcome is a collection of cash assistance programs that is complex and confusing because the country's leaders have not decided between a public policy that is neutral on the dominant issue

8. Jack Tizard, "Nursery Needs v. Choices," draft of Wolfson Lecture, 1976; the quotation is from page 28. Tizard here undertakes "to restate the case for comprehensive nursery services, forming part of a comprehensive family policy for parents and children." See also J. Tizard, P. Moss, and J. Perry, *All Our Children: Preschool Services in a Changing Society* (London: Maurice Temple Smith, 1976).

9. Nicole Questiaux and Jacques Fournier, "France," in Kamerman and Kahn, eds., *Family Policy*, p. 135.

of female labor force participation and a policy that encourages defined sex roles, the women's role being childbearing and child rearing. French policy does, however, appear to be moving toward giving women greater freedom to choose between homemaking and joining the labor force—a policy that is less than equality but more than patriarchy—but it moves at a stumbling rather than a brisk pace.

At the same time, French early childhood policy, which has emphasized the *école maternelle*, a kindergarten available to children between two and one-half and six years old, confronts the problem of overcrowding, a legacy of the ambivalent public policy reaction to increases in female labor force participation. By 1977 the kindergarten system accommodated 94 percent of five- and six-year-old children; 90 percent of four- and five-year-olds; but only 60 percent of children two and one-half through four, although children are technically eligible at age two for a program that offers both cognitive development and child care—and is free. In the absence of a comprehensive plan that views working mothers positively rather than passively and expands *école maternelle* facilities accordingly, pressures on the system now result in adult-child ratios of about 1 to 35 or even 1 to 40, far beyond the ratio of 1 to 20 that is the goal of French unions and professionals in the business. The French *crèches* provide full-day care for a small fraction of all children under two and one-half, a fraction that becomes more significant—perhaps one-half—when the calculation is limited to infants whose mothers work. If or how much the number of working mothers would increase if the *crèches* could accommodate more children remains an imponderable.

In the complex world of French family allowances, a basic benefit has long been provided to about 85 percent of French children up to the age of nineteen; only first children are excluded—a sign of continued pronatalist influence. The basic allowance, which is inadequate to meet actual child care costs, insufficient as a substitute for the income of a working mother, and discriminatory in its treatment of single-child families, is evenhanded in respect to working and nonworking mothers. Evenhandedness on that score also characterizes a new family supplement that since 1978 has replaced two supplements formerly paid to low-income families: one that was paid to single-wage-earner families only, and another that went to working mothers for child care expenses. On the face of it, the new policy would appear to be pronatalist above all—a clear encouragement to procreate without regard to labor force participation, since the benefit extends to children of working and nonworking mothers alike. But policy is really ambiguous because the base from which the allowance is calculated has been fixed by the government at a point that is too low to have a real bearing on individual decisions whether to have children or not.

Ambiguous government policy is again manifested in a proposal that was meant to underscore President Valéry Giscard d'Estaing's stated interest in strengthening the family. Adding on to the Swedish leave-for-childbirth model, the proposal would have provided mothers a two-year leave of absence from work, without pay but with guaranteed reinstatement. Rather than viewing it as progress, feminist groups fought the idea, fearful that it would result in widespread discrimination by employers against women of childbearing age.

What is clear is that the French have simply not decided for or against any family policy consistently applied. Andrée Michel, a thoughtful family sociologist, attributes the absence of a holistic policy in this area to the existence of two pressure groups with separate ideologies and goals—one dedicated to maintaining family life based on paternal authority, another committed to women's rights—each of which is satisfied by a particular government action on its behalf. Michel speaks of "a family policy of compromise which throws a few crumbs to each of the two opposing groups" while making plain her personal preference for a comprehensive policy based on the rejection of the male-dominated family.

Some others who watch French family policy developments either out of academic or bureaucratic interest see more than their own preferences suffering because of government ambivalence. For example, the research director of the French social insurance system—La Caisse Nationale d'Allocations Familials (CNAF)—worries about the effects of a complex, overlapping system of family benefits on the potential beneficiaries, and particularly on their ability to understand as many as twenty family benefit programs, some limited, some universally applicable. In language reminiscent of that heard at American welfare reform hearings, this thoughtful bureaucrat describes the complex system as "overwhelming" to clients, and expresses anxiety about the gap between the bureaucracy and its clientele. Do families get the allowances to which they are entitled? Who helps them at the local level? How well informed are most families about the range of benefits to which they may be entitled? Academic researchers ask whether programs of social services are well suited to the needs of and are understood by clients. What families use homehelpers and what families do not? How well known is the existence of the service and conditions for its use? How good is the fit between the services home-helpers can provide and the needs of clients?

The importance of the questions far outstrips the support for the research to answer them. An inquiry into the homehelper service, regarded as one of the three major research efforts of the CNAF, depends on responses from fifty families in Lyon who constitute the total national sample. Researchers and bureaucrats understandably deplore the lack of public support for social policy research in France and observe that in a real sense much French social policy is social experimentation. A different way of putting it is that French taste favors nibbling from a smorgasbord of family policies. The result is a good deal of uncertainty about which sample is indigestible and which is nutritious.

Sweden: Equality Is the Goal

The tilt in Sweden—and also in Denmark—continues to be away from any public policy that directs women exclusively to homemaking roles.[10] The tilt is less sharp than it might be, however, and so is the implementation of a formal commitment to equality.

Some attention has been directed to the six-hour workday as a possible mechanism for achieving greater equality and more equitable distribution of family responsibilities between men and women. But although the six-hour day idea is frequently put forth as an option acceptable to many of the interests involved, the rate of economic growth in Sweden argues against its realization in the near future. If the current economic growth rate continues through the 1980s, and if all that growth were dedicated to the achievement of a six-hour day, no increase in real wages would be possible before 1986. Since such an outcome is regarded as intolerable for low-paid workers, no government support developed for the Commission on Family Aid's 1975 proposal that parents of young children who reduce their workday to six hours be compensated for loss of income by means of partial benefit from the social insurance system.

Instead, the government has emphasized the expansion of day-care facilities for children under six. To accomplish stated goals will require

10. Rita Liljeström, "Sweden," in ibid., p. 29.

decisions about staff–child ratios, about efforts at cognitive development of children in nursery school settings, and about greater involvement of men in what has been a women's field. Substantial effort will be needed to meet the goals of the 1975 preschool act, which calls for community care of preschool children for all working parents who want it. Out of all women with children of preschool age, about 37 percent worked part-time and 28 percent full-time in 1977. The assumption is that those figures will continue to increase over the next decade. With 134,000 places in day nurseries and 77,000 in family day care in 1979, some public child care is provided for 27 percent of the preschool population of about 770,000. Only one child in six, however, can get care in a day nursery, which leaves a large unmet demand for this preferred form of child care. If private arrangements for care decline and demand for participation in community care exceeds the predicted rate of 50 percent of the preschool cohort, the number of new places needed would be that much larger.

Substantial gaps between stated need and available places in preschool are not unique to Sweden. The substitution of relevant numbers would make the story applicable to the United States and other Western nations. What is unique is the statutory commitment to plan for the expansion of preschool activities to cover anticipated demand. First reports were not encouraging. The initial government suggestion to the municipalities was for 100,000 new day-care places by 1981. But if the municipalities are required to plan for child care, they were not obliged to build day-care centers. And whether they would meet the ambitious goal of 100,000 new places remained uncertain as the deadline approached.

For over forty years Swedish social policy has included equality between the sexes as a goal, but the real test is only now at hand. Children's allowances, housing allowances, maternal and child preventive health care, school meals, health insurance, and home help are cited to illustrate Swedish progress toward equality over the years. So is the 1975 law granting free abortion up to the eighteenth week of pregnancy. The improved parental insurance scheme is similarly highly touted as a sign of shared responsibility for children that reflects the equality principle. A statutory provision that originally allowed a mother to draw social insurance in lieu of earned income after the birth of a child now allows the nine-month benefit period to be shared between mother and father or to be used by the father alone. The final three months may be used bit by bit until the child's eighth birthday and may even be used to shorten working hours. These flexible arrangements might be expected to attract more fathers who are or claim to be unable to separate themselves from work for sustained periods.

A Swedish journalist who monitors the progress of women's liberation and who has described herself as "less pessimistic than some academic women" nevertheless volunteered that "the difference between Swedish ideology and Swedish practice is very great." Neither children's allowances nor other child-related benefits ensure either equal distribution between men and women of home and child responsibilities or equal labor force opportunity. Five years after "mother's insurance" became "parent's insurance," 10 to 12 percent of eligible fathers participated—a figure judged by some as "failure," by some others as "an encouraging increase from the first year's 2 percent," by none as "success." Amendments extending the insured period by a couple of months, but generally on terms still likely to result in disproportionate use by mothers—rather than equal division between parents—were interpreted as evidence of backward drift both in thinking about equality and in government action. An alternate interpretation suggests, of course, that the real preferences of the Swedish people are different from those espoused by social engineers.

If there is backward drift, a political explanation attributes it to the fall of the Social Democratic government in 1976 after forty-four years in power, and the inability of the Liberal forces in two subsequent "bourgeois" coalition governments to lead Conservative and Center party colleagues on family policy matters.[11] Of the latter two parties—especially strong among high-level white-collar employees, entrepreneurs, and farmers—one favors sending women back to the home, the other is not uncomfortable with the idea. A matter of ideology for the Conservatives, the Center party's emphasis on freedom of choice rather than affirmative action inevitably reduces women's labor force participation, according to legislative specialists on family issues. Liberals—a party of white-collar employees and small-business owners—join Social Democrats in taking a contrary position. The result is said to be reflected in the one-step-forward, two-steps-backward extension of parental insurance and cut in benefits at the margin. What can be anticipated in light of the outcome of the 1979 parliamentary elections

11. Lillemor Melsted, *Swedish Family Policy*, Swedish Institute, Election Year '79 Series, no. 4 (New York: Swedish Information Service, 1979).

is a continuing demand for day nurseries at odds with the disposition of the government to pay women to stay at home. Resistance to the latter is much greater than in the Federal Republic of Germany, but if the day nurseries are not built, many women feel they will have to be at home anyway. So Sweden offers a test of the ability of a rich nation to fulfill its stated ideals in early-childhood and family policy.

Modest Lessons for America

During a meeting in 1977 of European scholars and American scholars and bureaucrats, a Swedish sociologist expressed curiosity about the timing of the American interest in family policy. One answer relates the timing of interest in any social problem (and of research on the problem) to the need of political leaders for new issues. Family policy was prominent in 1977 because Jimmy Carter took it up in 1976, three years after Walter Mondale—then a senator in search of his own issue—gave family policy its initial exposure. Since a political leader seemed interested, detailed analyses of marital instability, abortion, adolescent pregnancy, runaways, child health, children without parents, domestic violence—all family-connected phenomena that predated discussions about family policy—thereupon assumed a new status. Put differently, when politicians are perceived to be interested in a subject, scholars who share the interest undertake to prepare backup packages for them. With family policy, the package included inquiries into whether there is a full-blown and crystal-clear family policy technology in Europe suitable for importation to America.

Although Americans hoped European experience might reveal some comprehensive approach to dealing with family problems, Europe may be more advanced than America only in identifying the components of the family problem and assigning priorities to them. The American family policy debate is a muddled one that lumps together concern about child development; about day care for children of mothers who must work; about day care for children of mothers who want an alternative to uninterrupted child care; about changes in family structure, especially the escalating divorce and remarriage figures; about cohabitation; about abortion; and about the implications of the women's movement for family life. The European conception of family policy is more sharply focused on the protection of children and on the possible conflict between the protection of children and women's drive for equality. For example, cohabitation, divorce, and marital questions in general are not part of Swedish family policy, which has as its goal the protection of children, not the stability of marriages.

Thoughtful politicians and thoughtful scholars on both continents worry about finding ways to ease problems of families without destroying the privacy of the institution. Ethical and philosophical aspects of public intervention in family relationships are first-order concerns in Great Britain. An emphasis on preserving the privacy of the family institution stands out as the British contribution to the family policy debate. In West Germany, the memory of how the state can wean children away from family values is strong enough four decades later to discourage important new departures in family policy. In France, on-again, off-again family policy activity, manifested particularly in family allowances, reflects uncertain goals and techniques.

No comprehensive family policy technology is available for America to import from Europe, but several European practices might be eventually adopted. A family policy–minded administration should create a way to observe, for example, the Swedish parental insurance program, the parenting demonstrations in Britain, the French single-wage-earner allowance, and any continuing German *Tagesmütter* activity in hopes of detecting the possible benefits or uncovering the hidden costs of these programs if launched in the United States. Similarly, as changes in work rules—a flexible work schedule (flexitime), job sharing, and the six-hour day—directed to amending the traditional distribution between husband and wife of economic support and family-care responsibilities become subjects of private and public experiments in Europe, an active effort should be made to capture, record, and evaluate their development.

There is nothing uniquely European or uniquely American in experiments at and away from the work place, in other isolated responses to the needs of working women, or in the study of child development. Among the industrial democracies, Britain, France, West Germany, and the United States, at least, share the same inconsistent goals—to minimize state intervention in family life, yet to maximize the number of compatible, self-sufficient, two-parent families as units for the nurturing of children. The European lesson for the United States is that no country with which the United States identifies closely knows how to achieve those goals either.

CHAPTER SEVEN

Many Causes with Many Votaries

FAMILY POLICY too quickly became a fad in American social policy, enthusiastically embraced without attention to the difficulties of developing, enacting, and implementing a public program. One of these difficulties involves spelling out objectives without losing support. Votaries of many of the separate causes massed behind the pro-family banner are each persuaded of the singular importance of their particular cause. Economic assistance to poor families preoccupies some. For those who see family policy as a way to preclude unwanted family formation, population control, family planning, and abortion as a right are all-consuming goals. Their antitheses are all-consuming for those who argue that family policy should both protect the rights of the unborn fetus and preserve adequate freedom for individual couples to conceive and support whatever number of children they desire. For feminists and their sympathizers, the family policy ideal is equality of employment opportunity, equal sharing of parental responsibilities, and preschool child care. But mother-in-the-home as "every child's birthright" is also argued as family policy. Although families with physically, mentally, or emotionally handicapped members divide over public support of high-quality institutional care and public support of home care, each position is rooted in a perception of family policy as government help to special families.

Since family policy is viewed differently from each of these perspectives—by no means the full range of perspectives—it is clear that the transformation from concept to program can be troublesome. History is not reassuring: the modern precursors of family policy—the war on poverty, welfare reform, child development—each generated internecine warfare as each impeccable theme was advanced to the messy and divisive stage of specific proposals. Some critical questions of family policy like abortion, income support, and foster care have already produced their own controversies.

A Flexible and Fuzzy Concept

Evidence presented earlier in this book invites impatience, suspicion, and doubt about family policy. I am impatient with the entrepreneurs of family policy, finding it a concept without a clear content; suspicious of politicians, bureaucrats, or scholars who participate in the movement without pinpointing its objectives; and doubtful whether family policy, no matter if described as comprehensive or partial, implicit or explicit, is a useful or practical theme. Its sloganeers might more profitably concentrate on health, education, and welfare programs to serve children in need or older Americans. In those programs the tools available to government are better suited to the job to be done.

Attention has been focused on family policy because of the belief that public programs to strengthen families would mitigate the social disruption apparent since the mid-1960s. But there can be unanticipated consequences of public policy designed to achieve an objective like stronger families—an objective with many intangible and emotional components. For example, recall the unanticipated, troublesome effects on marital stability of the negative income tax experiment. Touted as family-strengthening, income guarantees to poor families appear to increase family dissolution. Or, on another level, consider the hope once expressed by President Carter that his staff members would marry rather than "live in sin."[1] (Neither an administrative order nor a legislative proposal, it nonetheless carried more weight than any casual expression of prejudice on that subject by any private citizen.) If the president's preferences were adopted by his staff and by others, no one knows whether the resulting formal unions would be strong families or unhappy ones that might otherwise never have been formed.

Clearly, too, family policy is a complicated problem because families are neither monolithic nor unchanging. I have noted earlier that the four-person family composed of father, mother, and two children with the father as sole earner—often referred to as "typical"—described only 7 percent of husband-wife families in the late 1970s. What is generally overlooked is that at some point in their lives a majority of

1. *New York Times*, July 1, 1977. Many months later, the president's press secretary claimed the remarks were made in jest. *Washington Post*, January 26, 1978.

Americans do live in a family with those characteristics. Thus no family policy is realistic if it is based on that kind of four-person group as the typical beneficiary, nor is it realistic if it fails to recognize the sometime typicality of that grouping. Family policy that begins with a perception of two adults sharing responsibility for one or more children will reflect the situation in which almost five-sixths of children under eighteen live. It will not reflect the living arrangements of 11 million children living with only one parent. So it becomes necessary to invent ways of strengthening different family structures. A flexible work schedule, for example, that permits one working parent to leave relatively later in the morning and the second to arrive home relatively earlier in the day is irrelevant for the single-parent family. By the same token, an after-school group-care facility may be invaluable to the single parent—and of no value to the nonworking mother in a two-parent household.

There is no sure-fire policy prescription to strengthen families. Although elegant social science analysis might provide some surprises, rational thinking would posit that peace, full employment, income support, ready access to health care, convenient transportation, decent, safe, and sanitary housing, clean air and water, and good schools are more conducive to strengthening family life than their opposites. But families dissolve notwithstanding all these and myriad other exemplary public achievements, and families hold together—providing for their members, maintaining Lasch's haven in a heartless world—under conditions of war, economic depression, slum living, environmental pollution, and educational jungles.

Idiosyncratic and even perverse effects on family stability characterize sundry other public policies, including some public action first designed and perceived to be pro-family. One well-publicized example is federal income tax rates. Rates fixed to give most married taxpayers an advantage over most single taxpayers with identical incomes can be disadvantageous to some families when both husband and wife work and have approximately equal incomes—an increasingly common phenomenon. A December divorce and January remarriage becomes rational economic behavior.[2] Again, in half the states, public assistance

2. The government's position, according to an Internal Revenue Service official, is that "the law does not allow tax divorces." The issue was joined when the IRS challenged the tax-filing status of a Maryland couple who had been divorced three times and remarried twice, admittedly to take advantage of tax rates for single persons. Each earned about $30,000 annually. The couple calculated that filing as single persons saved $2,800 over filing a joint return. "Many corporations merge and diverge strictly for tax benefits

to dependent children requires absence of the father from the home. Common sense says that an informed, rational, desperate father unable to provide for his family will desert in order to qualify the family for assistance. But after a decade of preoccupation with welfare reform issues, there are still no research findings to sustain that hypothesis. So some politicians and some analysts worry about the possible desertion-incentive effects of the absence-from-the-home proviso, and others worry about the possible work-disincentive effects if the proviso were eliminated. Which position is pro-family and which antifamily is far from certain.

The idea of public policy to strengthen the family gives rise to exhortation on behalf of imprecise goals. To espouse "the principle of supporting family vitality" provides little help to the public official or concerned citizen who might like to do just that. To ask that the nation develop a family policy as comprehensive as its defense policy leaves unresolved the question whether some family policy equivalent of the B-1 bomber, enclosed within the comprehensive package, is critically necessary to the country or an unnecessary and undesirable extravagance. No evidence suggests that a comprehensive family policy will endow its components with greater independent validity than they otherwise might enjoy. A child care program is the leading example. It can be argued that public child care is pro-family because it offers women an opportunity to combine family and work, or antifamily because it invites second-class child rearing. Both positions were taken before family policy became a fashionable topic. Either position could be accommodated by a comprehensive family policy, and either could be correct or incorrect. In effect, there is no way to turn a pro-family ideal into legislation or administrative regulation without making some judgments about specifics. Making those judgments means benefiting some families while implicitly asking others to wait in the queue, meeting some families' needs, disappointing others. What starts as comprehensive family policy inevitably becomes selective policy after all.

---

and nobody questions it as a sham," said the man involved. "Why should couples be treated differently than corporations?" *New York Times*, September 11, 1979. For a discussion of the trade-offs between progressive rate schedules and a "marriage-neutral" approach, see Michael J. McIntyre and Oliver Oldman, "Treatment of the Family," in Joseph A. Pechman, ed., *Comprehensive Income Taxation* (Brookings Institution, 1977), pp. 208–17.

Since family policy has no consistent, accepted meaning, there can be no valid way for either true believers or skeptics to distinguish the accomplishment of family policy from its absence. Politicians, family service practitioners, and some analysts are less specific when they come to the substance of a national family policy than when they affirm or deny the need for one. "It is clear that the national government should have a strong pro-family policy," Jimmy Carter has said, "but the fact is that our government has no family policy, and that is the same thing as an anti-family policy."[3] Robert M. Rice, the director of policy analysis of the Family Service Association of America, wrote in 1977 that it is "crucial to the welfare of both families and the society-at-large that private interests and government begin the long and difficult process of formulating such a national [family] policy."[4] But in the foreword to Rice's book, A. Sidney Johnson III, the director of the Family Impact Seminar who has staffed congressional, executive, and educational family policy inquiries—including one that led to a Carter position paper—disassociates himself from "any implication that we should seek to develop a single, national, comprehensive family policy."[5] In each case, just what it is that the nation lacks and should or should not have is left more fuzzy than clear.

Infinitely flexible, family policy can be whatever the particular discussant wants it to be. "Family policy means everything that government does to and for the family," either explicitly (by design) or implicitly (by chance), Sheila Kamerman and Alfred Kahn told an international conference group. Neither that explanation nor alternative suggestions by Kahn and Kamerman that family policy may be defined as a field, an instrument, a rationale, or a perspective allay suspicion that family policy can be everything or nothing, that it is an all-purpose rallying cry to which no specific meaning attaches.[6]

Since everyone is, was, or will be part of a family, and all government activity bears on at least some of the population, the Kahn and Kamerman definition of family policy as everything that government does to and for the family comes close to including all government action.

3. "A Statement in New Hampshire," August 3, 1976, *The Presidential Campaign, 1976*, vol. 1: *Jimmy Carter* (Government Printing Office, 1978), pt. 1, p. 463.

4. *American Family Policy: Content and Context* (New York: Family Service Association of America, 1977), p. 94.

5. Ibid., p. x.

6. *Family Policy: Government and Families in Fourteen Countries* (Columbia University Press, 1978), pp. 3–16; the quotation is from page 3.

Family policy would be everything. But given the tradition of family privacy and the division of power in the federal system, a more limited definition encompassing only actions expressly intended to affect families in general or specific ways would mean that precious little federal policy would fall in the net. As Laurence Lynn, an economist who has been chairman of the National Research Council's committee on public policies affecting families and children, told another international conference group, family policy is a term "as amorphous and unyielding to precise analysis" as any term in current policy debates.[7]

One way to avoid the everything-or-nothing dilemma is to acknowledge that the crisis of the family is actually the crisis of poor families and dysfunctional families, and to define family policy as public programs to aid parents and children in poor or dysfunctional families. Sensitive to the tradition of family privacy, this definition is also the one most likely to be taken seriously by policymakers because it focuses on identifiable problems. In the Alva Myrdal tradition, it would make income maintenance the first-order concern of family policy, then add to that concern both parental dysfunction and child dysfunction because they are impediments to the parental nurturing of children.

Throwing the cloak of family policy over these substantive questions, however, will not assure sympathetic attention to them. Since it is not self-evident that intractable problems of family dysfunction can be overcome through government action, policymakers may choose to do their policymaking where payoffs seem more likely. The wave of the future is gray, as Lynn has also pointed out,[8] and in the inevitable conflict between the needs and purposes of the aged and the needs and purposes of family policy, especially of that narrow, troublesome part encompassing parental and child dysfunction, the aged will win. They have apparatus in place, they have members, and they have precedent. In any event, many family policy activists seem unwilling to accept dysfunction as a limitation on the scope of family policy. But if they push unfocused demands for comprehensive policy, and others urge specific efforts that cannot be guaranteed to overcome dysfunction, family policy will be more discussed at conferences than in Congress.

From the time Jimmy Carter as presidential nominee mentioned family policy until the star-crossed White House Conference on Fami-

7. "Fiscal and Organizational Constraints on Family Policy," paper prepared for the International Seminar on Family Policy, University of Notre Dame, March 1978.
8. Ibid.

lies, influential sponsors and specialists sustained demand for family policy. But no detailed prospectus on family policy as a public issue has been written. Ultimately, however, a prospectus should explain exactly what is asked of government in the name of family policy. A public issue depends for its continued existence on the mobilization of groups seeking a benefit for themselves or for others that is within the power of government to award by legislation, administrative order, or court decree. Whether the benefit is money, regulation of individual or official behavior, or special assistance to a particular class, it must be translatable into the output of government—statute law, administrative interpretation, or judicial determination. In this sense, kindness, compassion, and happiness, for example, are not public issues. Good health care is a public issue, but good health is not. Nor are strong families. They cannot be mandated by a governmental entity. Groups do not mobilize to request or demand them as formal products of governmental activity.

Social causes with measurable goals do become public issues. Equal employment opportunity for women and for blacks and Hispanics, for example, can be measured, though imprecisely; can be both legislated and adjudicated; and is a public issue. Universal access to health care involves a measurable goal and is a public issue. So is the protection of a woman's right to abort a fetus or of a fetus's right to protection against abortion. In each case, groups mobilize in support or opposition, and the public issue remains on the agenda as the effort goes on to achieve passage of a bill, or persuade a court, or influence an administrative interpretation. A loss in one arena invites a shift to another. The substantive goal of group activity is specific, and the process involved in achieving it is identifiable.

Unifying Theme, Divisive Specific

Unless family policy is broken into component parts, it is only an abstract theme that neither blesses nor damns, neither rewards nor punishes. Only the components of family policy are susceptible to legislative action or administrative order. Mobilizing groups on behalf of family policy is a code for mobilizing groups on behalf of a particular approach to some component that is reducible to government action. At that point, however, family policy begins to bite.

Delineating components invites disaster. Assume, for example, that family policy advocates delineate one high-priority component as federal subsidies to child care facilities that are available on demand, at nominal cost. Some who think of family policy as a way to minimize, not facilitate, out-of-home child care will line up in opposition. Some others, for whom family policy means above all a program that will depopulate institutions and try to put all children in permanent family settings, will give the child care component of family policy only casual support. And still others, for whom family policy means improved opportunities for three-generational housing arrangements, will simply be indifferent to child care. The clear self-interest necessary to develop enough group support to transform a dream into a public issue—or to suppress it—does not attach to family policy. Organized self-interest does attach to discrete entities that may collectively be termed family policy.

This explains why family policy is irresistible in the abstract and impossible in the particular, at once unifying and divisive. For example, Daniel Patrick Moynihan and the critics of his celebrated report both wanted a family policy. Moynihan, having found a "tangle of pathology," saw family policy as programs to overcome black illegitimacy. Black groups denied that black illegitimacy was a pathology and specified equal opportunity and job creation for blacks as their priorities. Sharing a dedication to family policy, Moynihan and his black critics diverged on its purpose—whether family policy is remedial ("to establish a stable Negro family structure"), or supportive (to recognize the strengths of black families).

Richard Nixon described his family assistance plan as the ultimate family policy. "The new plan," Nixon said, "rejects a policy that undermines family life." Besides increasing the will to work, the plan would result in "the survival of more marriages, the greater stability of families."[9] Others did not agree. Conservatives viewed the plan as a subsidy to the unworthy; liberals regarded it as antifamily because of a bias in favor of work over child care. Although the family assistance plan lost, a coalition of civil rights and women's groups advanced a child development program as a great breakthrough in family policy. Nixon vetoed the bill, and couched his action as a defense of "family-centered" child rearing over the bill's "communal approaches."

9. "Welfare Reform Message from the President," *Congressional Record* (August 11, 1969), p. 23144.

Jimmy Carter made "the American family is in trouble" a recurring theme in his campaign. Without limiting the judgment of a "steady erosion and weakening of our families" to any ethnic or economic group, he stated his intention "to construct an administration that will reverse the trends we have seen toward the breakdown of the family in our country." That sounded good even to an activist not easily beguiled by vague promises. "I am very pleased," Marian Wright Edelman of the Children's Defense Fund said in August 1976, after a meeting with Carter, "that we now have a voice that is going to be an advocate for families and children."[10] Subsequently, many groups enlisted in support of an undefined White House conference and in support of objectives like family policy and family impact analysis, all presumably means to a desirable end.

But the nearly four years spent in preplanning, planning, unplanning, and replanning a White House Conference on Families benefited not a single dysfunctional family. Nor are there present or obvious potential beneficiaries of a prolonged family-impact analysis that after three years was still engrossed in considering what is a family and what is an impact. Too many good minds have spent too much time in conferences looking for definitions of fuzzy terms.

The persistent issues of family dysfunction have little to do with whether the family is suddenly in trouble as an institution or whether it is here to stay. A thoughtful, scholarly inquiry leading to the here-to-stay conclusion and a politician's assertion that "the American family is in trouble" may not represent incompatible positions as much as different preoccupations.

On the one hand, it can be persuasively argued that instead of declining, the extended family never existed; that instead of increasing, family disruption has only changed in character; that instead of indicating a less stable family life for children, the growth of single-parent families indicates the reverse, because it means that single mothers are keeping their children rather than farming them out; that instead of harming children, changes in maternal work habits are mostly without effect. On the other hand, there is cause for anxiety about the percentage of children who live in poverty, about the helplessness of some victims of domestic violence, about the child support problems resulting from unmarried motherhood, desertion, separation, and divorce.

10. *The Presidential Campaign, 1976*, vol. 1, pt. 1, p. 385.

The choice is not between pollyannaism and alarmism. The family can be both here to stay and in trouble. That some families survive domestic violence is no justification for the failure to develop a shelter program. Out-of-wedlock births and consequent single-parent households may be a workable family form that is preferable to out-of-wedlock births and institutional care, but to be workable is not necessarily to be best. Varieties of life-styles, changes in family form, and changes in family function, in short, should be separately examined for what they are rather than collectively deplored or accepted.

By the same token, if new technology or new resources or new organizational arrangements can be brought to bear on persistent and agreed-upon problems associated with family life, the new devices should not be set aside because the problems are old. Whatever the definition of a workable family, the conception and birth of an unwanted child is an undesirable event rendered no less so by an awareness that there have always been unwanted pregnancies and births. The same can be said of adolescent pregnancies, wanted or unwanted, in that the health risks to mother and child are substantial and adolescents are not likely to be ready emotionally to care for an infant. Without belaboring the illustrations, let it be acknowledged that the institution of the family has adapted to these events and continues to do so. But it should also be acknowledged that the pregnancy rate of young teenagers is evidence of trouble. For some, it will appear to be a health problem, because of the high risk of morbidity. Others will see an economic problem, because of the unlikelihood that the parents can support themselves, let alone a child. To categorize it as a family problem is surely not unreasonable, because "family" conjures up images of maternal and child health, self-support, emotional interdependence, and intergenerational relationships, all of which are involved.

In sum, whether the erosion of the nuclear family is a myth or not, the many problems that can be labeled family problems do not vanish. If those problems affect a large or growing segment of the population, anxiety about them can be expected to increase. If the notion of public policy to enhance family stability is a misguided notion because the family is not decaying, the notion of nonintervention is also misguided because there are circumstances associated with family life that government action can improve. Identifying the appropriate issues and applying the appropriate remedy should be the essence of family policy.

Interventionist Cause, Noninterventionist Era

If 1973, the year of the first and only congressional hearing on families, is taken as a benchmark, subsequent years are characterized by a continued discussion of family by politicians but by no important increase in either legislative products or executive proposals designed to benefit families. Both welfare reform and the war on poverty had different histories. When Lyndon Johnson endorsed the discovery of poverty in America, it brought proposals, programs, agencies, and evaluations. When Richard Nixon took on welfare change, that subject took on immediate urgency. But the joint Carter-Mondale awareness of the family problem stimulated little more than the organization or renaming of family policy centers by universities eager to attract support from government agencies and philanthropic foundations. Family policy stalled at the discussion stage.

The Absence of Theory

Family was unveiled as a major policy area without a theory to explain and guide public intervention. Again in contrast with the approaches to poverty, civil rights, or welfare, no tentative explanation of just how government action could effect change accompanied the call for family policy. The poverty program's community action agencies and its Head Start program were to empower the powerless and make it possible for poor people to have a hand in changing the quality of their communities and their lives. Whatever the later problems and defects in implementation, the conception seemed to hang together, to be directed in a logical manner toward a reasonable objective. Similarly, civil rights enforcement and equal employment opportunity pointed toward the environment depicted in Martin Luther King's "I Have a Dream" speech. In both cases, causation and program were tied together as they were, too, in welfare reform, where the welfare system's perceived incentive for paternal desertion served as the reformers' point of departure.

But when Jimmy Carter announced that the American family was in trouble, he proposed no more of an explanation-cum-remedy than Walter Mondale had when he announced years before that "it all begins with the family"—a conclusion Mondale himself judged "not very profound." Why the family is in trouble, if indeed it really is, and just how remedies would act on troubles are not explained. Policymaking depends on at least an implicit theory. Without one, politicians who call for government action are guilty of bad planning. There is an instructive contrast between Carter's call for family policy and Moynihan's earlier presentation of his theory about the Negro family. Black scholars and activists at the time described Moynihan's theory as wrongheaded, but it was an explanation leading to an emphasis on particular programs. If Carter began with an implicit theory of the nuclear family as the norm, he undermined it by shifting to an acceptance of the diversity and pluralism of families.

Some of the consequences of the absence of a Carter plan might have been overcome by sure-footedness in seeking out some specific areas where agreement on program development was most likely. Johnson's response to the antipoverty planners had been, in essence, full steam ahead with exploration and planning until we are ready to unveil a package. Nixon showed impatience during the months it took his welfare reform planners to work out a program. Both waited, however, until they could say more than that there are too many poor people in America or that the welfare system is unsatisfactory. Rather than wait for a plan, Carter went public with his family-in-trouble conclusion first, either assuming the remedies would readily fall into place or failing to understand the complexity of family forms and life-styles. After offering only an emotion-laden judgment, whatever the depth of conviction on which it was based, Carter ought to have made sure that backup work on the family problem got done. But that work, it will be recalled, was allowed to drift in HEW, to the point where the responsible assistant secretary's written testimony on progress was conceded to be "misleading" in oral testimony by the same assistant secretary.

Moreover, administration leaders did not encourage congressmen concerned about the family problem. John Brademas and Alan Cranston, House and Senate subcommittee chairmen with appropriate jurisdiction who might have assisted or led joint legislative-executive planning efforts, were each embarrassed and irritated by some of their dealings with the administration on family policy matters. Both publicly deplored the administration's disregard for its campaign promises on the subject.

Family policy in the form of a reasonably well developed approach to a perceived national problem has not been rejected nor has it been tried and found wanting. It does not exist. Those who raised the issue had no ideas or plans under wraps, have not subsequently generated ideas or plans from their subordinates, and have more often than not turned away from ideas or plans originating in Congress.

Timing

Most of the reasons for concern about families are not tied to the social upheavals of the 1960s. Poverty, unemployment, discrimination, unattended children, inadequate housing, abortion, adolescent pregnancy, prolonged foster care, child support delinquency, consignment of handicapped children to institutions rather than crash efforts at adoption, domestic violence—none are inventions of the last decade. Some big issues like unemployment in families with dependent children, and some narrower issues like child support delinquency, have been on the policy agenda for at least the past quarter-century. What is new is the discovery that all these depressing problems can be gathered under the heading "decline of the family," and that family policy is the key to arresting the decline.

Whatever the validity of the discovery and of the family policy prescription, the timing is wrong. Family policy implies intervention, regulation, public assistance, manipulation of individual choice—all difficult under any circumstances, since family issues carry a traditional protection against such government activity. Yet family policy has been offered when, in nearly all respects, the national swing is to nonintervention, deregulation, fiscal restraint, reliance on market forces.

To overcome the formidable barriers to making family a public issue, all the conditions would have to be right—for example, proposals would have to test out, trust in government would have to be high. But family policy has come on the scene as a collection of controversial proposals: as out-of-home child care that may be good for both mothers and children or may be good for mothers and not so good for children or may be good for neither; as freedom of choice on abortion, perhaps the most divisive social question of the seventies; as income guarantees that test out to have peculiar effects on family stability; as shelters for abused women, privately seen by some congressmen as publicly sponsored lesbian centers. The proposals lack the elegant appeal of Head Start, say, with its promise of organized centers that would teach deprived preschool children such basics as colors. With such an appeal, family policy proposals or a family policy package might, in an era of high trust in government, break through the door that separates family life from government. But this is not an era of high trust in government, and the elements of family policy, as nearly as those elements can be identified, are far from being sure remedies for family problems.

Exactly these judgments were reflected in testimony given at pre-conference hearings of the White House Conference on Families. The testimony, said the conference chairman, indicated a popular mistrust of government and a concern about the perceived intrusion of government between parents and children.[11] Hearing the message, conference leaders announced six months before the first of the three regional conferences assembled that "modest recommendations" were their goal. Though the noninterventionist era could not be made an interventionist era, somewhat belatedly the interventionist cause could be adjusted to conform to the era.

Turning Homilies into Policies

Actually designing public policy to support the pluralism and diversity of family life is harder than deploring family instability and government's seeming insensitivity to it. The principal elements of the Carter administration's family policy were a willingness to endorse and to cooperate with congressional initiatives in child support enforcement, belated support of congressional initiatives in foster care and adoption, an impetuous call followed by inadequate planning for a White House conference, and sympathetic interest at least in sharply restricting federal payment for abortion procedures. Hand-wringing aside, the Carter record on family policy is not very different from the records on family policy of other postwar administrations. What that conclusion demonstrates is the complexity of family as a public policy problem and the fierce resistance engendered by almost any intervention proposal.

Virtually all recent experience with political interest in family stability indicates that as a political issue the family problem can be deceptive. In an easy sense, family policy is an inchoate, universally admired cause like peace, justice, or equality. In a harder sense, family policy is a collection of controversial programs to deal with the needs of people

11. Child Welfare League of America, Hecht Institute for State Child Welfare Planning, *Child Welfare Planning Notes*, vol. 4 (December 10, 1979), p. 91.

who have stopped caring for each other or who lack the ability to care for each other. Only the desirability of child support enforcement programs produces anything close to a consensus, and even on this subject there are dissenters who insist, with logic on their side, that although child support enforcement may save public money and may be ethically defensible, it does nothing to maintain family stability.

It is no service to emphasize the easy sense of family policy while avoiding the hard. The vision of a nation of strong, happy families should not substitute for government activity to protect or compensate as best it can troubled members of dysfunctional, unhappy families. Useful first steps in the latter direction would be fact gathering and in-house advocacy.

Unimpeachable data and built-in advocacy are important in the movement from a place on an agency's legislative agenda to the president's program, and to the congressional calendar. Neither data needs nor structured advocacy within decisionmaking channels has been accorded the attention necessary to move the family problem politically from a subject for homilies to a subject for practical policy-making and implementation. The minimum conditions for success in developing public policies as remedies for family dysfunction are reliable data about dysfunction and an effective apparatus within government for receiving the data, formulating programs based on them, and lobbying for adoption of plans and program proposals. These conditions have not been satisfied.

Data

Some family data are very good. Invaluable for policy planning in a variety of fields from education to housing to taxation, official vital statistics on marriages and births, and on divorces and deaths—the formal beginnings and endings of families—are compiled and reported regularly by the Public Health Service. Further reliable detail having to do with leading causes of death and with age-adjusted death rates for those leading causes in turn guide various aspects of health policy. In recent years data revealing an increase in divorce rates, especially, have been viewed with alarm, and are one stimulus to the interest in social policy that might strengthen families. Among other stimuli to policy initiatives, adolescent pregnancy and birth data are significant despite indications that births to teenagers are a declining phenomenon rather than a growing one. Adolescent suicide data were cited by President Carter in one of his early "I'm worried about the family" speeches as one of the reasons for his worry, although no policy initiative ever followed. Other public health data provide intelligence about child health, and regular monthly reports of the Social Security Administration detail numbers of families and of individual children benefiting from aid to families with dependent children.

For all of that, the data are poor from which to address family dysfunction as a public policy problem. The high degree of emotionalism injected into the family policy discussions serves as a surrogate for information and knowledge in both old and new areas of concern like foster care, child support, and domestic violence.

The size of the foster care population is a leading case. Over the years it has been variously estimated that from 250,000 to 350,000 children were in out-of-home care; more recent extrapolation from sample data suggests half a million. Yet even the Child Welfare League—as if unwilling to believe the HEW estimate—in 1979 reported a different and lower figure.[12] If there is no firm handle on the total number of children in foster care, it must follow that there is no firm knowledge of their geographical distribution, the reasons for their placement in foster care, and the actual time spent in such care.

A consortium of private groups—the American Public Welfare Association, the National Council of Family and Juvenile Court Judges, and the Child Welfare League—now handles the issue of foster care data through the Child and Youth Centered Information System (CYCIS), financed by a substantial grant from the Edna McConnell Clark Foundation. A principal purpose of CYCIS is to use modern computer technology to keep track of children, whether neglected, abused, or delinquent, in twenty-four-hour out-of-home care, and to show that privacy and security of data can be maintained. If fully implemented nationally, CYCIS should answer the numbers question, and by revealing, for example, the characteristics of children longest in care, suggest specific priorities for policy. CYCIS would also help to guard against the sorriest element of the foster care system in operation—the haphazard manual selection of cases for review leading to ignored children who are victims of caseworker turnover, caseworker inexperience, or caseworker values. Though a well-endowed founda-

12. Child Welfare League of America, CYCIS-DATA Project, *Using CYCIS to Achieve Permanence for Children* (CWLA, 1979), p. 4.

tion and five cooperating states can point the way, CYCIS's ultimate value as an information bank depends on nationwide implementation, which, in turn, depends on continuing pressure from the federal government for state monitoring systems.

Child support enforcement is another example of a problem of family dysfunction about which the data are still inadequate in important respects. It is known that in 1975 only one-fourth of the 4.9 million divorced, separated, remarried, or never-married women with a child or children in the home received child support. Two out of five AFDC families with a court order or parent's voluntary agreement for child support received no payment from the absent parent, and irregular, partial, or short-term payments were common among those families who did receive payments.[13] Presumably, the child support enforcement legislation subsequently enacted eased that problem, if not for all single mothers, at least for welfare-dependent women whose participation in the enforcement program has been uninterruptedly mandated by statute. Or did it? Most of the amount collected—reported by HEW to total about one-half billion dollars annually—goes to meet administrative expenses and to reimburse federal and state governments for their payments to AFDC cases. Part of the federal share is paid to states as an incentive for them to collect on behalf of other states. Collections nationally are said to represent about 5 percent of the total amount paid recipients, yet virtually none of the collections on behalf of AFDC recipients affects the individual's AFDC grant itself. Whatever net fiscal benefits accrue are fiscal benefits for federal and state governments. Whatever costs accrue are emotional costs to the AFDC mother and her children, as well as economic costs to a second family. Neither of these costs is reported or calculated. If they are inconsequential, as they may well be, the case for child support enforcement as a deterrent to delinquency in meeting support orders would be further strengthened. If they are not inconsequential, the paltry fiscal benefits to government may not be worth the consequences to family tranquillity. Sophisticated survey research can surely produce appropriate data.

13. U.S. Bureau of the Census, *Current Population Reports*, series P-23, no. 84, "Divorce, Child Custody, and Child Support" (GPO, 1979), p. 15; U.S. Department of Health, Education, and Welfare, Social Security Administration, Office of Research and Statistics, *Aid to Families with Dependent Children: 1975 Recipient Characteristics Study*, pt. 2: *Child Support Enforcement*, DHEW (SSA)78-11777 (HEW, 1978), p. 11.

Finally, the use of obviously uncertain data bearing on domestic violence confused that issue. Apparently caught short by the sudden appearance of congressional interest in domestic violence, public officials treated second-rate data as if they were unimpeachable. One result was justifiable skepticism about the relevance of the prescription to the dysfunction portrayed. If episodes of domestic violence are characteristic of over 15 percent of American couples, a congressional response that authorizes limited-term $50,000 grants here and there can be defended as an emergency stopgap, but cannot be taken seriously as the total public policy response. Yet HEW officials, who were responsible for supporting the limited field research and simultaneously queasy about their information, found themselves not only without an explanation of the tie between domestic violence and family policy but also without an explanation of how proposed policy would meet the assumed problem. The legislation ran into trouble, but the problem—whatever its real incidence—continues.

In-House Advocacy

Like families, other social groups or institutions—say, the aged or women or racial minorities or colleges and universities—incorporate an economic mix, religious diversity, and a range of social classes. Unlike families, each of the others can claim important successes in social policy. Those who urge family policy—implicit, explicit, comprehensive, or whatever—often trace their problems to the pattern that distinguishes policymaking for families from policymaking for these other groups. Family policy, it is said, has had no anchor within the executive branch. Family has no real analogue to the old Children's Bureau, the Women's Bureau, the Civil Rights Commission, the Equal Employment Opportunity Commission, or the Bureau of Higher and Continuing Education, a circumstance that reflects continuing ambivalence about the status of family policy.

Without a bureau on families or a practical surrogate, the argument goes on, no internal advocacy of policies for families is discernible, nor is there continuing attention to what family policy should include. Instead, the agenda of policies for families is an amalgam of proposals to advance the children's cause, like child health assessment; proposals to advance an administration's image as the solver of big problems, like welfare reform; and proposals that are spin-offs of the women's movement, like child care. Whether any of these proposals are incorporated into an administration's family policy—indeed, whether an administration claims to espouse a family policy—depends on chance factors rather than on the discharge of assigned responsibility. According to proponents of a families bureau, bureau status connotes legitimacy: the cause that "owns" a bureau need not first establish its right to be heard somewhere along the line on the merits of its program.

The idea of a bureau is anathema to other ardent family policy proponents who correctly view with alarm the possible substitution of an agency for a program. According to this view, the inevitable legacy of a bureau for families would be busy work rather than forthright advocacy. All the evidence suggests that that depressing vision could accurately describe the role of an administration or bureau on families. Believers in family advocacy from within government should be closely monitoring the consequences of a gesture twice made by the Carter administration. First, apparently stimulated by the positive reaction to the family issue that he raised during his campaign, President Carter early in his administration gave families formal recognition as a national government concern. HEW's Office of Child Development became the Administration for Children, Youth, and Families. But it was only a titular change, not a substantive one. About thirty months later, sounding for all the world as if he had no idea of the existence of ACYF, the president told the National Conference of Catholic Charities that he was creating an Office for Families in HEW to be involved in developing "new ideas on a continuing basis." Staff members at ACYF described themselves as "surprised" to hear of the president's plan to create an agency for which they had been working since he created it the first time.

The oddity of a born-again bureau invites attention to the willingness of family organizations and family policy proponents to allow the F in ACYF to wither during the thirty months after its creation in 1977. In that period, before Carter announced his new Office for Families, neither groups in government nor outside groups proposed using ACYF as the lead agency in a family-related initiative. At least until John Calhoun's appointment as commissioner at the beginning of 1980, ACYF was lightly regarded and little consulted. The Office for Families, brought into being as an office within ACYF but without an assigned mission other than to develop new ideas on a continuing basis, defined its role in language reminiscent of the Family Impact Seminar. What the new agency will be doing, an ACYF deputy commissioner explained in February 1980, is focusing attention on the impact that federal policies and programs have on the family and examining selected policies to determine how they help or harm families.[14] If it takes ACYF's family program and the Family Impact Seminar as models, the Office for Families will be more cipher than advocate.

There is a better model. A small agency isolated from the mainstream of department activity can make a dent on policy development if its leader has independent strength and its program is organized around a set of specific priorities within the power of government to satisfy. The early leaders of the Children's Bureau, Julia Lathrop and Grace Abbott, whose collective service as chiefs extended over a quarter-century, managed to avoid the trivia of administration. Instead they emphasized the bureau's investigating and reporting work. When the New Deal arrived, the bureau was ready to propose ideas, especially in child health and aid to dependent children. Later, when other leaders began to avoid decisions about priorities, the bureau spread itself too thin. In the end, the bureau was enveloped by the Office of Child Development, where social, emotional, and cognitive development of disadvantaged children, especially, was to be the emphasis. But President Nixon's veto of child development legislation left Edward Zigler, the OCD's director, in an untenable position, and he returned to academic life. The OCD took on the same drift and diffusion that had characterized the Children's Bureau in the fifties and early sixties. It is time now to focus again on children in need—those who are homeless, without adequate support, badly nourished, in need of physical or mental health services. While an Office for Families searches for a function, a revived Children's Bureau might get on with useful work.

The Coming Fracture

Good data and internal advocacy can facilitate informed policymaking, but informed policymaking will not resolve differences between the children's advocates, women's advocates, welfare advocates, sen-

14. *Children, Youth, and Family News*, HEW Office of Human Development Services (February 1980).

ior citizens' advocates, and civil rights advocates who found family a cause they could share—until the time for establishing priorities.

Just before Christmas 1979, leaders of a national children's advocacy group met to consider some political realities of family policy. After several years of intensive lobbying, Congress seemed ready to enact two measures accorded highest priority by most child and family advocacy groups and embraced by the Carter administration as cornerstones of family policy. One bill would have extended medicaid coverage to millions of additional children and added services deemed critical to improved child health. In child advocacy circles its adoption would be considered a major triumph. But the House of Representatives had added to the bill restrictions on the use of federal funds to pay for abortions and a new freedom for states to strike all abortions—including those to save the life of the mother—from their lists of medicaid services.[15]

A second bill would have moved toward reform of foster care and adoption practices by providing adoption assistance payments and probably increasing federal grants for child welfare services especially to inventory and track the placement of children in foster care. Because the bill put emphasis on permanent family settings for children adrift in foster care and on preventing indiscriminate use of foster care, it had also been accorded a very high priority by child and family advocates. To this bill, however, the Senate had attached changes in how the income of AFDC families was to be calculated—changes that would probably have reduced the number of eligible families.[16]

In both cases—the antiabortion provision on the child health bill and the income-calculation change on the foster care bill—legislative sponsors could readily argue pro-child and pro-family purposes. None, in any event, claimed antichild or antifamily intent.

But tying the abortion and welfare questions to child health and foster care fractured the family and child advocates. All would support the original child health and foster care measures. Some would abide and some would support either abortion restraints or particular welfare eligibility restraints or both. Some would support neither of the latter. But at the next level, among those who opposed either the abortion or the welfare item, some favored abandonment of the basic legislation if

15. *Congressional Record*, daily edition (December 11, 1979), pp. H11770–76.
16. *Adoption Assistance and Child Welfare Act of 1979*, S. Rept. 96-336, 96 Cong. 1 sess. (GPO, 1979).

it could not be stripped of the unwanted addition, whereas others found the basic legislation of such singular importance that even "bad" family policy amendments should not lead to abandonment of the bill.

This fracturing of the family policy interest is inevitable. Competing ideologies—in abortion, pro-choice versus pro-life; in welfare, more income assistance versus more pressure for self-sufficiency; in foster care, unlimited spending on foster care of poor children versus pressures for permanent placement; in adolescent pregnancy, "secondary prevention" versus primary contraceptive efforts—claim or are thought to be able to "fix" family problems. But the superior validity of one or another ideology is not established. In none of the family policy issues can it be said that only one side is the pro-family side. Confronted with the cold reality of social policy dilemmas, rather than the warm glow of families walking in the woods, the family interest fractures. Family policy evokes visions of social programs that will benefit all persons in all families. In some cases, however, the interests of parents and the interests of children will not overlap. In other cases, the interests of some parents and children will not overlap those of other parents and children. Ultimately, advocates for children, for women, for the aged, and for special groups among them will go their separate ways.

Judgment

The judgment on family policy is yes and no. On the one hand, it is yes, problems of families are identifiable, if not solvable. Family dysfunction leaves helpless and unloved people dependent on public programs to save them from disaster. Some of those programs are clearly in need of improvement. Family policy is simply a description of a bundle of government programs, and hence inevitable.

On the other hand, it is no, its inventors have not described their invention nor have they shown a working model. Conferences and seminars have not helped clarify the concept. The facts about families are not well enough known to make policy. Congress is not much interested, and the executive agencies involved have made no progress in assembling a family policy package. The attention devoted to the term and its possible meaning has not benefited the groups assumed to be its probable beneficiaries—children, women, perhaps the poor.

Family policy is not a coherent program awaiting formal approval. Organizing on behalf of family policy is not feasible, because it is more like peace, justice, equality, and freedom than it is like higher welfare benefits, or school busing, or medical care for the aged.

Family policy is unifying only so long as the details are avoided. When the details are confronted, family policy splits into innumerable components. It is many causes with many votaries.

Index